Germany's Foreign Policy towards Poland and the Czech Republic

A thorough examination of critical aspects of Central and Eastern European history, this book explores historical legacies and contemporary dynamics in the relations between Germany, Poland and the Czech Republic. The authors provide a comparative assessment of Germany's post-reunification relations with the Czech Republic and Poland from the perspective of a social constructivist theory of foreign policy analysis. Identifying the key actors and factors, they examine the long-standing continuity in the norms and values that underpin German foreign policy and explore the issues of borders, territory, identities, minorities and population transfers. Paying particular attention to the process of European integration and the role of the new Germany within Europe, the authors identify how new possibilities for co-operation might finally overcome legacies of the past.

This pioneering study will be of particular interest to students of European Politics and International Affairs.

Karl Cordell is Principal Lecturer in the Department of Politics, University of Plymouth, UK.

Stefan Wolff is Professor of Political Science, University of Bath, UK.

Routledge Advances in European Politics

1 **Russian Messianism**
Third Rome, revolution, Communism
and after
Peter J.S. Duncan

2 **European Integration and
the Postmodern Condition**
Governance, democracy, identity
Peter van Ham

3 **Nationalism in Italian Politics**
The stories of the Northern League,
1980–2000
Damian Tambini

4 **International Intervention in the
Balkans since 1995**
Edited by Peter Siani-Davies

5 **Widening the European Union**
The politics of institutional change
and reform
Edited by Bernard Steunenberg

6 **Institutional Challenges in the European
Union**
*Edited by Madeleine Hosli, Adrian van
Deemen and Mika Widgrén*

7 **Europe Unbound**
Enlarging and reshaping the boundaries
of the European Union
Edited by Jan Zielonka

8 **Ethnic Cleansing in the Balkans**
Nationalism and the destruction
of tradition
Cathie Carmichael

9 **Democracy and Enlargement in Post-
Communist Europe**
The democratisation of the general
public in fifteen Central and Eastern
European countries, 1991–1998
Christian W. Haerpfer

10 **Private Sector Involvement in the Euro**
The power of ideas
*Stefan Collignon and
Daniela Schwarzer*

11 **Europe**
A Nietzschean perspective
Stefan Elbe

12 **The European Union and e-Voting**
Addressing the European Parliament's
internet voting challenge
*Edited by Alexander H. Trechsel and
Fernando Mendez*

13 **European Union Council Presidencies**
A comparative perspective
Edited by Ole Elgström

14 **European Governance and
Supranational Institutions**
Making states comply
Jonas Tallberg

15 **European Union, NATO and Russia**
Martin Smith and Graham Timmins

16 **Business, the State and Economic Policy**
The case of Italy
G. Grant Amyot

17 **Europeanization and Transnational
States**
Comparing Nordic central governments
*Bengt Jacobsson, Per Lægreid and
Ove K. Pedersen*

18 **European Union Enlargement**
A comparative history
*Edited by Wolfram Kaiser and
Jürgen Elvert*

19 **Gibraltar**
British or Spanish?
Peter Gold

20 **Gendering Spanish Democracy**
*Monica Threlfall, Christine Cousins
and Celia Valiente*

21 **European Union Negotiatons**
Processes, networks and institutions
*Edited by Ole Elgström and
Christer Jönsson*

22 **Evaluating Euro-Mediterranean
Relations**
Stephen C. Calleya

23 **The Changing Face of European Identity**
A seven-nation study of (supra)national
attachments
Edited by Richard Robyn

24 **Governing Europe**
Discourse, governmentality and
European integration
*William Walters and
Jens Henrik Haahr*

25 **Territory and Terror**
Conflicting nationalisms in the Basque
Country
Jan Mansvelt Beck

26 **Multilateralism, German Foreign Policy
and Central Europe**
Claus Hofhansel

27 **Popular Protest in East Germany**
Gareth Dale

28 **Germany's Foreign Policy towards
Poland and the Czech Republic**
Ostpolitik revisited
Karl Cordell and Stefan Wolff

29 **Kosovo**
The politics of identity and space
Denisa Kostovicova

30 **The Politics of European Union
Enlargement**
Theoretical approaches
*Edited by Frank Schimmelfennig and
Ulrich Sedelmeier*

31 **Europeanizing Social Democracy?**
The rise of the party of of European
Socialists
Simon Lightfoot

Germany's Foreign Policy towards Poland and the Czech Republic

Ostpolitik revisited

Karl Cordell and Stefan Wolff

Routledge
Taylor & Francis Group

LONDON AND NEW YORK

First published 2005
by Routledge
2 Park Square, Milton Park, Abingdon, Oxon OX14 4RN

Simultaneously published in the USA and Canada
by Routledge
270 Madison Ave, New York, NY 10016

Routledge is an imprint of the Taylor & Francis Group

Transferred to Digital Printing 2009

Typeset in Sabon by
Florence Production Ltd, Stoodleigh, Devon

British Library Cataloguing in Publication Data
A catalogue record for this book is available
from the British Library

Library of Congress Cataloging in Publication Data
Cordell, Karl, 1956–
  Germany's foreign policy towards Poland and the
  Czech Republic: Ostpolitik revisited/Karl Cordell &
  Stefan Wolff.
      p. cm. – (Routledge advances in European politics; 28)
    Includes bibliographical references.
  1. Germany – Foreign relations – Poland. 2. Germany –
  Foreign relations – Czech Republic. I. Title: Ostpolitik revisited.
  II. Wolff, Stefan, 1969– III. Title. IV. Series.
  DD120.P7C67 2005
  327.4304371–dc22   2004024934

ISBN10: 0-415-36974-6 (hbk)
ISBN10: 0-415-49957-7 (pbk)

ISBN13: 978-0-415-36974-9 (hbk)
ISBN13: 978-0-415-49957-6 (pbk)

For
Jenny and Gunnel
and
Lucy and Sigrid

Contents

Acknowledgements   x

1 The German question and German foreign policy:
   a conceptual introduction   1

2 A usable past? German–Czech and German–Polish
   relations before the Second World War   16

3 An insurmountable legacy? Invasion, occupation,
   expulsion and the Cold War   30

4 German–Czech and German–Polish relations since
   the end of the Cold War: an overview   50

5 Foreign policy and its domestic consumption: the
   German political parties and Ostpolitik   62

6 Domestic constituencies and foreign audiences:
   the *Landsmannschaften* and their impact on
   German–Polish and German–Czech relations   82

7 The role of the minority populations   106

8 Ostpolitik: continuity and change   131

9 Towards a common future?   155

   Notes   166
   Bibliography   171
   List of interviews   177
   Index   179

Acknowledgements

This book has been a truly collaborative effort and is the result of our co-operation on this inherently complex subject matter of 'the German question' that dates back around seven years. Apart from this book, we have, individually and jointly, published a number of books and articles on this topic, and have freely drawn on previously published and published research. At the same time, this book represents a departure for both of us. In the past, our concern had been primarily with ethnic German minorities in Europe, and to a lesser extent with the German refugee and expellee communities. Only sporadically had we touched on more comprehensive assessments of the various dimensions of the German question. In following and analysing political developments over the past fifteen years, we came to realize that the German question, declared resolved by many in 1990, continued to remain a significant factor in European politics at least and in particular in Germany's relations with Poland and the Czech Republic. In this triangle of fate, we witnessed remarkable change and stagnation, continuity and innovation, as well as compromise and confrontation. In this volume we attempt to analyse its causes and consequences.

No work like this is merely the product of its authors' efforts. We have many people to thank for their comments on earlier drafts, for corrections of factual errors, for the time they made available for us to interview them. We benefited greatly from a research grant awarded by the British Academy (LRG 35361), which allowed us to engage two very able research assistants in Poland and the Czech Republic: Andrzej Dybczyński and Zdeněk Hausvater; and from the equally generous support of our departments at the University of Plymouth and the University of Bath. Without the encouragement of Heidi Bagtazo, Grace McInnes and Harriet Brinton at Routledge, we may never have started writing this book. Special thanks are due to our family and friends who created the environment in which we were able to finish this book. In particular we would like to thank Jenny Hedström for her comments on early drafts of the manuscript, Professors Elżbieta Stadtmüller and Beata Ociepka for the loan (again!) of their office at the University of Wrocław, Robert Stradomski for sorting things out in Poland, Sandra Barkhof for her assistance in the drafting of requests and letters in German, and last but by no means least, many thanks to Marta Urbanek for acting as chauffeur and minder in Poland.

As our analysis shows, there is little doubt that some aspects of the German question will continue to play a role in European politics. As we go to press, a new war of words has erupted between some in Poland and Germany regarding restitution and compensation for losses and damage incurred during the Second World War and in its aftermath. The German question is no longer open, but neither has it been fully resolved. In this volume we hope to explain why this is so.

Karl Cordell and Stefan Wolff
Plymouth and Bath, February 2005

1 The German question and German foreign policy
A conceptual introduction

Introduction

During his historic visit to Warsaw in December 1970 to sign the second of the so-called *Ostverträge*, German Chancellor Willy Brandt made a historic and unprecedented gesture. During a commemorative act for the victims of the Warsaw Uprising of August–October 1944 he fell to his knees in an act of apology for what Germans had done to Poland during the Second World War. Some twenty-four years later, in August 1994 on the occasion of the 50th anniversary of that same uprising, German President Roman Herzog also apologized for German actions during the war in a speech in Warsaw and expressed Germany's unconditional and strong support for Poland's accession to NATO and EU. A further ten years later, German Chancellor Gerhard Schröder paid respect to the heroism of those that participated in the Warsaw Uprising and to the contribution they made in liberating Europe from the Nazis. His speech, however, dealt also with a different kind of past and present. In categorically ruling out German governmental support for any claims for either restitution of property or financial compensation on the part of the Polish state to Germans expelled from Poland in the aftermath of the war and in denouncing plans to create a Centre against Expulsions in Berlin, Schröder took the opportunity to reassure Poles that, from a German perspective, there was no longer a German or any other question related to the consequences of the Second World War that remained open.

These three events, stretching over a period of three decades and across two distinct periods of European post-war history, are highly indicative of the change and continuity that characterizes German–Polish relations in particular, and Germany's relations with the countries of Central and Eastern Europe in general. They emphasize the significance of history to contemporary bilateral relations and they highlight, in the public debates preceding and following each individual event, the persistence and consistency of specific norms according to which Germany has conducted its foreign policy towards Central and Eastern Europe despite problems and discord at the bilateral and German domestic levels. To the extent that these problems and divisions continue to exist, they also highlight that despite the enormous progress that has been made in achieving reconciliation between Germany and its Eastern neighbours, several aspects of the so-called German question are still of political significance with regard to Germany's relations with some of its neighbours in Eastern and Central Europe.

Their significance, however, is also of another kind. Each of the events referred to in the previous paragraph self-evidently refers to Germany's relations with Poland. For reasons that are elaborated upon elsewhere in the book, there is no single comparable event of similar nature and significance in German–Czech relations. This is astounding in more than one way. When compared with Poland, the rifts between Germany and Czechoslovakia (as of 1993, the Czech Republic) were similarly deep, the wounds inflicted by Germany on that country in the context the Second World War were as painful, and the magnitude of the post-war expulsion of ethnic Germans were, proportionately, at least as great. Yet, it took until 1973 until a treaty similar to that with Poland was concluded (and only after Soviet pressure on the Czechoslovak regime) and afterwards there was no measurable improvement in relations between the two countries. Since 1990, relations have been at best civil, and at times openly hostile, with a low point being reached with the cancellation of an official visit by Chancellor Schröder in 2001. If anything, and in clear contrast to German–Polish relations, the state and development of German–Czech relations seems to underscore the continuing significance of the so-called German question rather than its resolution even at the level of political elites.

Taking these observations as a starting point, this book explores the main determinants of German foreign policy-making and implementation in relation to Poland and the Czech Republic. Our main aim is to show the basic continuity of German Ostpolitik since the late 1960s to the present and to explain it in terms of the development of, and adherence to, a set of norms to which the overwhelming majority of the German political class and public subscribes, regardless of changes in the broader regional and international context in which Ostpolitik is formulated and implemented. This is not to say that Ostpolitik has not been affected by such changes. It fared better during periods of détente during the Cold War and has had unprecedented success since the end of the Cold War. Rather our point is that German Ostpolitik priorities – peace, reconciliation and 'change through rapprochement' – have remained largely the same while the opportunities for them to succeed have at times gradually and at other times rapidly increased. Focusing on two distinct cases – Poland and the Czech Republic – allows us also to determine the degree to which opportunities created in a broader regional and international context are used to pursue the priorities set and accepted by Ostpolitik and to explain the somewhat different outcomes that they generated in relation to the current state of German–Polish and German–Czech relations.

In this first chapter, we will set out a theoretical framework for a foreign policy analysis of Ostpolitik. However, as this is intrinsically linked with the German question as such, we first need to explore the conceptual context to which this theoretical framework is then to be applied in order for it to be relevant for our subsequent analysis.

Conceptualizing the German question

From about the time of the French Revolution in the late eighteenth century to the present, the history of Europe could be told as a history of different national questions large and small. Many are and were intimately linked to one another. Most at some point caused conflict and sometimes full-scale warfare, and all, in one way or another, related to questions of nationhood and territory. In this sense, the German question is not very different from, say, the Russian or Albanian questions. However, what distinguishes it from any other national question in Europe are the sheer extremes to which the German question has driven the continent, and on two occasions ultimately the entire world.

A single German question as such has never existed; rather, a multitude of issues have arisen from a fundamental problem of European politics, namely the fact that the territory of any German state or states has never included the entirety of the German nation. A unified German state only came into existence in the second half of the nineteenth century, stretching from Alsace and Lorraine in today's France all the way across Central Europe to East Prussia, known today as District Kaliningrad and as such part of the Russian Federation. Although this German state included some 60 million Germans at the time of its foundation, large groups of ethnic Germans remained outside the territory of the state. This was most obviously the case with Germans in the Austro-Hungarian Empire, who, although not a majority in numerical terms and widely dispersed outside the territory of today's Republic of Austria, played a dominant role in the empire. A third group of Germans, who hardly ever figured in the national or territorial calculations of German nationalists, were the Germans of Switzerland. They had entered into a confederal state with three, significantly smaller, other ethnic groups (of French, Italian and Romansh origin) several hundred years earlier. Following a short civil war-like conflict in 1848, the Swiss federation as it exists today was formed. The only other significant group of ethnic Germans living outside the confines of these three states were those Germans who had emigrated to Russia since the middle of the eighteenth century and lived there as colonists, enjoying specific privileges granted by imperial decree.

Quite clearly, the German situation, or rather the situation of Germans, is no exception in this respect. The demarcation of borders in Europe, and particularly in Central and Eastern Europe, happened according to the interests of the great powers rather than according to the apparent distribution of ethnic groups. From the late nineteenth century, the gradual withdrawal from Europe of the Ottoman Empire and the dissolution of the Austro-Hungarian Empire in the early twentieth century created a series of new states, hardly any of which was either homogenous or contained all members of the titular ethnic group within its boundaries. The settlement patterns of diverse ethnic groups that had grown over centuries of imperial hegemony in Central and Eastern Europe would, at best, have made it extremely difficult to create states in which political and ethnic boundaries would coincide. The fact that borders were established in accordance with the interests of the great powers rendered any such attempt impossible. In addition, even though a Romantic version of nationalism had become a powerful ideology in the region, not all ethnic groups had a well-established national identity in the sense of expressing a preference for their own or any specific state at all. Instead some of them had developed strong regional identities that were, in the first instance, not focused on ethnicity. Nevertheless, nationalism had a tremendous impact on inter-ethnic relations in the region, and the three waves of state 'creation' – at the Congress of Berlin in 1878, after the First and Second Balkan Wars in 1912/1913, and after the First World War in 1919 – left their mark in Central and Eastern Europe by establishing ethnically plural states whose constituent ethnic groups were ill at ease with each other.

The Romantic conception of the nation held by increasing numbers of people at both mass and elite level throughout Central and Eastern Europe additionally complicated matters. It defined the nation as being based on shared cultural, linguistic and customary traits within a geographic and demographic context in which migration, colonization and conquest more than anything else had shaped the ethnic composition of the four empires. The Russian, German, Ottoman and Austro-Hungarian Empires were truly multi-national entities. The German Empire stood out among them as it was a latecomer in the sense of nation-state building. By the time the first German nation-state was founded in 1871, an understanding of what the German nation was had existed for much longer: and this leads us to the 'first set' of German questions.

'Where and what is Germany?' is a common way of paraphrasing the German question, focusing on the nature and content of a German national identity, and thus on a question that is primarily directed at the Germans themselves. At the same time, however, it also gives rise to broader considerations about Germany's place and role in European and world politics. These are considerations that have been made by Germany's neighbours, and that more often than not in the twentieth century, amounted to serious concerns for the security and stability of the European and international orders. From that perspective, the German question is also about how Germany can fit into any system of states without threatening, or being perceived as threatening by, its neighbours. Many answers have been given to this particular dimension of the German question.

A loose confederation of states was the answer of the Congress of Vienna in 1815. A German nation-state excluding Austria was the answer provided in 1871. A state truncated territorially and burdened by reparations was the solution decided upon in the Treaty of Versailles in 1919. An enlarged Germany was the answer provided by the Munich Agreement of 1938. An occupied and subsequently divided state was in effect the chosen solution of the Potsdam Conference of 1945, and a unified Germany firmly integrated in NATO and the EU was the answer in 1990. In the long term, with the exception of the latter (so far), none of these proposed solutions to the German question proved to be stable, or even viable, although the reasons for the eventual collapse of each settlement varied considerably over time. What they all had in common was that they only partially addressed the complexity of the German question.

This complexity arises from the fact that the German question is a multidimensional phenomenon. It has been, and to some extent still is, first and foremost a political problem. As such, the German question has been about whether there should be one German nation-state or more, what the borders and internal political structures of such a state (or states) should be, with which methods nation-state building should be achieved and what consequences this would have for Europe and the world (Geiss 1990: 22). At the same time, the German question is also a cultural problem, or, more precisely, a problem of defining German culture. Related to this is the question of how to define a German identity and thus determine who is German. Obviously, the cultural and the political dimensions of the German question are inextricably linked through time, albeit in different ways.

A foreign policy analysis approach to the study of the German question

The complexity and multidimensionality of the German question manifests itself in the (long-term) links between domestic and international dimensions. Political and ethnic aspects of the issue originate from the fact that the essence of the German question is the incompatibility between (the borders of) its territory and (the perceived size of) its nation, and the way in which Germany and European/world powers have responded to this problem. This complex and multidimensional context thus forms the background to our analysis and simultaneously defines its parameters. Focusing on Ostpolitik as a specific instance of German foreign policy, the German response to the incompatibility of territory and nation becomes the object of our analysis. In other words, what we are examining is the factors that determine the course of German foreign policy towards Central and Eastern Europe, specifically towards Poland and the Czech Republic. We limit ourselves to developments in the period after the Cold War, but make a case for the explanatory value of historical developments that reach back much farther. The bottom line of our argument is that long-standing links between the three states and nations, and especially events immediately before, during, and after the Second World War and the interpretation of those relations on the part of the German political elite have given rise to a set of norms that have governed the conduct of German foreign policy since the late 1960s in the sense of setting out the objectives of Ostpolitik and the appropriate means with which to pursue them.

Our approach is thus informed by both foreign policy analysis and constructivist international relations theory. Exploring the main tenets of both and establishing links between them is the task of the remainder of this chapter that will allow us to develop an analytical framework that we can subsequently apply to our comparative study of German policy towards Poland and the Czech Republic in the post-Cold War period.

The study of foreign policy

There are many definitions of foreign policy. In a very broad approach to foreign policy analysis, Mark Webber and Michael Smith consider it to be composed 'of the goals sought, values set, decisions made and actions taken by states, and national governments on their behalf, in the context of the external relations of national societies' and to constitute 'an attempt to design, manage and control the foreign relations of national societies' (Webber and Smith 2002: 9). Christopher Hill, in a more succinct definition, sees foreign policy as 'the sum of official external relations conducted by an independent actor (usually a state) in international relations' (Hill 2003: 3). Comparing these two recent definitions to one developed by George Modelski almost four decades earlier, reveals that the understanding of the object of foreign policy analysis has not changed significantly since the early 1960s. According to Modelski, 'foreign policy is the system of activities evolved by communities for changing the behaviour of other states and for adjusting their own activities to the international environment' (Modelski 1962: 6ff.). Even though the conceptualization of the object of foreign policy analysis itself has not changed much over the years, the context in which it is studied has undergone profound changes that James N. Rosenau described in the introduction to a volume on *New Directions in the Study of Foreign Policy* (Herman, Kegley and Rosenau 1987) as follows:

> The study of foreign policy [has] become ever more challenging and intriguing ... not only because the danger of conflict and violence grows with the growing overlap of groups and nations, but also because the sources and consequences of foreign policy have become inextricably woven into the patterns of interdependence.
>
> (Rosenau 1987: 2)

Since Rosenau's observation this interdependence has, if anything, grown and has become a major cornerstone of foreign policy analysis in the age of globalization. Interdependence is clearly also a significant feature of the background of our own analysis in this volume. It manifests itself at different levels and in different dimensions. First and foremost, there is interdependence between the national, bilateral and broader regional and international levels of analysing German Ostpolitik. For example, during the Cold War, domestic debates over what was deemed acceptable in the efforts of West Germany to normalize relations with the countries of Central and Eastern Europe and achieve peace, reconciliation and change in the political regimes of these countries was inextricably linked with the room for manoeuvre that successive German governments had and claimed for themselves. West Germany's sovereignty and room for manoeuvre was in turn constrained by a geopolitical situation determined by relations between the Cold War superpowers, who exercised considerable influence on the policies pursued by their allies.

Interdependence is one key feature of what many scholars refer to as the foreign policy arena in which factors located in the international, governmental and domestic contexts interact with one another and determine the course and outcome of specific foreign policies (Webber and Smith 2002: 31). To place the illustration of the arena in which Ostpolitik was and is conducted given above into a more general and abstract context, one could say that the international context consists of military, political, economic and geographic factors that determine hierarchies of power and influence (ibid.). For its part, the governmental context is perhaps best described in terms of Mark Allinson's bureaucratic model of foreign policy analysis, i.e. a process of interdepartmental bargaining. The domestic context of foreign policy, especially in liberal democratic states, is determined by constraints that electoral accountability, the legal and constitutional order of a given country and the strength of particularist interests of specific pressure groups put on the autonomy of foreign policy decision makers (cf. Webber and Smith 2002: 70ff.). Contemporary foreign policy analysis thus stresses 'the open interplay of multiple factors, domestic and international' (Hill 2003: 8) as 'foreign policy has its domestic sources, and domestic policy has its foreign influences' (ibid.: 31).

The complexity and multidimensionality of the foreign policy process creates a number of conceptual and empirical problems. These include the delineation of boundaries between foreign and domestic policy, the distinction between grand foreign policy designs and the 'habitual responses to events occurring in the international environment', and the acquisition of accurate information on the foreign policy process (White 1989: 5–10).[1] These are challenges with which we were confronted when carrying out the research that underpins our argument. The delineation of boundaries between foreign and domestic policy was a key issue, especially given the context of our analysis in the German question, which, as shown earlier, is in itself a multidimensional phenomenon straddling the boundaries of the domestic and international spheres. Yet, just as much as the German question not only straddles these boundaries but also creates strong interdependencies between phenomena in both spheres, we found that a strict distinction between issues of foreign and domestic policy was either straightforward or unnecessary. For example, electoral considerations that German political parties have made in relation to the recognition or non-recognition of Poland's western border clearly fell into the area of domestic policy calculation with an impact on the content of foreign policy. On the other hand, the relationships that successive German governments developed with the main domestic pressure group in relation to Ostpolitik, namely the various expellee associations, were of themselves an issue that had both domestic and foreign policy implications. Rather than debating whether the expellee issue was a domestic or international factor, we decided to treat it as a distinct factor in its own right and explore both its domestic and international dimensions and the influence of the expellees upon Germany's foreign policy.

Ostpolitik is one of the few, if not the only quasi-autonomous, or unilateral, foreign policy contribution that the Federal Republic of Germany made between the 1960s and the end of the Cold War (cf. Allen and Webber 2002: 197). Our interest during this period and beyond is primarily in its grand design, in Ostpolitik as a broadly conceived strategy of foreign policy to achieve peace, reconciliation and regime change. While an analysis of this kind cannot ignore a consideration of the more mundane aspects of foreign policy, our argument that Ostpolitik is an example of German foreign policy continuity based on the persistence of and adherence to a set of norms is much better pursued in the context foreign policy as grand design.

The final challenge to foreign policy analysis identified by White – the acquisition of accurate information – is a problem that can only be partially avoided and addressed. While archival material for the post-1990 period is generally not yet accessible to researchers, many of the key players in Germany, Poland and the Czech Republic are still alive and their memories are fresh. Consequently, interviews became one of our main strategies by which information was acquired and through access to a multitude of actors in all three countries we were in a relatively good position to engage critically with the information provided by them and to judge its accuracy. Thus, the main elements, from a research design point of view, of our analytical framework for an analysis of Ostpolitik as a distinct phenomenon of German foreign policy can be located at different levels:

- The German domestic context: public discourse; political parties; expellee pressure groups.
- The German governmental context: individual political leaders and their skills and visions; specific features of the foreign policy making

system (including institutional culture and administrative capacity); availability and the commitment of resources to the pursuit of specific foreign policy objectives.

• The bilateral context: historical legacy of bilateral relations; perceptions of German intentions and actions in Poland and the Czech Republic; expectations about the course of bilateral relations in all three countries.

• The international context: constraints and opportunities in the regional (i.e. European) and wider international context (Cold War versus post-Cold War constellations).[2]

This general analytical framework provides only a partial foundation for the main argument that we develop in greater detail in subsequent chapters. That is, that long-standing links between the three states and nations, and especially events immediately before, during and after the Second World War and their interpretation by the German political elite have given rise to a set of norms that, since the late 1960s, have governed the conduct of German foreign policy in the sense of setting out the objectives of Ostpolitik and the appropriate means with which to pursue them. While this accounts for those elements of our argument that focus on the importance of German political actors and the nature and significance of bilateral relations in a wider regional and international context, it does not fully explain why a particular set of norms has governed this specific dimension of German foreign policy – Ostpolitik – rather than national and particularly security interests. In order to locate the missing element of the theoretical foundation of our argument and in order to be able to comprehensively test our proposition, we must now turn to more general conceptions and theories of international relations and link them with the analysis of foreign policy in our specific case.

The constructivist theory of international relations and foreign policy analysis of the German question

Since the early 1990s, constructivist international relations theory has emerged as a major third school of thought set against (neo-)realism and (neo-)liberalism. It derives from a metatheory of social constructivism (e.g. Berger and Luckmann 1966), that seeks to explain 'how agency and interaction produce and reproduce structures of shared knowledge over time' (Wendt 2001: 421) in the conduct of international relations. Constructivist international relations theory, therefore, is not a foreign policy theory. The best effort to create a constructivist foreign policy theory was undertaken in an essay by Henning Boekle, Volker Rittberger and Wolfgang Wagner (2001), in which they proceed from the basic constructivist assumption that 'actors follow a logic of appropriateness rather than a logic of consequentiality' (ibid.: 105). A constructivist foreign policy theory, naturally builds on the two foundational principles of constructivist international relations theory – the claim 'that the fundamental structures of international politics are social rather than strictly material ... and that these structures shape actors' identities and interests, rather than just their behaviour' (Wendt 2001: 417). In the specific context of our analysis, we share Boekle, Rittberger and Wagner's (2001: 105) assumption that 'social norms rather than other ideational factors are best suited to explain foreign policy'. This assumption does not contradict constructivist international relations theory which places significant emphasis on the fact that the objectivity of social structures 'depends on shared knowledge' (Wendt 2001: 419). Rather, it identifies one key component of shared knowledge – social norms – that are 'seen as the more influential the more they are shared among the units of a social system and the more precisely they distinguish between appropriate and inappropriate behaviour' (Boekle, Rittberger and Wagner 2001: 105). As such they have 'an immediate orientation to behaviour' (ibid.: 107). By referring to a set of widely shared norms, actors are able to choose *appropriate* courses of action in a given situation that are congruent with preferences defined 'in accordance with the goals that have been designated as legitimate' (ibid.) on the basis of social norms. In other words, because social norms rule out the pursuit of certain goals as illegitimate, they prescribe appropriate courses of action on the basis of value-based expectations of behaviour.

The link between social norms and actual foreign policy behaviour is seen in the socialization processes that foreign policy decision makers undergo both domestically and internationally, i.e. they learn what kind of foreign policy behaviour is expected of them in the domestic and international arenas in which they have to make choices (Boekle, Rittberger and Wagner 2001: 105ff.) Against the background of our conceptualization of the German question, it is easy to see why both societal and international norms are relevant to discussion of German foreign policy in general and in particular in relation to Ostpolitik as one of its distinct manifestations. We stated earlier that Ostpolitik was the only unilateral foreign policy contribution that the Federal Republic of Germany made between the 1960s and the end of the Cold War, which could, quite easily, be interpreted within a neo-realist conception of international relations theory. This is so because the strategy was developed as a consequence of the prevailing balance of power rather than as a result of a conscious course of action with regard to West Germany's relations with the countries of Central and Eastern Europe. However, if balance-of-power considerations had been the driving force behind Ostpolitik during the period between the late 1960s and the end of the Cold War, one would have had to expect a change in Ostpolitik from the early 1990s onward. Within a neo-realist conception of international relations, the significant change in Germany's foreign policy arena, and especially the increase in power that it experienced following German unification, would have inevitably led to a more assertive Ostpolitik.[3]

Instead, as we argue below, the goals of Ostpolitik remained broadly speaking the same, as did the means by which they were pursued, precisely because the societal and international norms determine which courses of action are appropriate in the context of Ostpolitik.

In order to develop a persuasive argument to this effect, however, we first of all need to identify the relevant social norms at the domestic and international levels. Here we can again rely on Boekle, Rittberger and Wagner (2001: 124–132), who suggest the following indicators of international and societal norms:

- indicators of international norms
  - general international law
  - legal acts of international organizations
  - final acts of international conferences

- indicators of societal norms
  - constitutional and legal order of a society
  - party programmes and election platforms
  - parliamentary debates
  - survey data.

While our study examines these different categories in order to demonstrate that the norms that guided German Ostpolitik decision-making during the Cold War period have not changed since the end of the Cold War, we need to show first of all that the indicators identified by Boekle, Rittberger and Wagner at a more general level bear relevance for the study of the specific foreign policy area of Ostpolitik. As far as general international law is concerned, this category primarily refers to treaties, customary international law, general principles of law, and to judicial decisions and opinions (Boekle, Rittberger and Wagner 2001: 124–127). The relevance of this category for our discussion is obvious. Since the early 1970s Germany has entered into several legally binding treaties with Poland and Czechoslovakia/the Czech Republic and is also bound by the obligations that derive from its membership in the United Nations, Organization for Security and Co-operation in Europe (OSCE) and the EU. These include limitations placed on the use of force, the respect for other states' sovereignty and territorial integrity. Germany has always been an advocate of the employment of peaceful and diplomatic means for the resolution of disputes, and in particular in relation to Ostpolitik, judicial decisions and opinions at domestic and European level have been signifi-cant in determining (and post hoc confirming) the appropriateness of specific courses of action taken by successive governments. As a member of the EU, Germany is bound by legal acts of this organization that at the same time it shapes significantly. The critical role that Ostpolitik has played in making the process of the Conference on Security and Co-operation in Europe (CSCE) possible and the mutually sustaining relationship that the two have had since the Final Act of the Helsinki Conference of the CSCE of 1975[4] indicates the significance that can be attached to this process and the principles upon which it was founded in shaping norms that have guided the formulation and implementation of Ostpolitik.

In the light of the multidimensional nature of the German question explored at the beginning of this chapter, it is also easy to see how societal norms, manifest in the German constitutional and legal order, in party programmes and election platforms of the major political parties, and in parliamentary debates and survey data will be relevant for our analysis. We also examine the significance of Germany's constitutional imperative to secure the nation's reunification in peace and freedom and the constitutional definition of the entitlement to German citizenship that have been important factors in shaping Ostpolitik. We assess how these and other widely accepted and respected foundational principles of the West German post-war constitutional and legal system and their foreign policy implications for Ostpolitik have been reflected in party programmes, election platforms, parliamentary debates and survey data. Yet, by no means do we suggest that there has always been a complete all-encompassing consensus about Ostpolitik in German society or even among its political class. Rather, we aim to show that this consensus developed during the 1960s and 1970s and only gradually began to encompass ever wider sections of the political class and the general public in the Federal Republic. This became possible only because despite the re-orientation towards a more active policy aimed at peace, reconciliation and regime change within the relatively narrow confines of the Cold War order, the architects of Ostpolitik never questioned another fundamental norm with which German foreign policy had to comply – to maintain the close and permanent ties with Western political, security and economic structures that had been established since the early 1950s. Thus, the gradual development of a consensus on the value-based norms governing Ostpolitik was only possible as a double consensus on *Westbindung* and Ostpolitik (Erb 2003: 48).

This also illustrates the close and dynamic relationship between societal and international norms. These were very clear at the international level with regard to what appropriate West German foreign policy behaviour should look like. These norms were by no means identical, but they overlapped on crucial issues, such as territorial claims and the use of force. Eventually, the success of Ostpolitik in establishing a modus vivendi that allowed both *Westbindung* and the pursuit of a policy of reconciliation, peace and regime change towards the countries of the communist bloc in Central and Eastern Europe contributed to the broadening consensus on the norms that governed Ostpolitik. In other words, our argument is not that certain norms suddenly appeared on the horizon of German foreign policy and were immediately embraced by political elites and the general public, but rather that:

[a] number of factors combined during the late 1960s to transform the context of German foreign policy. The most deliberate was the reorientation of policy on reunification ... The formulation of an active Ostpolitik, and Willy Brandt's determined diplomacy ... succeeded over a period of years in reconciling West Germans to the reality of two German states and in re-establishing a modus vivendi with Bonn's eastern neighbours.

(Wallace 1978: 40)

If we briefly return to the levels of analysis that we identified earlier as relevant for our examination of Ostpolitik in relation to German diplomacy vis-à-vis Poland and the Czech Republic, we can quite easily demonstrate that indicators of societal and international norms such as those suggested by Boekle, Rittberger and Wagner (2001) can be shown to be present at all levels of analysis:

- in the German *domestic context* in the form of public discourse, survey data, party programmes and election manifestos, as well as election results;
- in the German *governmental context* in the form of parliamentary debates and judicial decisions of the constitutional court;
- in the *bilateral context* in the form of treaties and declarations;
- in the *international context* in the form of the CSCE/OSCE process and in German participation in the EU and the endorsement of EU enlargement.

Examining the relevant indicators of norms at all four levels during the Cold War period and since the early 1990s enables us to present a conclusive argument as to why, despite changes in the domestic and international environments, German Ostpolitik has remained remarkably consistent.

Accounting for difference in outcomes: German–Polish and German–Czech relations compared

We stated earlier that the essence of our argument is that the principal course of Ostpolitik has not changed with the advent of the post-Cold War era because, in accordance with the constructivist outlook on foreign policy analysis, the norms underlying Ostpolitik – peace, reconciliation and regime change – have remained the same. Consistency in policy goals and means, however, is no guarantee of identical or at least similar policy outcomes. This is particularly the case for such foreign policy outcomes that depend not only on decisions made and implemented in one country, but also on the response to them in the country targeted by these decisions. Specifically with regard to our comparison of German–Polish and German–Czech relations, reconciliation is not something that can simply be willed about by decisions made in Bonn or Berlin, but requires a specific response in order for it to succeed.

Within a research design influenced by constructivist international relations theory, different policy outcomes can be accounted for by the presence of different social norms. As we noted earlier, Germany, Poland and the Czech Republic form what we refer to as a triangle of fate, i.e. a regional substructure 'in which interactions [are] more intense than at the global level' (Allen 1989: 68). This has several implications for the establishment of any causal relations between norms and policy outcomes. First, it means that international norms, especially in the post-Cold War period and the context of EU enlargement are likely to be very similar, while differences in norms at domestic, governmental and bilateral levels are not precluded. Therefore, we need to consider whether, within the broad general framework of Ostpolitik, there are different norms in relation to German policy towards Poland compared to the Czech Republic, and we need to examine whether there are differences in norms at any of these levels in the two target countries of German Ostpolitik.

This would suggest that, in order to find an answer to our second question concerning the reasons for different policy outcomes vis-à-vis Poland and the Czech Republic, the detection of differences in norms might be sufficient. Yet, while this might be satisfactory within a framework that establishes the applicability and validity of foreign policy analysis informed by constructivist international relations theory, it is in itself not an answer that fully explains outcome differences as it says little about why there are, if any, different norms. Subsequent to demonstrating the existence of different norms at the domestic, governmental and bilateral levels in the three countries, we will therefore probe deeper into the chain of causality and examine the reasons for this in both historical and contemporary developments.

The research design implemented

In the chapters that follow we undertake a comprehensive comparative analysis of German Ostpolitik vis-à-vis Poland and the Czech Republic by examining societal and international norms and their impact on foreign policy making in Germany, as well as the significance of relevant norms in Poland and the Czech Republic for the outcomes of Ostpolitik. The next two chapters provide an overview of the historical background to German–Polish and German–Czech relations and place the subsequent analysis in its contemporary, post-Cold War environment. Following on from these more historical observations, Chapter 4 looks at developments in the three countries' relations since 1990. We then focus on the German domestic context and its international and bilateral settings by exploring the role of the major players in Germany – the political parties and the expellee organizations – and the way in which they have contributed to the formulation and implementation of Ostpolitik. The combined focus on actors and issues then continues in Chapter 7 when we turn to the role of ethnic German minorities in Poland and the Czech Republic. Here, as in the preceding chapters, we identify the impact of different norms on policy formulation and implementation in Germany and its two eastern neighbours, as well as considering the dynamism in bilateral relations against the background of changing international conditions. Combining historical narrative with empirical analysis, the material presented in these chapters has enabled us to summarize and conclude our discussion in Chapter 8 – demonstrating, on the one hand, that German Ostpolitik has remained norm-consistent throughout the period under examination, and that the norms themselves have remained largely identical, thus accounting for the basic continuity of German Ostpolitik. On the other hand, we will show in this penultimate chapter how subtle and not so subtle differences in societal norms in all three countries and in relation to their bilateral relations provide a convincing argument accounting for the somewhat different policy outcomes of post-Cold War Ostpolitik vis-à-vis Poland and the Czech Republic. The final chapter assesses what the future is likely to hold for the relationships between the three countries.

2   A usable past?

German–Czech and German–Polish relations before the Second World War

For hundreds of years, ethnocultural differences between people(s) were neither a problem between individuals, nor a source of mass political mobilization. Yet, with the emergence of nationalism as a political ideology and the emergence of the nation-state as the primary principle of political organization and of regulating relations between such entities, ethnicity became a factor in domestic and international politics. Rival nationalisms clashed as demands for the creation of nation-states resulted in different aspirant national movements laying claim to identical stretches of territory, and sometimes to the same groups of people.

In Central, Eastern and South-eastern Europe, the rise and demise of empires, migration within and between them, and the inevitability of incompatible ethnic and political borders provided the background against which such clashes happened. One example of such a clash was the ensuing and gradually escalating tension between Germany and the nascent Polish and Czech(oslovak) national movements. The question of Germany and its relationship with the Czech Republic and Poland is central to this volume. Not only is Germany an obvious component of this 'triangle of fate', disputes between Poland and Czechoslovakia (as was) on one side, and Germany on the other, have often been centred upon a contest for territory, and in the case of Poland and Germany especially, for hearts and minds.

The multifaceted and complex relationship that began to develop between the three entities can, from a German perspective at least, be illustrated quite vividly with the example of citizenship. For most of the twentieth century, German citizenship was to all intents and purposes determined according to descent. The 1913 *Reichs- und Staatsange-hörigkeitsgesetz* (Reichs Citizenship Act) determined that only descendants of those defined as Germans in German law, irrespective of whether they felt themselves to be German or spoke German, could be German citizens. As we shall see in the case of Upper Silesia, many of the locals did not feel themselves to be German, despite fulfilling the legal criteria, and in Masuria, many nationally conscious Germans in fact spoke only the local form of Polish. The 1913 Act deliberately adopted the principle of *ius sanguinis* in order to promote and preserve the ethnic tradition of the German nation-state established in 1871, and to maintain links with ethnic Germans who lived outside its political boundaries. The complexity of this issue is reflected in the difficulty that exists in identifying exact English terms for the three key concepts of German legal and political thought in this respect. These are: *Staatsangehörigkeit* (defined as the formal legal relationship between citizen and state); *Staatsbürgerschaft* (defined as the participatory membership in a polity or commonwealth) and *Volkszugehörigkeit* (defined in terms of ethnocultural identity) (Brubaker 1992: 50ff.). Until the changes in German citizenship law at the end of the twentieth century, this meant that conscious possession of a German ethnocultural identity normally was an essential condition for full political participation within the political process. In turn, the link established between *Volkszugehörigkeit*, on the one hand, and *Staatsbürgerschaft* and *Staatsangehörigkeit*, on the other, was problematic inasmuch as it gave rise to potentially conflicting loyalties. The inter-war period is probably the best-documented example of how such conflicting loyalties were instrumental and eventually became self-fulfilling prophecies. The rise of the Nazis in Germany and the way in, and purpose for, which they established links with ethnic Germans across Europe was perceived as a threat by many (neighbouring) governments. The response of these governments was to curtail the rights of German minorities. This in turn encouraged ever greater numbers of people from the minority communities to put their faith in Hitler, as was most obviously the case with the Sudeten Germans, but to a lesser extent also with German minorities elsewhere in Central and Eastern Europe. Thus, the ethnonational foundations of *Staatsangehörigkeit* and *Staatsbürgerschaft* indirectly had disastrous consequences for those groups of people they were designed to protect. It was precisely some of these consequences, namely the expulsion of, and subsequent discrimination against the remaining members of German minorities in Central and Eastern Europe that made it apparently impossible and politically undesirable to change German law in this respect. Any such change could have deprived the *Aussiedler* (ethnic Germans who emigrated to the Federal Republic from Central and Eastern Europe between 1950 and 1993)[1] of their entitlement to German citizenship, the possibility of migration and the consequent availability of full civil rights and liberties in Germany. At the political level it was also important for the Federal Republic to employ such legal devices in order to demonstrate to Germans at home and abroad that those left behind had not been abandoned. In the case of Czechoslovakia/the Czech Republic, the ethnic/national identity of the residual German population has not been subject to the same level of dispute as has the national provenance and consciousness of their counterparts in post-war Poland. This difference between the Czech and Polish cases is but one of many we shall encounter in this volume. Bearing such dissimilarities in mind, we now need to examine in more detail the roots of the contemporary relationship.

The origins of German minorities in Central and Eastern Europe

If we talk about the complexity and multidimensionality of Germany's relationship with Poland and the Czech Republic, we must acknowledge the (long-term) link between domestic and international dimensions and between the political and ethnic aspects. In different ways, this link has persisted throughout the existence of the German question, particularly during the inter-war period and since the end of the Second World War. Yet, post-1945 developments can only be understood fully and properly on the basis of the historical developments that 'created' ethnic Germans outside Germany.

Before turning to an examination of Czech–German and Polish–German relations since 1990, it is therefore necessary to take several steps back and explore the origins of ethnic German minorities in Central and Eastern Europe. In so doing we will be able to trace the multiple developments that gave rise to their settlement across this part of the continent. This is of importance to our theme because these minorities and their relationship with their (putative) kin- and host-states played a crucial role in the creation of the circumstances that have shaped Germany's post-Cold War relationship with the Czech Republic and Poland.

The origin of ethnic German communities lies in three distinct, but often inter-related, processes, namely conquest and colonization, migration and border changes. The latter is primarily a phenomenon of the twentieth century, connected most obviously with the peace settlements of Versailles (with Germany) and St Germain (with Austria) in 1919. The re-ordering of Europe after 1945 had a similarly profound territorial, demographic and political impact. Territorially it did so in relation to the expansion of the Soviet Union, the westward shift of Poland and the truncation of Germany. In demographic terms it did so in relation to movements of populations that resulted in the creation of ethnically more homogeneous states. Politically it did so through the determination of zones of influence in the context of the emerging bipolar world order.

If we turn the clock back even further, we find that Germanic colonization and migration to what are now Poland and the Czech Republic dates as far back as ninth-century Moravia (Otter 1994: 12). Similar processes became evident in the twelfth and thirteenth centuries in Pomerania, East Brandenburg, Bohemia and Silesia where local aristocrats were keen to develop their vast lands. To this end they actively sponsored immigration of Germanic settlers and gradually, for the most part, freely entered into the orbit of the Holy Roman Empire (of the German Nation). The ensuing Germanization process occurred at both mass and elite levels, through migration and cultural assimilation of the host-communities into the migrant communities, and quite unusually, not the other way round.

As for conquest, in the thirteenth century, the *Deutscher Ritterorden* (Teutonic Order) conquered most of today's Baltic states, i.e. Lithuania, Estonia and Latvia, as well as former East and West Prussia. As with the German colonists in other parts of Central and Eastern Europe, the Teutonic Knights had been invited by local aristocrats, in this case in 1225 by the Polish Prince Konrad of Masowia. As had earlier been the case in Central and Eastern Europe, religion played an important role in the politics of migration. The Roman Catholic Church was an important factor in promoting German cultural penetration and later identity shift. The Christian mission to areas such as Bohemia and Silesia was largely spearheaded by Germanic clergy. Having said that, elements of the Bohemian nobility tended towards Byzantium as a means of checking the influence of German-speaking aristocrats. It was only with the collapse of the Greater Moravian Empire between 903–906 and Bohemia's subsequent rapprochement with the Holy Roman Empire after 928 that the Catholic Church began to gain the upper hand in the battle for influence, hearts and minds. By 975, Byzantine influence had been completely eradicated from the area (Otter 1994: 13ff.).

Despite these and other rivalries, in Central Europe unlike in the Baltic area, conversion was achieved fairly peacefully, and German (or variants) of it, was established as the lay clerical language (Seibt 1997: 40–58). Over the generations, German as a language of communication spread from the clergy to the aristocracy and then throughout much of the rest of society. The spread of the language, combined with Germanic immigration, was crucial in facilitating an identity shift among the indigenous populations of the aforementioned areas. For example, Germanic merchants first took up residence in Prague as early as the eleventh century, and by the end of the thirteenth-century Germanic migration into Bohemia and Moravia reached new heights, as local landowners sought to improve their often under-populated lands (Otter 1994: 29ff.). As a consequence, the cultural and political orientation of Bohemia and Moravia changed even further. The formal accession of the Bohemian Crown to the Holy Roman Empire in 1356 was merely the logical culmination of this process.

Returning to the Teutonic Knights, we find that they were charged by local aristocrats with the task of subduing the non-Christian Baltic tribes, converting them and colonizing their lands. As a reward for their services, they were promised sovereignty over the conquered territory. However, unlike their counterparts in Central and Eastern Europe, the Baltic Prussians resisted violently, and it took the Knights almost forty years to 'pacify' them. Simultaneously, the Teutonic Order sought to free itself from Polish suzerainty and establish a Crusader kingdom along the Baltic littoral. Inevitably, they came into conflict with the Polish and Lithuanian kingdoms, and this dispute was settled only in 1410, with the defeat of the Knights at Grunwald/Tannenberg by the forces of the nascent Polish–Lithuanian Commonwealth.

The initial phase of colonization and conquest came to an end in the middle part of the fifteenth century. It was to re-commence at various times thereafter, as plague and warfare rendered vast areas almost totally devoid of human inhabitants. Although the region was wracked by religious wars and fell prey to Swedish and Russian imperial pretensions, few tangible signs of national antagonism can be discerned, irrespective of modern ideological interpretations of these conflicts. Despite the protestations of modern Romantic nationalists, no attempts at deracination took place. For example, in Bohemia and Moravia (as elsewhere in Europe), the population was differentiated in terms of estates. Of course, linguistic and cultural change demarcation also existed. It was, however, linked to movement from one estate to another (Hilf 1986: 19). Some consider the Hussite Wars of the early fifteenth century to be a partial exception to this rule. During the nineteenth and twentieth centuries, Czech(oslovak) nationalists were keen to portray the Protestant reformer Jan Hus as a proto-Czech(oslovak) nationalist. Although his movement gained more adherents from the 'Czech' population than the 'German' population, Hus had many supporters among the latter (Otter 1994: 46ff.). If nothing else, the Hussite Reformation serves as a useful example of how modern nationalist movements seek to re-interpret the past in order to render it useful. Similarly, others take the forcible re-Catholicization of the Slav population of Bohemia and Moravia by the German Habsburgs in the seventeenth century as being integral to the development of Czech national consciousness (Žák 2004). Such views contrast sharply with the post-modern orientation of contemporary German politician Antje Vollmer, who sees modern (i.e. post-1789) nationalism has having destroyed a previously harmonious relationship between Czechs, Slovaks and Germans, regardless of religious denomination or (proto-)national provenance (Vollmer 1997).

Although the exact point in time in Europe at which modern national consciousness began to develop may be open to debate, what cannot be disputed is that from the late eighteenth century onwards, the situation began to change. The age of nationalism had dawned. National identity, as opposed to religious denomination or feudal obligation increasingly became the marker of individual and collective differentiation. Some see the rise of nationalism as having disturbed a certain pre-existing inter-ethnic harmony in Europe (Vollmer 2002). This is undoubtedly true, but we should not lose sight of the various wars of religion that wracked Europe prior to the rise of nationalism.

Equally crucial to the changed situation in Europe was the rise of Prussia to great power status and the several wars fought by the kings of Prussia that resulted in territorial changes that affected the ethnic balance across Central Europe. In some areas, such as East Pomerania, and in parts of Upper Silesia and Bohemia, Germans, as a result, found themselves in a numeric minority where they had previously been part of larger areas in which they belonged to the ethnic majority. In addition, Germans and other ethnic groups in these areas were subjected to countervailing nationalist pressures with the German and Polish national movements competing with one another in a struggle for territory and very often the same hearts and minds.

Although the partitions of Poland between Germany, Austria and Russia in the late eighteenth century may not have been conceived as a nationalist enterprise, they did, however, provoke a nationalist backlash. Throughout the nineteenth century, in Russian and Prussian Poland in particular, various attempts were made to either Germanize or Russify the Polish population. In Prussian Poland, both inward migration from 'core' Prussian, and after 1871 German, territories coincided with rapid industrialization and helped to facilitate this programme. Paradoxically, the modernization process simultaneously stimulated the dissemination of the written Polish word and assisted the growth of a Polish national movement. The movement that emerged was split between two competing visions of who was a Pole and who should be considered to be a full citizen of the hypothesized Polish state. Leftists of various hues tended to hark back to the markedly cosmopolitan Polish–Lithuanian Commonwealth where ethnicity had played scarcely a role in the determination of social status. The political right, however, sought to create a Poland in which ethnic Poles would predominate both numerically and culturally. This contest was not settled until the late 1940s, when, as in Czechoslovakia, right and left united behind the exclusivist option of ethnically homogenized nation-states.

Although the ethnic boundary between German and Slav tended to be less blurred in Bohemia and Moravia than in Poland, what all the Czech and Polish lands had in common during the nineteenth century was internal and inward migration. Germans, Poles and Czechs from the geographical, ethnic and political centres migrated to newly industrializing areas. The results of this process were uneven. Nevertheless, it is true to say that the ethnic balance began to tilt away from Germany and towards the embryonic Czech and Polish national movements (Kořalka 2001: 40ff.). As a consequence of these changes the previous social status associated with being or becoming a German began to be called into question, and relations between Germans and other ethnic groups and emergent nations became more fraught. The reasons for these increasing tensions were many, and they differed across the region. Among the most prominent was the rise of competing doctrines of nationalism that resulted, among other things, in demands for an end to political privileges based upon linguistic and religious criteria and in the increasing appeal of the concept of popular sovereignty. To some extent, there was also growing competition for scarce economic resources. In areas that the Polish national movement laid claim to, and where there was a large German presence, Germanization had been a traditional route towards modernization. Similarly, conversion from Roman Catholicism to Protestantism was seen as being advantageous.

In Bohemia and Moravia, there was a similar crude equation between the adoption of German language and culture and religious discrimination.

In Bohemia and Moravia this trend had become particularly marked following the destruction of the indigenous Czech and German Protestant aristocracies at the Battle of the White Mountain in 1620. The Catholic Habsburgs discriminated against Protestant Slavs and Germans alike. They encouraged Catholic German migration, and Czech was reduced to the status of a peasant language. It was only in the wake of the Enlightenment that (modern) Czech began to re-appear as a literary and later (quasi-) official language (Otter 1994: 77ff.). In the nineteenth century, partly through mutation and partly as the result of a conscious political programme, the legitimate cultural, linguistic and religious grievances acquired a decidedly national flavour. František Palacký's rejection of Czech participation in the Frankfurt Parliament in 1848 marks the definitive parting of the ways that no subsequent half-hearted moves towards reform on the part of the Habsburgs could prevent.

During the nineteenth century, as ethnic and cultural markers and borders came to be defined and refined, the German and Czech populations homogenized as such and began to develop an increasingly antagonistic collective relationship. The process of industrialization is of importance here. It first became marked in Bohemia in the 1860s. The entrepreneurial or capitalist class was overwhelmingly German-speaking, of both Christian and Jewish denomination. Skilled workers and artisans tended also to be of a German background. This left the unskilled and semi-skilled who were disproportionately Czech speaking. Put crudely, the class hierarchy tended to re-enforce the ethnic pecking order. Not only that, huge numbers of Czechs migrated to previously compact German areas of settlement. As a result, the ethnographic map of Bohemia and Moravia began to alter. The changing ethnic composition of Prague is a primary, if largely forgotten example of this phenomenon. Czechs came to form a kind of national proletariat, many of whom had been uprooted from there isolated small towns and villages. They had then been thrust into alien cosmopolitan urban centres and usually into conditions worse than those they had left behind. Small wonder they became willing targets for propagandists who sought to simplify reality and to provide answers in terms of national difference and historic right. Society became divided into two mutually antagonistic camps, the Czech and the German (Hilf 1986: 50ff.). In Poland, the situation was broadly similar.

In Germany, Otto von Bismarck's response to problems with the Catholic population and the Polish element of that minority was one of repression. The government launched the *Kulturkampf* against its own Catholic citizens and against its Polish minority in particular. Moreover, under a law of 1886, the Prussians sought systematically to reduce the Polish element of the population in areas in which they formed a majority (Ther 2001: 48). Poles found themselves to be the object of officially sanctioned discrimination particularly in the spheres of education and agriculture. Indeed, 30,000 Poles were expelled from the *Provinz Posen* alone on various pretexts. Given such experiences of political and economic discrimination and of cultural and religious persecution at the hand of Germans, it should come as no surprise that, among both Czechs and Poles, the apostles of the new doctrine of nationalism questioned the legitimacy of Prussian and Habsburg rule and the pre-eminence of the German language and culture, and sought to return people to their 'original roots'.

The age of nations

The status of ethnic German communities as members of the dominant ethnic group in the German and Austro-Hungarian Empires was revoked unequivocally and finally only at the end of the First World War. Apart from anything else, the peace settlements of Versailles and St Germain resulted in the re-creation of Poland and the foundation of Czechoslovakia. The Polish politician Roman Dmowski had been proved correct: the re-establishment of Poland could only come in the wake of war between Germany and Russia. He was also, at least in part, correct in his belief that although there was a clash of interests between Russia and Poland, it was nothing compared to the antagonism between Germany and Poland (Walicki 2000: 26). With the re-creation of Poland, and the establishment of Czechoslovakia, two new states found themselves host to sizeable German minority populations. Given the demographic dynamics, the presence of a German minority in Czechoslovakia was, if anything, more problematic for the new Czechoslovak state than the corresponding minority was for Poland. In Czechoslovakia, a mix of four major population groups with none of them in an absolute numeric majority, dominated the scene. Czechs formed the largest group, followed by Germans, Slovaks and Hungarians. In addition, there was a sizeable number of Jews and Roma, not to mention Ruthenes. Apart from the Jews and the Roma, all lived territorially concentrated in distinct parts of the country and in such a way that irredentist claims by Germans and Hungarians constituted a significant factor in Czechoslovak politics from the day of the inception of the state.

In typical fashion, the settlement at the end of the First World War had addressed some aspects of the German question, ignored others and created new ones. This becomes apparent if we compare Eastern with Western Europe. In the west the emphasis had been on securing territorial changes that would increase the military capabilities of, and compensate France, Belgium and Italy. Placing Germany under unprecedented reparation payments and curtailing its industrial and military capacities was meant to prevent it from re-emerging as a, if not the, major economic, political and military power in Europe. In Central and Eastern Europe, the intentions were somewhat different. Here, the peace conferences sought to establish a new order that would satisfy the demands of the multiple national movements for the creation of independent nation-states. The great powers simultaneously sought to establish a regime under the auspices of the League of Nations that could ensure that those ethnic groups that were either not granted their own nation-state or that did not live on its territory would be sufficiently protected. In addition, considerations about the 'economic viability' of Poland and Czechoslovakia had led to the territories of these new states being rather ill defined in terms of their ethnic composition. Thus, not only was a situation created in which any stable political and economic development in Germany was precluded almost from the outset, but revisionist politicians in Germany were also given plenty of ammunition to hype up domestic (and, for example, in 1938 even international) political support for their revisionist goals. At the same time, some members of the increasingly dissatisfied German minorities in many of the states in Central and Eastern Europe served as willing agents of destabilization in the region. The rise of Nazism in the Weimar Republic was one of the first signs, albeit hardly a direct consequence, that the settlement of 1919 had, if anything, exacerbated the German question as a problem of European and international security.

Under the Treaty of Versailles, Germany lost substantial amounts of territory to Poland. The so-called Polish Corridor, which gave Poland access to the Baltic Sea, separated East Prussia from the rest of the territory of the Weimar Republic and contained large numbers of Germans who had been citizens of Germany before 1919. Upper Silesia was divided between Poland and Germany, thereby creating another significant ethnic German minority in Poland. Disputes over identity were by no means the sole province of governments – they even broke out within single families. In all, the territorial changes in Central and Eastern Europe after the end of the First World War left approximately 5 million ethnic Germans in countries outside Germany, Austria and Switzerland.

In 1931, Poland's German minority was calculated conservatively at 784,000. At the end of the First World War, Polish uprisings in Upper Silesia and Poznania had combined with a favourable diplomatic climate that resulted in Poland being able to push its westward boundary further than had originally been envisaged by the victorious Allies. In terms of population, this policy resulted in Poland acquiring more Germans than it had bargained for. However, as many of these Germans were considered by the Polish authorities to be Germanicized Poles, there was an assumption that they could easily be returned to the 'fabric of the nation'. Yet, there were also those whom the Poles did not necessarily want, and who themselves were not reconciled to Polish sovereignty. To complicate matters even further, many 'Germanicized Poles' were either actively hostile towards Poland, or at best ambiguous in their attitudes. For a variety of reasons through to 1939, the number of declared Germans living in Poland declined. Whatever the causes of this decline, it would not be correct to

say that this reduction was achieved as the happy consequence of socialization into the 'Polish hearth'. In fact, the bulk of the reduction can be
accounted for in two ways. The first is emigration to Germany – in part
voluntary and in part 'induced' – that happened in the wake of economic
and political problems in Poland. The second is the fact that many of the
remaining Germans switched nationality between censuses. Only in a
minority of cases was this as a result of the successful application of the
aforementioned socialization process. More commonly, however, it was
because people realized that by switching identities they would be regarded
with less suspicion and avoid discrimination. It is also important to note
that, in Upper Silesia in particular, identity was fluid and identification
with Germany, Poland or indeed Czechoslovakia was often situational,
conditional, flexible and contradictory.

In Czechoslovakia inter-communal tensions developed in a very similar
fashion as they did in Poland. After the First World War in Central and
Eastern Europe, the right to self-determination for Germans (and Hungarians) was applied only selectively. The Czechoslovak national movement
had the ear of the power brokers and thus gained a more sympathetic hearing at St Germain. Like virtually all of its Slavic counterparts, the Czechoslovak national movement was something of a paradox. Essentially
anti-German, it employed classic Herderian principles. Dominated by its radical wing, led, among others, by Tomáš G. Masaryk and Edvard Beneš, it
embodied stereotypical Romantic notions concerning the provenance, nature
and geographic extent of the Czechoslovak nation and its hypothesized state
(Gordon 1990: 102ff.). In the end, the national movement cast its maximal
demands to one side, and on 28 October 1918 Czechoslovakia was proclaimed, two weeks before the conclusion of the First World War. The circumstances surrounding the state's foundation were hardly auspicious.
Germans, Poles, Ukrainians, Jews and Hungarians were excluded from the
revolutionary assembly of November 1918 (Hilf 1986: 63). If, for example,
Vollmer (1997) claims that a Czechoslovak nation-state was created in 1918,
it was a state that from the moment of inception had a problematic relationship with its various ethnic and religious minorities, precisely because
they did not see themselves as Czechoslovaks either in terms of civic or ethnonational principles. Czechoslovakia could only survive on the basis of
mutual accommodation. Given the geopolitical realities, immediate attempts
by German-populated areas to secede from the new state were doomed to
failure. Although areas totalling around one-third of the newly-created
Czechoslovak state tried to opt out, neither Germany nor Austria were in
any position to support them, and the Allies would not tolerate any unilateral border revisions in favour of either German state (Otter 1994: 129).
The result was that although a Czechoslovak state was created within the
borders acceptable to the elder Masaryk, it was a state that contained huge
numbers of disaffected citizens, predominantly Hungarian and German.

There were more than 3 million ethnic Germans in Czechoslovakia, a figure that made them the second largest ethnic group in the country. Their relative importance within society was distorted by the fact that Czechs and Slovaks were lumped together as Czechoslovaks, despite the absence of a common language (Leff 1997: 24). The sheer size if not the actual presence of the German minority presented a huge problem to the Czechoslovak authorities. For the most part, they were settled in territorially compact areas adjacent to Austria and Germany; they were economically advanced, and were generally alienated from the state from the moment of its inception. Had they been awarded the autonomy that they, alongside the Hungarians and Slovaks, believed was on offer, it is possible that some of the sting might have been drawn from the arguments of ultra-nationalists. However, the dominant Czech political elites feared German economic power, and they were worried that if areas that contained substantial minority populations were granted autonomy, the state would collapse (Leff 1997: 39). On the other hand, from 1926 onward, centre-right Czech parties were prepared to share power with German parties. This new approach, which was built upon the realization that previous strategies of domination and exclusion were simply not working, brought three benefits. First, it, at least theoretically, helped promote identification with the state on the part of ethnic Germans. Second, it reduced the appeal of German revisionists. Third, it kept the communists, who were in fact the only mass inter-ethnic party in the country, at bay. However, as was to become apparent, all such measures came far too late in the day to be of any long-term benefit.

League of Nations guarantees concerning minority protection that the Czechoslovak government had freely entered into were not applied in the letter or spirit of either domestic or international law. Germans (and others) found themselves systematically excluded from the public service. In addition, the government embarked upon various strategies designed to reduce the influence of domestic German capital upon the economy. In the agricultural sector, these moves were supplemented by a policy of land reform aimed at redistributing German-owned land to Czechoslovaks (*Historikerkommission* 1996: 25).

Such measures, combined with the haphazard application of the principle of self-determination in 1919 ruled out any possible subsequent rapprochement between either Czechoslovakia or Poland on the one side and Germany on the other. Instead, Czechoslovakia and Poland looked to France as their ultimate guarantor against a resurgent Germany (Kubů 2001: 72). Any possibility of sustained bilateral co-operation between Czechoslovakia and Poland, however, ceased as early as 1918 when a dispute broke out between the two. It concerned the ethnicity of the population and delineation of the border between the two newly established states in the formerly Austro-Hungarian Silesian districts of Český Těšín/ Cieszyn and Hlučín. Fighting between irregular units, sometimes backed by regular armed forces, acts of terror, civil unrest, rioting and intervention by the Allies were the order of the day. After numerous attempts and local and international mediation, the result was an affirmation of the original border, which, from a Polish perspective, unduly favoured Czechoslovakia (Kacíř 2000: 112–126). The dispute, however, permanently soured relations between the two, and provided another flash point in 1938 (in the context of the Munich Agreement) and between 1945 and 1947.

Despite their failure to co-operate with one another, both the Polish and Czechoslovak political elites were aware of the difficulties of the situation in which they found themselves. The question was how to address them. By and large the liberal and socialist left were in favour of strategies of accommodation that might encourage integration. The communists regarded such questions as being barely relevant. On the other hand, the right saw the presence of ethnic Germans as an unwelcome reminder of 'centuries of oppression'. What the right sought to do was create states that, if not ethnically homogenous, were at least much less diverse than at the point of their inception. The question would then become one of how this process of homogenization was to be implemented, and what the reaction above all of Germany would be.

In Poland the German minority carried little substantive political weight. German political representatives remained marginal to the wider political process. The same was not true of Czechoslovakia. Here the party system had immediately polarized around ethnic lines. Initially German parties fell into two broad camps: those, such as the *Deutsche Nationalsozialistische Arbeiterpartei* (German National Socialist Worker's Party/DNSP), who were implacably opposed to the Czechoslovak state, and those such as the *Deutsche Christlichsoziale Volkspartei* (German Christian Social People's Party/DCVP), who were prepared to enter into (grudging) co-operation with the Prague authorities. However, it was not until 1926 that the DCVP together with another German party, the *Bund der Landwirte* (Farmers' League/BdL) actually entered government as part of a centre-right coalition. In 1929, they were followed into government by the *Deutsche Sozialdemokratische Arbeiterpartei* (German Social DemocraticParty/DSAP), but by this time Konrad Henlein's *Sudetendeutsche Heimatfront/Sudetendeutsche Partei* (Sudeten German Homeland Front/Sudeten German Party/ SdP) had emerged as the dominant force on the German political scene (*Historikerkommission* 1996: 28ff.). At the general election of 1935 its blunt and strident demands for *Anschluß* to Germany, attracted the support of 64 per cent of ethnic Germans voting.

It is self-evident that in circumstances such as these, as the major kinstate, the position of Germany would be crucial. In a nutshell, the issue was one of whether political elites in all three countries were prepared to coax the wider population towards accommodation. However, through a combination of both endogenous and exogenous factors, polarization rather than accommodation was the order of the day. Although Czechoslovakia fared relatively well during the economic crises of the 1920s and 1930s, the German minority in Czechoslovakia was disproportionately affected by the slump of the 1930s, a fact that contributed further to their increasing radicalization. As for Germany, it suffered first from hyperinflation in the early 1920s and then from mass unemployment and deflation a decade later. The economic situation in Poland was little better, and in some ways even worse given the low level of industrialization and widespread poverty, especially in the east of the country. In all three countries, demagogues gained greater currency and nowhere more so than in Germany. As the economic crisis deepened so the appeal of radicals widened, and society, if such a thing can said to have existed at all, continued to fragment under the pressures of polarization and radicalization. Centrifugal forces grew apace, and the ethnic core separated from the ethnically distinct periphery. This process, coupled with the intensification of class struggles, served to hasten the final fragmentation.

In Poland, minorities, principally the Jews and Germans, together with Poland's historic enemies Germany and Russia were labelled as the main sources of Poland's misery. In Czechoslovakia, Germans and Germany fulfilled the same role. In Germany, anti-Polish and anti-Czech sentiment was complemented by increasing anti-Semitism and hypernationalism. These messages were articulated most graphically and successfully by the Nazis, who turned the revision of the Versailles Treaty, especially regarding borders and Germany's military capacity, into a fetish. Any chance of the region avoiding the abyss was lost in January 1933 when Hitler came to power. Although tactics and priorities varied from time to time, the fate that was to befall Jews, Poles and Czechs was clear to anyone who had read *Mein Kampf*. Between 1933 and 1939 the three states entered into a courtship of death. An increasingly belligerent Germany was faced with a Polish government less and less inclined to enter into all but short-term compromises. In the case of Czechoslovakia, the League of Nations proved to be useless in terms of engineering a solution that would allow all sides to retain credibility and legitimacy. Not that the Nazis, in particular, were interested in compromise. In Czechoslovakia, German-populated areas had been particularly badly hit by the depression of the 1930s, and it was not until 1937 that serious attempts to alleviate the economic situation were made (Otter 1994: 137). By that time it was far too late. The Sudeten German population, pro-Nazi or otherwise, overwhelmingly sought a solution in terms of secession. Certain in the belief that the Czechoslovak armed forces would not (be allowed to) defend the state, in September 1938 the UK, France, Italy and Germany connived in the secession of the heavily German populated Sudetenland from Czechoslovakia. As if to demonstrate to Czechoslovakia just how friendless it was, Hungary and Poland subsequently helped themselves to (disputed) Czechoslovak territory as well. The final humiliation came in March 1939, when, in the wake of a German-backed coup in Slovakia, Germany occupied the remains of Bohemia and Moravia and sponsored the creation of a clerical-fascist independent Slovakia.

This left Poland. From the perspective of a huge majority of Germans within and without Germany, the post-First World War territorial losses to Poland were insufferable. Neither is there any doubt that a large majority of these Germans was not particularly concerned that the self-confessed racist Nazis had incorporated the re-acquisition of former German territories within their mission. Ostensibly, the dispute concerned the Free City of Danzig, the Polish Corridor and other territories in Pomerania, Upper Silesia and a small part of East Prussia all of which had been lost between 1918 and 1921. In reality, the struggle was about something else entirely. What was central to the Nazi objective was not the simple territorial expansion of the state, the fabled *Lebensraum* of *Mein Kampf*, or the restoration of 'just' borders. The invasion of Poland was in fact the first step in a race war in which the Jews, as 'mortal enemies of the Aryan Germans' were to be exterminated, and Poles were either to be exterminated or enslaved. The only exceptions to this grisly fate were to be those few Poles who were deemed to be of sufficient Aryan extraction. In September 1939, with the active participation of the Soviet Union in the wake of the Molotov–Ribbentrop Pact, Poland was once again wiped off the map. Germany's resultant territorial gains extended the borders of the state far beyond those of 1914.

3 An insurmountable legacy?

Invasion, occupation, expulsion and the Cold War

Introduction

In the previous chapter, we examined the development of bilateral relations in the German–Czech–Polish triangle of fate from their very beginnings to the aftermath of the First World War and saw how history, interwoven with myth, reinterpretation of historical facts and then utilized in various nation-building projects, had become a key factor in the justification of particular policies, in the three countries concerned and beyond. While historical developments from that period still play a role in the contemporary context of German–Polish and German–Czech relations, they only take second place to the events that we are about to explore, namely the Second World War and the subsequent expulsion of ethnic Germans from Poland and Czechoslovakia. Before turning to Ostpolitik, we need to examine the policies, or lack thereof, that West German post-war governments pursued towards East-Central Europe until the mid-1960s as this will enable us to demonstrate the sea change that was to come about in 1966 with the accession of Willy Brandt to high office.

War and its consequences

The wartime German occupation regime treated ethnic Poles brutally. The Nazis' views of Poles are as well known as is the vigour with which they implemented them. Apart from those who were spared on the grounds of temporary expediency, the elite was subject either to summary execution or imprisonment, and the mass of society was reduced to a life of slavery. Inevitably such brutal treatment provoked resistance and a desire for revenge. By way of contrast with Poland, in Czechoslovakia the Nazi approach was more nuanced. As in Poland, resistance of course brought reprisal. Nevertheless, given that the Nazi hierarchy viewed a large minority of Czechs as being 'capable of Aryanization', the ordinary Czech population was not subjected to the same degree of random and organized acts of brutality as was their Polish counterpart (Seibt 1997: 335–342). This is most emphatically not to say that the Czechoslovak population was treated lightly. It is currently estimated that in occupied Czechoslovakia around 70,000 ethnic Czechs and Slovaks died directly or indirectly at the hands of the occupation forces (Kárný 2001: 143). Total Czechoslovak wartime losses totalled some 250,000, including some 70,000 Jews who perished at the hands of the Nazis. Polish losses totalled 6,000,000, including 3,000,000 Jews, and over 1,000,000 non-combatant deaths of non-Jewish Poles in German-occupied Poland. In both instances the Nazi objective was to establish Aryan racial supremacy. The difference was that in the Polish case, few Poles were considered to be capable of Aryanization. Correspondingly, in the educational sphere for example, opportunities for Poles to receive an education were even more limited than they were for Czechs (*Histori-kerkommission* 1996: 47). In sum then, the occupation regime was even tougher in Poland than in Czechoslovakia. By recognizing and accepting that fact, it is possible to better understand the long-term consequences of each occupation regime as one among several factors that shape contemporary German–Polish and German–Czech relations.

Unsurprisingly, both the non-communist and increasingly powerful communist resistance movements came to reach a common view with regard to Germany and the Germans. This was that Germany should be rolled back to its 'Carolingian core' and that ethnic Germans should be 'sent back' to the truncated German state. As early as 1942, the Allies had agreed in principle to dismember Germany. In light of the failure of the Versailles settlement, they were determined that there would be no repetition of 1919. At its broadest level, a decision was taken to truncate Germany territorially, decrease ethnic heterogeneity by mass population transfers westwards and thus render nation and state more congruous. In other words, the Allies were keen to learn from the past. So, the failure of the peace settlement after the First World War, and the (partial) recognition of this failure, heavily influenced the approach to the German question during and after the Second World War. Equally important, however, were individual aspirations of the Allied powers, their conception of what precisely the German question was, and the relationship that they had with each other and with Germany.

Thus, the lessons learned from the inter-war period were only one among many factors that shaped Allied policies towards Germany. Crucially, the learning process had been highly selective. At one level, the Western powers seemed to believe that the key to maintaining peace in Europe was to 'disentangle' the various population groups (Kramer 2001: 6). The occupation of Germany and the strict control of its political and economic processes by the Allies complemented this belief and constituted part of the wider learning process. Over the course of a few years, these policies led to the division of Germany into two states, the development of very different political regimes in each of them, and their integration in the two opposing world systems during the ensuing Cold War. Ironically, in the last decade of the twentieth century these decisions helped to revive an aspect of the German question that politicians in Germany and Europe had not had to confront since the second half of the nineteenth century – German unification. The geopolitical reality of superpower dominance during the Cold War made the German question more easily manageable, if only by embedding it within the struggle for global dominance and spheres of interest waged by the US and the USSR.

In the early years of the Cold War, the most dramatic way in which lessons had been drawn from the failure to solve the German question in 1919 was the expulsion of more than 10 million ethnic Germans from Central and Eastern Europe. This included some 3 million from Czechoslovakia, and approximately 7 million from territories that were annexed to Poland and the Soviet Union. This expulsion constituted the most dramatic episode of the new learning process because of the sheer magnitude of the migration it implied and because of the brutality with which it was carried out. This was particularly so in the immediate aftermath of the war before the Allies had reached a formal consensus on the 'orderly and humane' transfer of ethnic Germans at the Potsdam Conference in July and August 1945. Nonetheless, the expulsions have to be seen in the context of the Second World War. In Central and Eastern Europe, German occupation policy had been particularly vicious, and many members of ethnic German minorities in the countries affected had played an active role in the oppression of their (former) co-citizens.

It is important to note that the expulsions, although occurring in unprecedented magnitude, were in fact selective, and that the processes were not identical in the two countries. In both Czechoslovakia and Poland, exceptions were made for those who had actively fought against the Nazis. They were few in number, and not even all of them were or could be, protected from expulsion. Nor were all of those who could have claimed exemption keen on staying behind. Second, some ethnic Germans who had married into Czech, Slovak or Polish families were allowed to remain, but many of them chose to emigrate either during the period of expulsions or in later years. Third, 'essential labour' was exempted from expulsion. Finally, in Poland in particular, large numbers of people who had been claimed as German by successive German governments, were exempted from expulsion, in theory if not always in practice, on the grounds that they were in fact Polish.

As the war drew to a close in Poland, the communists were in formal coalition government with the *Polski Stronnictwo Ludowe* (Polish Peasant's Party/PSL) led by wartime London-based prime minister Stanisław Mikołajczyk. In effect, and unlike in Czechoslovakia, the communists thus became the dominant power even before the war ended. During the early phases of the war, the Polish communist leadership relegated questions of territory and ethnicity to the back burner. However, with the ascent of Władysław Gomułka to the post of first secretary in November 1943, a new course was adopted. In essence in terms of ideology, rhetoric and organizational incorporation, the communists successfully made the national programme of the pre-war Dmowoskiite right their own (Curp 2001: 575ff.). With regard to ethnic Germans, the aim became to get rid of as many as possible, and by all means necessary. The first mass incarcerations of ethnic Germans took place in February 1945, in the wake of the collapse of the German front in central Poland one month earlier. What then followed has direct relevance to this volume, as, to this day, its legacy still casts a shadow over bilateral inter-state and inter-personal relations. We find that the Poles simply took over the German concentration camp system and filled the camps with ethnic Germans and indeed anyone else they felt might be opposed to the evolving communist regime. With regard to the *Volksdeutsche* (ethnic Germans who had been Polish citizens in September 1939), and who were collectively accused of treason, the *Volksliste* introduced by the Germans was turned on its head. Thus, the lower individual's ranking on the four-tier list, i.e. the less German the Nazis had classified them, the more likely they were to be offered the return of their Polish passport. With regard to the large numbers of *Reichsdeutsche* who now found themselves under Polish rule, immediate mass deportation, as opposed to mass incarceration followed by deportation, was the rule. In both cases, it is important to note in this context that all the Potsdam Communique did was sanction ex-post facto Germany's territorial losses (despite the fact that it referred a final settlement to a future peace treaty) and the mass deportation of Germans to German territories under Allied control. The expulsion process was not completed until 1950. By then, approximately 1.2 million former German citizens were either given Polish citizenship or right of abode in Poland (Kulczycki 2001: 215), an indication that the criteria for expulsion were progressively enforced with less rigour, often because local officials found them incomprehensible and illogical.

So in Poland, and despite the protestations of non-communist politicians such as Stanisław Mikołajczyk, that Germans should live in Germany (Kersten 2001: 79), communists and their opponents, shared a fairly broad definition of who was a Pole. In addition, it was important for Poland to promote speedy economic recovery, and in order to facilitate this process, Germans were needed as specialists in industry and mining, or simply as labourers. Thus, many thousands of Germans who had been citizens of the Third Reich (*Reichsdeutsche*), were forbidden to leave Poland for several years. Initially they were often placed in labour camps where many of them experienced conditions not dissimilar to those in the former German concentration camps.[1] By 1950, with the expulsion and camp system all but wound up, remaining Germans who were classed as essential labour were allowed to reside along with their dependants among the Polish host-society.

This policy of mass expulsion also helped to solve another question. In the wake of the expulsions, land-hungry peasants, the homeless from central Poland and ethnic Poles expelled from parts of pre-war Poland that Stalin awarded himself could be given relatively sizeable grants of expropriated land. Given the widespread fear of renewed German aggression, the ruling communist elite was thus able to tie the fate of large numbers of people to that of the overall political system. This particularly applied to the peasantry. By June 1947 the authorities had created well over 400,000 new farms (Ther 2001: 59). Communism and close ties to the erstwhile arch enemy Russia (now the Soviet Union) were seen and, to some extent, accepted as the final guarantor of the continued existence of the Polish state. Obviously, the insistence by many vocal (often wrongly equated with influential) politicians in West Germany, based on the final communiqué of the Potsdam conference, the final border between Germany and Poland would only be established with the signing of a general peace treaty, made this an easy exercise. The consequence was that mutual German–Polish perceptions remained distorted, delaying and subsequently complicating the process of reconciliation between the two countries.

With regard to Czechoslovakia similar factors were at play. The expulsion of Germans again afforded the possibility of awarding land to landless peasants, including to those Czechs and Slovaks who had been deported from Romania, Poland and formerly Polish areas that had become part of the Soviet Union (Otter 1994: 157), as well as from territory annexed to the Soviet Union which had previously been part of eastern Slovakia. The parallel with Poland becomes even more exact when we consider the fact that until the 1960s the Federal Republic refused publicly to state that the Munich Agreement of September 1938 was completely null and void. The end result was that the communist authorities in Prague, like their counterparts in Warsaw, were able to present themselves as the guarantors of national independence against a vengeful Germany.

Again, there are a number of differences between the Polish and Czechoslovak cases. The criteria under which ethnic Germans were permitted to stay were stricter and more rigorously enforced in Czechoslovakia than in Poland. In essence, exceptions were made only for those who had a consistent anti-fascist and pro-Czechoslovak record; those with close Czech or Slovak family ties and those that were deemed to be essential labour, such as the German miners of the Zips area. Exceptions were also made for some who had switched nationality during the period of German occupation, but who now sought the return of Czechoslovak citizenship on the basis that they were not ethnically German. Interestingly, refugees from the disputed (with Poland) Upper Silesian areas of Český Těšín/ Cieszyn and Hlučín, who professed themselves to be German were not counted as such. Just how many Germans were affected by this process is still a matter of dispute. This is true with regard to the overall number of Germans who were resident on Czechoslovak territory as the war drew to a close, the provenance of that population, and their fate. Detail to one side, in absolute and percentage terms, the expulsion of Germans from Czechoslovakia was more comprehensive than it was from Poland. It was also more brutal. On one occasion the wartime Minister of Defence, Sergei Inyr, expressed the objective in a particularly vivid manner. In a radio broadcast from London on 3 November 1943, he urged his compatriots by invoking the alleged ideological mission of the Hussites: 'When our day comes, once again our whole nation will chant the Hussite slogan: "Kill them, skin them, spare no-one"' (Staněk 2001: 217).

In order to provide a resolution of the Sudeten German issue, the Czechoslovak government-in-exile led by Edvard Beneš, at first actually subscribed to the possibility of border change and population exchange with Germany. However, as the War dragged on, the Czechoslovak position, and that of the Allies in general, began to harden, becoming explicitly anti-German, which, given the circumstances, is hardly surprising. By early 1943, Beneš had swung his support behind those, principally the communists and the internal resistance movement in general, who advocated comprehensive and swift expulsion (Lemberg 2000: 185ff.). The final details appear not to have been worked out until the conclusion of the Košice Programme of 5 April 1945, by which time the civilian population and resistance had begun to take matters into their own hands. As in Poland, the process of flight and expulsion began before the cessation of hostilities, and, prior to the autumn of 1945, was marked by unbridled criminality on the part of some civilians acting in concert with civil and military authorities. Towards the end of the war, the Beneš government complicated the issue by proposing that (parts) of German Lusatia either be ceded to Czechoslovakia or placed within a Czechoslovak–German condominium. Matters were made even more difficult by suggestions that large chunks of Lower Silesia that had been placed under Polish administration at Potsdam should in fact be assigned to Czechoslovakia. In both cases, the reasons given were couched in ethno-cultural and historical terms (Kučera 2001: 58ff.). In addition, the territorial dispute with Poland concerning Upper Silesia continued to fester. It was only in January 1947 that the Czechoslovak government came to accept its post-war borders with Germany and Poland as definitive. It did so following the direct intervention of Stalin in the matter (Kučera 2001a: 67). It is unlikely that Beneš's apparent determination to revive his pre-1919 schemes for a territorially enlarged Czechoslovakia did anything to endear him to the Soviet dictator.

One of the most important differences between Poland and the Czech Republic is the fact that in the former country no single package of legislation could be pointed to as having sanctioned and 'regulated' the expulsion process. This difference is not only important in terms of history. It is of relevance to contemporary German–Polish and especially

German–Czech relations. Moreover, in Poland all legislation concerning the expulsion of ethnic Germans from post-war Poland has now either been repealed or has been voided by superior EU law (*Dialog* 2002: 61). By way of contrast, the contemporary Czech state draws its legitimacy from the short-lived post-war Beneš-led government. The so-called Beneš Decrees, issued in 1945 and 1946 in part dealt with the fate of the remaining German population and granted amnesty to anyone who had committed a crime during the expulsion process. Successive Czech governments have stated that these elements of the Decrees are now defunct. Yet, as the entire package is seen as forming an indissoluble element of the constitutional bedrock of the contemporary Czech Republic, it inadvertently serves to complicate relations with Germany.

By late 1946, the process of mass expulsion and flight from Czechoslovakia was by and large completed. Thereafter, remaining emigrants increasingly came to be comprised of skilled workers and anti-fascists who left under the aegis of family re-unification programmes, and people of mixed descent who had opted for Germany. Ironically, the last wave of forced migration from Czechoslovakia into (West) Germany occurred in 1948 in the wake of the communist take-over in February 1948. Following the communists' accession to sole power in Prague, around 30,000 non-communist Czechoslovak citizens fled to Germany. Despite their protests and those of German refugees and expellees, they invariably found themselves sharing transit camps with German deportees from Czechoslovakia (Hoffman 1996: 80ff.).

As we mentioned earlier, in Poland, by 1949 there remained approximately 1.2 million former *Reichs-* and *Volksdeutsche*. In Czechoslovakia the corresponding figure was approximately 220,000. In Poland, the overwhelming majority of 'former Germans', were in fact regarded as 'Germanicized Poles' and as such were subjected to a campaign of 're-Polonization'. The remainder were permitted a degree of cultural autonomy, although they were not awarded explicit minority rights until mid-1956, at which point they mostly opted for the newly accorded possibility of emigration to Germany. In Czechoslovakia, the minority was expected to assimilate into the host-society, and they were not recognized as constituting a national minority until the political changes introduced in 1968/1969 during and following the Prague Spring. Paradoxically, in the intervening period, by a process of drip feed, they were accorded a limited amount of cultural autonomy. In 1948 and 1949, it had been made easier for Germans (and Hungarians), to re-acquire Czechoslovak citizenship, and in 1953 it was summarily and compulsorily restored. From the mid 1950s, cultural restrictions were gradually eased, as a limited German-language press was allowed to circulate and ethnic Germans were granted a small number of opportunities to express and preserve other aspects of their ethnocultural identity (Rouček 1990: 201ff.)

Stalemate and recrimination

The forced migration of more than 10 million Germans from Poland and Czechoslovakia to occupied Germany at the end of the Second World War added an entirely new dimension to the German question. Despite the politicized rhetoric of the expellee organizations and their opponents inside and outside of Germany, German society as a whole has never fully acknowledged the suffering of the expellees. Nor has it been able to embrace the history and cultural traditions of former and extant German minorities as part of a German cultural identity. This failure to acknowledge history for what it is – something that cannot be reversed, but needs to be appreciated in order to prevent its repetition – has extended beyond Germany into Central and Eastern Europe where the issue of the postwar expulsions impinged upon the EU accession negotiations.

The inability of German society post-war and post-unification to deal with the expulsions from the perspective of their impact (or lack thereof) on German identity has also meant that some of the expellees and their descendants persist in their own selective view of history. They choose the expulsions as their starting point, thus almost completely denying the contextual, if not causal significance of any events predating the expulsions. As such, the expulsions and their aftermath constitute an almost classic example of the multidimensionality of the German question. This is also true from the point of view that the expulsions did not solve the German question, and perhaps did not even contribute to this process. In fact, they created a small, and perhaps decreasing, but nevertheless vocal political group in Germany that lets no opportunity pass to call for a return to the Federal Republic of the former *Deutsche Ostgebiete*. Since 1990, the official representatives of the German expellees have denounced these demands on various occasions, and within wider German society support for this extreme position is less than marginal. A larger segment, but again by no means a majority even among the expellees, continues to demand the collective right of return to their ancestral homelands from which they were expelled after the Second World War. The problem here is not so much how serious these demands are or how many people support them, but the perception that they created, and still create, in Poland and the Czech Republic. These claims can be used as welcome 'proof' of German revisionism by nationalists and Eurosceptics alike. From that perspective, too, the German question has not lost any of its domestic, bilateral and European relevance.

Naturally, German aggression and occupation and the post-war expulsions cast a giant shadow over bilateral relations between the Federal Republic in its dealings with Poland and Czechoslovakia. To make matters worse, for both emotional and political reasons, the governments of Konrad Adenauer (1949–1963), stuck to various political fictions. These included the position that the Potsdam conference had not finalized

Germany's border with Poland; that ethnic Germans had the automatic 'right of return' to their former homes; and that only the Federal Republic, as opposed to the communist *Deutsche Demokratische Republik* (German Democratic Republic/GDR), had the right to act on behalf of residents of both German states. In addition, Bonn refused to enter into diplomatic relations with either Poland or Czechoslovakia on the grounds that they maintained such relations with the 'illegal and illegitimate' regime in East Berlin. The Prague Declaration of 1950 that affirmed the GDR's acceptance of the consequences of Hitler's aggression towards Czechoslovakia served to re-enforce Bonn's hardline position (Rouček 1990: 19). Throughout the 1950s, contacts between the Federal Republic and Czechoslovakia, were either conducted through diplomatic back channels, or through international organizations such as the Red Cross, just as they were between Poland and the Federal Republic. One of the few serious attempts to break the impasse came in 1955 in the wake of the limited rapprochement between the Federal Republic and the Soviet Union. In turn, Prague embarked upon a diplomatic offensive aimed at securing full diplomatic recognition from Bonn. It came to nothing, but did at least result in the release of the last German POWs still being held in Czechoslovakia (Rouček 1990: 23).

In effect, the Bonn government did not have an Ostpolitik (policy for Eastern Europe) at all. Instead it had a series of non-negotiable points and a policy of non-recognition (Loth 1989: 173). There were a number of factors that lay behind Bonn's attitude. The Federal Republic regarded itself as the only legitimate German state on the grounds that its citizens had exercised their right to self-determination through a free and fair general election. Moreover, Chancellor Adenauer was a convinced anti-communist who was not prepared to undertake risky initiatives with any communist country lest they weaken the security relationship with the United States and embryonic (West) European unity. He was also acutely aware of the fact that the huge number of refugees in the Federal Republic harboured the desire to return home. From his point of view the best way of keeping the situation under control was to get the economy going and promote Western integration. He hoped that if both goals could be achieved, then the refugees and their descendants would become better integrated within the society of the new state, and so gradually come to terms with political realities. Adenauer knew that the chances of any of this territory returning to German rule were remote. He felt that at best all that might be achieved at some point in the future was the creation of a united Europe in which nation-state borders would become irrelevant and where freedom of movement was a cardinal principle. However, he also was aware that to admit this in public would have incalculable consequences for the fragile democratic order of the Federal Republic. It is interesting to note that despite the transition from communism in Poland, the divergence of views that existed with regard to Adenauer persists. Some Polish academics remain unable to grasp the electoral and political logic of Adenauer's predicament. The result is that they persist in the reproduction of a stereotype that views him as some kind of 'chancellor of the expelled' (Sakson 2004). Such views contrast sharply with those of other Polish experts such as Witold Góralski. He argues that during the period of communist rule, wider Polish society was deliberately kept ignorant of the political situation in the Federal Republic as part and parcel of the strategy of presenting West Germany as a state permeated with the desire for revenge against Poland (Góralski 2004). Similarly, Józef Fiszer acknowledges that in private Adenauer recognized that the *Deutsche Ostgebiete* were gone, but to have acknowledged this in public would have been politically impossible for him (Fiszer 2004).

Adenauer also knew that the creation of a genuine European union was a far-off proposition. Neither should we forget the wider international environment within which he operated. Adenauer's entire strategy was predicated upon not only creating a West European anchor for Germany, but also upon enmeshing the Federal Republic within the wider Atlantic Alliance (Croan 1982: 355ff.). Reconciliation with France and alliance with the United States were Adenauer's paramount security concerns. This did not mean that he did not desire reconciliation with Poland and Czecho-slovakia. Rather it meant that under the prevailing political circumstances, East-Central Europe would have to wait (Byrt 2004).

Naturally enough, both the Polish and Czechoslovak governments had political and security concerns of their own. Not only did these involve strengthening the socialist alliance structure, they also focused upon the related aim of achieving security in the face of uncertainty over West German intentions. They were particularly worried about the possi-bility of the Federal Republic securing full American backing for a policy of re-annexation. Today such a view might sound fanciful or even para-noid. In fact, it could be argued that Adenauer was unnecessarily insensitive to Czechoslovak and Polish concerns. For example, in his cabinets of the 1950s, the presence of hardline figures with at best questionable pre-1945 records, such as Hans-Christian Seebohm and Theodor Oberländer, was rightly bound to enrage the authorities in Warsaw and Prague. The absence of regular formal diplomatic contact, the ideological disposition of the ruling elites in all three states and wartime memories meant that the wider populations of Czechoslovakia and Poland were fearful of German aggres-sion, and that this fear was reflected in the actions of their political elites. Furthermore, the domestic political priorities of the Adenauer government were not high on the agenda in Prague or Warsaw. In East-Central Europe, the general consensus was that Adenauer meant what he said when he refused to countenance the reality of the post-war borders and the related ethno-demographic changes that had taken place. After all, given their recent experience, there was no reason at all other than to take the chan-cellor at his word when he proclaimed his refusal to recognize in full the outcomes of the Second World War. Indeed, just as Adenauer had his own domestic priorities, so did the governments in Warsaw and Prague. These centered upon feeding and housing the destitute, and in getting the economy moving. A final factor that helped in the maintenance of negative stereotypes was the sheer lack of contact between the populations of the three states. Apart from visits by communist (front) organizations, almost the only contact came about through the visits of Germans to remaining family members in Czechoslovakia, and more especially Poland. On all sides, propagandists and Cold War warriors had effective control of the policy arena and the public discourse.

Indices of change

The first signs of change on the German side, the ill-fated *Politik der Bewegung* (Policy of Movement) aside (see Chapter 4), came in 1966 in the midst of what passed as an economic crisis, when the *Christlich Demokratische Union/Christlich Soziale Union* (Christian Democratic Union/Christian Social Union/CDU/CSU) formed a grand coalition with the *Sozialdemokratische Partei Deutschlands* (Social Democratic Party of Germany/SPD). This grand coalition, which lasted until 1969, similarly tried various initiatives of rapprochement, but again without achieving any major breakthroughs. One problem was the presence of CDU and especially CSU hardliners who were still loath to make concessions. The attitude of the government in East Berlin was also becoming increasingly problematic. In the absence of any serious attempts by Bonn to mend fences with the Soviet camp, the *Sozialistische Einheitspartei Deutschlands* (Socialist Unity Party of Germany/SED) had long proclaimed its desire to heal the inner German rift. However, when faced with the opportunity for genuine dialogue, they became obstructive. The attempts at a more constructive Ostpolitik thus began to run into the sand, and what sealed their fate was the series of developments in Czechoslovakia, known as the Prague Spring. The pre-Dubček leadership did evince a degree of flexibility in its dealings with the grand coalition (Skilling 1976: 380). Given Soviet and GDR concerns as to where reform might lead, it could be argued that the incoming Dubček government did not exercise enough caution in its dealings with the Federal Republic. The Federal Republic and Czechoslovakia did make progress with regard to bilateral issues during the Prague Spring of 1968. However, Moscow's and East Berlin's ultra-hardline approach eventually brought to a halt the nascent rapprochement between Bonn and Prague, and helped to bring about the destruction of the whole reform process in Czechoslovakia.

That communist hardliners perceived the Federal Republic to be a threat is beyond question. On the other hand, the extent to which it was seen as a genuine threat to the *Pax Sovieticus* is open to debate. Of course, in terms of power politics the Soviet Union was acting as any (quasi-)imperialist state would. It was seeking to preserve its strategic interests. On the other hand, in 1968 the Soviet Union was led by men who had fought the Germans between 1941 and 1945, who were ultra-conservative by nature and who genuinely doubted that non-communist Germans had come to terms with the border or indeed had even changed their basic attitudes towards Slavs. In other words, accusations that the Federal Republic was abusing its 'open' border with Czechoslovakia, that it was trying to entice Czechoslovakia with easy credits, and that Prague was keen to settle with the Sudeten Germans (Skilling 1976: 54), were actually made in all seriousness. It must also be noted that neither the government in East Berlin nor its Warsaw counterpart were particularly enamoured with Dubček's apparent willingness to deal with Bonn. The Poles had anxieties with regard to Poland's western border, and in East Berlin the SED was determined to pursue détente on its own terms and no other. The 'Prague Spring' foundered ultimately as a result of Moscow's reservations. It is important to note the role of the SED in the destruction of both the Prague Spring and the initiative of the West German grand coalition. The SED regime in East Berlin was petrified that if the grand coalition's initiative were to be well received among any of its allies, bloc solidarity would crumble in the face of West German 'psychological aggression'. From the SED's point of view, Dubček's coming to power just after the Federal Republic had embarked upon its first serious attempt at Ostpolitik represented a worst case scenario. From as early as March 1968, Walter Ulbricht demanded a Soviet-led military intervention and in August 1968 he got his way (Ivaničková 2001: 275).

With the crushing of the Prague Spring, an enforced pause for breath came into play. The next initiative came in 1969 with the *Machtwechsel* in Germany and the accession of the SPD's Willy Brandt to the chancellorship. Brandt had been foreign minister during the grand coalition, and had wanted to go further than the majority of his coalition partners in the CDU/CSU. Brandt also personified the spirit of détente, and his ideas chimed perfectly with those emanating at the time from Washington, London, Paris and Moscow.

Achieving dialogue with Moscow was of paramount importance, and the Soviet attitude was governed by three factors. The first was the strategic relationship with the US. The second was the fact that its Central European rear was now secure. Finally, the Soviet Union was wary of encirclement by the US in strategic partnership with an increasingly assertive China. Brandt had a vision of Europe, and he pursued Ostpolitik as a complementary adjunct to Westpolitik, leading him to develop a *Gesamteuropapolitik*. With regard to Poland and the Czech Republic, Brandt was prepared to talk without preconditions, and was prepared to drop the political and diplomatic baggage inherited from his predecessors. To that end, he, together with his Ostpolitik adviser, Egon Bahr, and his foreign minister Walter Scheel of the liberal *Freie Demokratische Partei* (Free Democratic Party/FDP), sought first of all to convince Moscow that things had really changed in Bonn. This was by no means easy. The Soviet leadership was still extremely wary of German intentions, and did not really believe that any non-communist German government, regardless of ideological stripe, could ever accept the territorial losses that Germany had experienced in 1945. Bahr did eventually succeed in convincing the Soviet government of the sincerity of the SPD, and the result was the Moscow Treaty of August 1970. The treaty was important for two reasons. The first was that it had been concluded with the Soviet Union itself. The second was that in the treaty the Federal Republic agreed to respect and leave undisturbed the post-1945 territorial changes in Europe.

Now that Moscow was convinced that Bonn was not pursuing a policy of re-conquest by other means, Warsaw received the green light to negotiate with Bonn. Today, the results of their bilateral treaty of November 1970 seem modest. At the time, however, they may be regarded as epoch-making, given the legacy of distrust and bitterness that existed throughout society on both sides (Góralski 2004). In fact, Brandt's visit was in itself epoch-making, not only because he was the first federal chancellor to visit Warsaw, but because of his famous and totally spontaneous *Kniefall* at the memorial to the Warsaw Ghetto (Sułek 2004). Brandt's remarkable action helped to convince his chary negotiating partners that he was genuine in his intentions. In the face of internal reservations, and acrimonious protests from the SED, which believed Bonn was bent upon the isolation of the GDR from its allies (Tomala 2004), Warsaw cautiously accepted Brandt's line that in the absence of a definitive peace treaty and conference wrapping up all residual issues outstanding from the Second World War, Bonn's hands were tied. Accordingly, and in line with the Moscow treaty, Bonn stated that it was unable to recognize Poland's border in international law. Yet, once again, within the terms of the treaty Bonn guaranteed that it respected the border according to the norms of international law, and confirmed that it had no intention of violating it. In return, Brandt and his team were told privately that a greater number of ethnic Germans would be allowed to emigrate from Poland to Germany. The Polish side also hoped that in signing the treaty, greater economic co-operation with the Federal Republic might result (Fiszer 2004). At this juncture it is important to note that by securing agreements with Warsaw, and more especially Moscow, the Four-Power Agreement over Berlin (1970), was facilitated. In turn, all these agreements helped to create the necessary conditions that allowed the two German states to sign the Basic Treaty of 1972, through which official, permanent, quasi-diplomatic relations were established between them (Bender 1986: 155ff.).

If we return to relations between the Federal Republic and Czechoslovakia, effectively, no progress was possible between the two until the process of 'normalization' had been completed in Prague, and the Husák regime had consolidated its grip on power. By 1970, the German political constellation was beginning to change. The SPD and FDP governed together. With regard to Ostpolitik this meant that Brandt and his allies had greater room for manoeuvre. By 1973, not only was 'normalization' all but complete, but the Kremlin had become more flexible in its stance, had ordered the removal of Walter Ulbricht in East Berlin, and had sanctioned his replacement with Erich Honecker as First Secretary of the SED. With the Moscow, Warsaw and Basic Treaties all in place and the Four-Power Agreement on Berlin concluded, there only remained the thorny question of bilateral relations between the Federal Republic and Czechoslovakia, and behind that the baleful shadow of Munich. The trick was to bridge the gap between the two sides' views of at which point the Munich Agreement had ceased to be valid. Prague's view was that as the Agreement had been signed under duress it had been void from the start. Bonn's view was that whereas the Agreement was indeed void, Hitler's subsequent actions had rendered it so. Regardless of the detail of timing, the important point was that both governments and all serious political observers recognized that it had lost whatever dubious legality it may have once had. Within the terms of the 1973 Prague Treaty both sides were keen to establish the grounds on which the Munich Agreement of 1938 was invalid, as much as anything else to forestall legal action on the part of disgruntled former Sudeten Germans. Unsurprisingly, given the greater prize of global détente a mutually acceptable compromise was found (Břach 2001: 298). This agreement was as important to the Czechs as Brandt's earlier concession with regard to Poland's western border had been to the Poles. Once again, the Bonn government was sending out a clear signal that it wished to re-build relationships, and that it recognized this could occur only if the German side explicitly refuted the policies of the Nazis and accepted the post-1945 and Cold War realities in Europe.

Naturally, the *Landsmannschaften* (German refugee and expellee associations) were less than happy with the terms of these treaties. The reality was, however, summed-up by Brandt with perfect accuracy when he said 'we are not giving anything up that has not already been gambled away'. For Brandt and his supporters the costs, i.e. abandoning untenable positions, were far outweighed by the benefits brought by détente, the diminution of stereotypes and the increased opportunities for ethnic Germans to migrate to the Federal Republic from Czechoslovakia and Poland. That this view was widely shared among the West German population became evident in the 1972 general elections, the first (and until 2002 the only) electoral campaign primarily fought on a matter of foreign policy. Yet, quite what ultimate benefits were supposed to arise from these and related treaties can only be speculated upon. Certainly, Brandt and his advisers hoped they would act as catalysts for a process they labelled *Wandel durch Annäherung* or 'change through rapprochement'. In a nutshell, they hoped that confidence-building measures would lead to a decrease in antagonism between the two blocks. A reduction in tension having been achieved, the next stage would be to enter into sustained and regular co-operation that would render the Cold War borders more malleable, with each bloc gradually disarming and opening itself to the other (Brandt 1967b: 7–8). The end game would have presumably resulted in the whole of Europe embracing social democracy, with the American presence reduced to symbolic levels, and with the Soviet Union also having reduced its presence within Europe, after having embraced a modified version of 'socialism with a human face'. As for Germany, in this scheme of things, the national question would then become redundant regardless of the existence or otherwise of two German states.

From grand design to pragmatic Ostpolitik?

These grand designs were of course never realized. With regard to Bonn's relations with Prague and Warsaw, the 1980s represented a partial return to the 1950s and early 1960s. Brandt's successor, Helmut Schmidt was more cautious and circumspect in his approach to East-Central Europe. He most certainly did not subscribe to the grand theorizing that had underpinned much of what the Brandt government had achieved. Although deeply sceptical of Soviet intentions, he also took the view that Moscow had legitimate security interests and that, like it or not, the Federal Republic had to view the Soviet Union as a major security partner. His attitude towards Poland and the Czech Republic was correspondingly less proactive than that of his predecessor. Apart from securing a large number of exit visas for Germans in exchange for the so-called jumbo credits to Poland in 1975/1976, little of note occurred. In fact, in the early 1980s, much of Brandt's legacy of goodwill towards the SPD was undone, when Schmidt among other SPD politicians evinced a degree of irritation with the emergent *Solidarność* (Solidarity) movement. In the Federal Republic, the independent Polish trade union was seen by some on the left as a potential threat to the security of Europe because of its 'unrealistic' demands, such as for the establishment of liberal democracy in Poland. However, with the coming to power of Helmut Kohl of the CDU in 1982, the whole situation changed in an increasingly dramatic fashion.

Kohl freely admits that prior to his ascent to power he was not particularly interested in Poland and Czechoslovakia. In so doing, he inadvertently illustrates an issue of importance to this volume. Although Kohl was sensitive to the experiences of German refugees and expellees, he showed little knowledge of, and interest in, two neighbours of Germany that had loomed so large in twentieth-century German history. Kohl's own disinterest perhaps masked certain, and in his case a long-discarded, antipathy towards both countries, that among many Germans manifests itself in disinterest in either. Such disinterest is by no means unusual in Germany, and it remains a problem because a lack of basic curiosity allows the easy reproduction of stereotypes. Paradoxically, in today's Germany some of those most knowledgeable concerning Poland and Czechoslovakia/the Czech Republic can be found within the ranks of the

Landsmannschaften. As for Kohl, at the time he was not merely expressing his sympathy with those who had experienced persecution; he was also demonstrating the aforementioned German trait of apathy and disinterest towards Czechoslovakia and especially Poland. The result is that in Germany there was and is something of a misperception concerning both Slavic countries. In turn, due to the pervasiveness of communist propaganda, and (enforced) insularity, up until the late 1980s at least, this misperception was more than matched in Poland and the Czech Republic. However, it is also important to acknowledge in this context that overall German policy towards Poland was, if anything, always more constant and consistent than that towards Czechoslovakia, based as it is and was on a mixture of a feeling of historic guilt and the greater geostrategic importance of Poland.

As for the East German SED, as was usual in such situations, it found itself in something of a bind. It wished to engage in a fruitful relationship with its communist counterparts in Prague and Warsaw. The SED's early acceptance of Czechoslovak perspectives on Munich forms one element of this strategy. Similarly, the official designation of expellees from Czechoslovakia (and elsewhere) as *Umsiedler* (re-settlers) fitted with the twin goals of reconciliation and socialist reconstruction. What is curious however is the SED's acceptance of the crudely deterministic arguments of the Czechoslovak communists, who saw their pseudo-revolutionary activity as representing the culmination of the Czech(oslovak) nation's long struggle with its German arch enemy (Ziebart 1999: 11ff.). Having said that, the GDR's role in the invasion of 1968 did nothing but re-enforce the negative image of Germans held by many Czechs.[2]

In both Poland and Czechoslovakia constant reminders of German atrocities coupled with a presentation of the Federal Republic that portrayed the Bonn government as being bent on revenge, simply served to re-enforce negative stereotypes. In both countries the wider population was presented with nothing more than a series of sharply-drawn caricatures. On the other hand, in the 1950s there were still many in Germany who not only hankered after the former *Deutsche Ostgebiete* but were also decidedly unfussy with regard to the means that should be employed in order to regain them (Sułek 2004). In Czechoslovakia, the communist party formed part of an 'extended negative discourse' with regard to Germany (Handl 2004). The situation was little different in Poland, which at the time was a heavily agrarian society with an ill-educated workforce. The only real alternative sources of information were church and state, except for those who had relatives abroad, principally in the US and Germany. The state's position has already been explored. That of the church also requires a degree of elucidation. Despite the obvious philosophical gulf between the two, in the 1940s communists and Catholics had been united in their desire to re-acquire 'ancestral Polish territory', expel as many 'real' Germans as possible, and to Polonize the so-called 'Germanicized Poles'

(Tomala 2004). This coalition of expediency broke down almost as soon as the task was accomplished. Yet, it was not until 1965 that the Polish episcopate felt secure enough to offer the hand of reconciliation to their Catholic co-religionists in Germany. The Catholic Church in Germany responded in kind, and in a sense the exchange between the two countries' leading clergymen can be viewed as having been the first step in the arduous process of German–Polish rapprochement. This momentous gesture was also a tacit admission on the part of the Polish church, that after the war, both Catholic clergy and laity on occasion had behaved in a less than Christian manner towards Germans of all faiths and none.

The extent to which this gesture and Brandt's policy of reconciliation had impressed the refugees, expellees, and those on the centre-right of the West German political spectrum is open to question. This can be shown by referring to Kohl's early relationship as chancellor with the *Bund der Vertriebenen* (Union of Expellees/BdV) and its constituent organizations. We find, for example, that despite all of the aforementioned measures and reassurances, when he addressed the annual conference of the *Landsmannschaft Schlesien* in 1985, what was of importance to Poles and Czechs watching the spectacle, was not the fact that he told them to moderate their demands, but the fact that he was there at all. His presence was enough to assure most Czechs and Poles that Kohl stood four-square behind the 'revisionists'. From their perspective, differences between Kohl and the hardliners were over tactics, not objectives. Nevertheless, despite this unpromising start, Germany did become engaged in Poland in the 1980s which by then was experiencing martial law and endemic economic chaos, but also significant political reforms that paved the way towards democratic transition. During the 1980s, the actions of the German Red Cross and other German charities possibly did more to break down stereotypes than did anything else in the previous forty years. During the 1980s, the SPD largely threw away the goodwill it had created in the 1970s through its constant demands that nothing be done that might undermine détente, or from 1985 onward that might destabilize the Gorbachev regime.

In sum, the 1970s and early 1980s were a time of halting rapprochement between the three states. Within the overall climate of détente, some progress was achieved. However, the environment in which this happened was heavily constrained by the pervasive atmosphere of the Cold War, and in particular the security interests of the Soviet Union and its East European allies. Given the apparent overwhelming power of that state, it was clear that major change in the wider region could only come about as a consequence of changes within the Soviet Union itself.

A new era

This is neither the time nor the place to deal with the Gorbachev regime. In essence, Gorbachev gave the green light to reform processes in the

Soviet bloc, and then refused to stop them when they proceeded in a direction that he opposed. He deserves full credit for facing down his own hardliners and letting events take their course.

During the 1980s, in Poland civil peace had never been fully restored. By 1988, the *Polska Zjednoczona Partia Robotnicza* (Polish United Workers' Party/PZPR) was exhausted and ready to talk to *Solidarność*. The result was the round-table agreement of 1989 that preceded the final fall of 'really existing socialism'. This agreement in turn spurred a flood of diplomatic and other activity between Warsaw and Bonn. It also helped to breathe life into the minuscule and struggling dissident movement in the GDR.

With regard to Czechoslovakia, we do not find the same level of interaction as we do between Germany and Poland. As in the GDR, the dissident movement was tiny, and media interest was constantly fixed upon Poland and then Poland and the Soviet Union. Neither was there a steady flow of refugees from Czechoslovakia into Germany as there was from Poland. It was only in the summer of 1989 that the Czech(oslovak)–German experience began more closely to parallel that between Poles and Germans in the 1980s. During this period, Czechoslovakia remained passive as it had throughout the post-1968 era. West Germans had not supplied food parcels to Czechoslovakia in the 1980s (as they had to Poland), because there had been no need for them. However, in the summer of 1989, GDR refugees were received with hospitality in Prague as they waited in tent cities for the two German governments to arrange their transit to the Federal Republic. Crucially, and despite this gesture of goodwill, Kohl and his government still failed to evince the same enthusiasm for Czechoslovakia as they were beginning to show towards Poland. This is not to say that he was hostile towards Czechoslovakia. Rather it is to say that Poland had become a personal and political issue, whereas Czechoslovakia had not. Crucially, with regard to Czechoslovakia, the Bavarian CSU, which had and has close links with the *Sudetendeutsche Landsmannschaft* (SdL), had a clear and well-defined, rather negative view of Czechoslovakia that they were not going to allow anyone to tamper with. The consequences of this state of affairs should not be underestimated. The goodwill created in the summer of 1989 between Czechs and Germans could have been built upon in order to create a climate similar to that being created between Poland and Germany. Yet, in accordance with the predominant pattern of German–Polish and German–Czech relations, the German chancellor, who was best placed to undertake some bold initiatives, did not accord Czechoslovakia the same priority as he did Poland (Handl 2004).

Ironically enough, when the Berlin Wall was breached, Kohl was actually in Poland at the embryonic German–Polish reconciliation centre at Krzyżowa with Polish Prime Minister Tadeusz Mazowiecki. With the fall of the Berlin Wall, the nature of the relationship changed radically. The great taboo of the post-war era was now exposed. Unwinding the broader division of Europe was one thing, restoring the unity of Germany quite another. Having said that, it quickly became clear to all that for the large majority of GDR citizens the state simply had no legitimacy, regardless of who happened to be in charge. The GDR had no future. By sanctioning unification, the Four Powers and the authorities in East Berlin were simply bowing to the inevitable, although both President Mitterrand and Prime Minister Thatcher accomplished passable imitations of King Canute in attempting to turn back the tides of history. There was, however, the question of the definitive delimitation of Germany's border.

The problem for the Poles was whether a united Germany would recognize Poland's western border in international law. Or would it seek to exploit the changed situation in order to either seek a revision of the border or some special status for those areas in which, according to the outlandish claims of the BdV and others, over 1 million ethnic Germans resided? It is important to recognize that whereas the Soviet political and military presence was not welcomed by a majority of Poles, they did at least feel that the small Soviet garrison acted as a tripwire against potential German aggression. This feeling was confirmed in 1990 by both outgoing communist politicians and their incoming *Solidarność* counterparts (Adomeit 1990: 15). It was not so much the case that the incoming government opposed the unification of the two German states. Rather, they were worried about the apparent ambiguities in the attitude of the German government towards the position of Poland's western border (Sanford 1999: 83).

The main problem for Kohl was how to persuade the *Landsmannschaften*, most of whose activists voted CDU/CSU, that the collapse of communism brought with it the possibility of a new era of co-operation, but that despite this it did not signal the possibility for a revision of borders. Kohl's initial hesitancy caused alarm throughout Poland. Luckily, the wider German public signalled its clear rejection of, or more accurately their almost total disinterest in the BdV's plans for a (further) referendum over Silesia, with a view to allowing some part of the former German province to accede to the Federal Republic in the same way that the GDR was about to. As a result, Kohl was able to proclaim that the unification of the two German states could be achieved. He was also adamant that in order for this goal to be realized, a fully sovereign Germany could and should recognize the existing border with Poland in international law. Although the BdV voiced its opposition to the plans, just as it had to the Warsaw Treaty of 1970 (Hupka 1971: 86ff.), their position and that of Germany's radical right-wing fringe held no attraction to the overwhelming majority of the German public. Indeed, such was the obvious political irrelevance of the BdV's attitude that the failed Silesian referendum campaign in fact helped to promote a change of leadership and leadership style within that organization. With the domestic front completely secure, Kohl was now able to push on and complete the 2+4 (plus on one occasion, Poland) negotiations and secure the unification of Germany.

As noted earlier, at this time the relationship with Prague was somewhat different. Even within the SdL calls for the revision of the Czechoslovak–German border were on the wane, although by no means absent. In reality, no German territory was at stake here. In theory, this should have made it easier for the two sides to settle their differences on an amicable basis. However, for Czechoslovak public opinion which for various reasons was prone to confuse wider German public opinion with the posturing of the SdL, uncertainties persisted (Handl 2004). By way of further contrast with Poland, neither was the ethnic provenance of Czechoslovakia's dwindling German minority in dispute. This absence of territorial and ethnographic disputes further serves to differentiate the Czech case from its Polish counterpart. However, within the SdL there was and remains a keen desire to obtain some form of recompense for what occurred during the years 1945 to 1949. However, just what is meant by recompense is a matter not only of dispute but also of interpretation. Some elements are keen to pursue the Czech government through various national and international courts. Others speak of the desire for a symbolic or figurative gesture of compensation by the Czech government (Rossmanith 2004). Hardliners further insist that the Czech Republic as a successor state to Czechoslovakia restore citizenship to those deprived of it under the terms of the Beneš Decrees. What did, however, unite the expellees from Poland and Czechoslovakia was the demand that Warsaw and Prague explicitly repeal all legislation prohibiting the right of return. As we shall see, these matters have had an impact upon the entire accession process. They have also had a visible impact upon domestic politics in Poland and the Czech Republic; and with regard to the Czech Republic, and to some extent Poland, accession has not necessarily solved all residual issues stemming from the period 1938–1949.

4 German–Czech and German–Polish relations since the end of the Cold War

An overview

The end of the Cold War presented a major watershed in international relations, especially on the European continent. The collapse of communism in Central and Eastern Europe in 1989/1990 presented the key actors in the region with a golden opportunity to enter into a new relationship. For the first time since the late 1930s, ordinary Czechs and Poles were afforded relatively easy access to the major capitalist state on their doorstep, namely Germany (Houžvička 2004). Access to western goods might have been the immediate issue, but there was of course a wholly novel political situation that was in need of care and attention. The question was really one of how best to proceed. As Wichard (1998) points out, the cornerstones had been laid many years ago in a series of gestures and statements. These included elements of the BdV's Stuttgart Charta of 1950, the initiatives undertaken by the churches in Poland and Germany in 1965, Brandt's visit to Warsaw in 1970 and in particular his spontaneous *Kniefall* at the memorial to the Warsaw Ghetto. Neither must we forget Václav Havel's denunciation of the expulsion of the *Sudetendeutsche* during his first visit to Germany in 1990, shortly after having become President of Czechoslovakia (Pick 2004). Those parts of Europe that had been divided from one another now had the opportunity to become re-acquainted with one another. However, for this process to begin certain issues and pre-conceptions had to be dealt with. As the former Polish foreign minister Władysław Bartoszewski expressed it:

> What must happen so that a real European togetherness between Germany and Poland is brought into train? Both peoples, the Poles and the Germans must throw the false pictures of one another into the dustbin of history, revise their preconceptions of one another, and through a reciprocal process of coming to know one another, break down reciprocal stereotypes.
>
> (quoted in Wichard 1998: 22)

These sentiments were widely shared in the Federal Republic. From almost the very instant that the Soviet bloc collapsed, the Federal Republic made it clear that it sought to include Poland and Czechoslovakia (as was), within the process of European integration. Germany thus came to play the classical role of ambassador with regard to both countries, and more especially Poland within the context of the EU accession process (Fiszer 2004). Others express it even more strongly, stating that 'the Polish road to Europe led through Germany' (Ociepka 2004).

Moreover, all three states now found themselves in a wholly new situation. Not only had 'really existing socialism' collapsed, Germany was on the road to unification. The Federal Republic was to have a common border with Poland, a situation that threw the dramatic changes in the geopolitical situation into sharp relief. Similarly, Czechoslovakia would find itself sharing a much longer border than previously with Germany (Meckel 2004). If nothing else, these obvious facts of political geography dictated that the relationship between Germany and its (new) neighbours had to enter a qualitatively new dimension. EU accession and German sponsorship of it was an obvious route to follow.

In order for either state to accede to the EU, and build a qualitatively new relationship with Germany, a number of preliminary steps had to be taken. First of all, the attitude of Russia had to be gauged and basic foreign policy options needed to be clarified (Barcz 2004). There was also a need for the three states to enter into a series of bilateral initiatives that would serve to establish the terms of their new, post-communist relationship. With regard to Poland, the most important of these were the 2+4 negotiations, the subsequent Border Treaty of 14 November 1990, in which Germany at last recognized Poland's western border in international law, and the Treaty on Friendship and Co-operation of 17 June 1991. From the Polish perspective, both treaties and the 2+4 negotiations were of equal importance (Góralski 2004). For Czechoslovakia, as it was at the time, a border question as such did not exist, but the regulation of its relations with Germany was of no lesser importance for the country than it was for Poland. The formalization of German–Czech relations took a somewhat different route – via the 1992 Treaty on Friendship and Co-operation and the 1997 and 2003 German–Czech Declarations. It is these treaties, declarations and the negotiation processes that preceded them, as well as their impact on bilateral relations, that we shall now examine in more detail.

The 2+4 Treaty

During the 2+4 negotiations, whose resultant treaties act in lieu of a peace treaty ending the Second World War (Barcz 2004), the Polish negotiating team sought to achieve a number of objectives.[1] The most important of these was securing definitive German recognition of Poland's western border (Barcz 2004). Other objectives included the resolution of issues concerning nationality and real estate. They were not dealt with in the 2+4 Treaty itself, but rather in letters appended to the main body of the treaty (Barcz 2004).

These negotiations were trickier than is widely assumed. Differences between Chancellor Kohl and his foreign minister, Hans-Dietrich Genscher, became quickly apparent to the Polish side, which was led by Prime Minister Tadeusz Mazowiecki (Anon. 2004b). Whereas Genscher had no problem with Polish requests that Germany recognize Poland's western border in international law, Kohl hankered for a much looser formulation (Anon. 2004b). Why he should wish for this is an interesting point. It may be that Kohl wished to avoid signing anything that might result in the government being challenged through the domestic courts. He may have still been wary of the residual influence of the BdV upon his own electorate. He and his advisers may simply have underestimated the extent to which the Polish side was keen to have the border recognized according to a tightly knit formula of words (Anon. 2004b). On the other hand, by delaying the issue of settling the border question, Kohl was able to present a clear choice to the expellee organizations: accept the border with Poland as is or forgo the once-in-a-generation opportunity to achieve German unification (Tewes 2002: 59).

Kohl remained committed to the established norms of Ostpolitik while simultaneously manoeuvring in the difficult governmental and domestic context with great success, he maintained the sustainability of the norm consensus, and in fact locked the expellee organizations within it. As we have just seen, this was not necessarily the dominant perception of Kohl's approach. During the 2+4 negotiations, he initially requested that the position of Poland's western border be left open until after the accomplishment of German unification (Anon. 2004c). This made the Polish side deeply suspicious of Kohl's true motives and position, especially as he had opposed Polish participation in the 2+4 dialogue (Anon. 2004c). For the outgoing communists (and others), who were by no means totally without influence or power even at this late stage, the attitude of the federal government was simply proof that in reality wide sections of both the German elites and wider public still sought a change in the post-war territorial status quo in Europe (Anon. 2004c).

Given geopolitical realities, the attitude of the US was bound to prove decisive. The Americans certainly took the view that the position of Poland's western border had been settled by a combination of documents comprised of the final communiqué of the Potsdam Conference, and the Görlitz and Warsaw treaties (Anon. 2004b). The Poles were, however, playing for higher stakes. Not only did they seek confirmation of the border according to a formula of words of their own choosing but they were also keen to demonstrate their new-found independence (Anon. 2004b). Eventually, in September 1990, after five months of negotiations, the 2+4 talks drew to a close, and Germany's post-war borders received final confirmation in international law.

The results of these deliberations and bilateral Polish–German treaties that flowed from them represent a high-water mark in terms of post-war contacts between the two sides (Byrt 2004). The way in which they reduced the psychological fear in Poland that one day the Germans might make territorial demands cannot be underestimated. Equally important was the fact that Poland was effectively locked into the 'West European orbit'. As such, the three treaties concluded in 1990 and 1991 provided a platform upon which more precise schemes for German–Polish co-operation could be pursued.

Clearly, at this time Poland was accorded far greater priority by Bonn/Berlin than was the Czech Republic/Czechoslovakia (Kafka 2004). Some Polish experts have claimed that the changes at that time caused Polish–German relations to enter a 'new historical dimension' (Sakson 2004). Such hyperbole could help to explain later Polish disappointment with subsequent developments (see Chapter 7). In public, Germany sought to draw directly upon the experience of Franco-German reconciliation through the establishment of the Weimar Triangle, together with France and Poland. However, although the three heads of government engage in regular summiteering, the benefits of the Weimar Triangle have been more symbolic than real, and as the collapsed EU Brussels summit of 2003 showed, no steadfast community of interests has arisen between the three (Schröter 2004). Then again, if we consider the view that the Weimar Triangle was offered up by the German side at a particularly tricky point in the 2+4 negotiations as an attempt to prevent the creation of a potential Franco-Polish alliance (Anon. 2004b), then the Weimar Triangle's subsequent failure to develop a policy-making capacity becomes clearer.

The development of bilateral relations in the 1990s: treaties and declarations

If we return to the 1990 German–Polish border treaty, we find that it was of particular importance to Poland because it was the means by which Poland became locked into the Four-Power negotiations on Germany and ensured definitive recognition on the part of Germany of Poland's western border. The German–Polish treaty of 1990 was also significant in as much that it finally destroyed the legal fiction that somehow Germany as an entity continued to exist within the boundaries of 1937, but in some way lacked the capacity to exercise sovereignty over its own territory, or even to assent to the creation of new borders (Adomeit 1990: 17). Neither was there much of a political price to be paid in Germany itself. Only the radical, right-wing fringe and the more antediluvian members of the *Landsmannschaften* opposed this encounter with reality. Conclusion of the treaty was problematic, not because the position of the border was called into question, but because of related issues concerning the loss of property. To cut a long story short, the Polish position was and is that Germany lost this territory under the terms of the final communiqué of the Potsdam Conference. In accordance with it, German property holders lost title to property held in the new territories of western Poland. The German position was that whereas Germany lost this territory under the terms of the Potsdam Conference, the final communiqué itself does not cover either the loss of property or whether or not compensation is payable for such loss (Ociepka 2004). The two sides agreed to disagree on the issues of property and compensation, and as we shall see, the issue refuses to go away.

The 1991 Treaty on Friendship and Good Neighbourly Relations proved to be more controversial, if not to lawyers, then at least in the public domain. For some of Germany's allies, it carried the potential to signal the re-establishment of a German presence in the east that might one day presage the re-awakening of dreams of *Mitteleuropa*. For some Poles the treaty was controversial for precisely the same reason. Whereas elements of both the right and left had earlier sought German recognition of Poland's western border, they saw no reason why inter-state relations should be anything other than correct. These groups were augmented by a much larger section of Polish society that was unhappy about a crucial concession that the Polish side had made. This was recognition of the fact that Poland had a fairly substantial German minority and that the Polish government would guarantee for that minority far-reaching rights (see Chapter 6). In fact, during the 2+4 negotiations, the Americans made it clear to the Polish team that Polish acceptance into the Atlantic Alliance would be contingent upon the Polish state embarking upon a wholesale change of attitude towards its German minority (Anon. 2004b).

Successive Polish governments had never denied the presence of such a minority. Indeed, the incoming post-communist government had no particular qualms in this direction. What had always been in dispute were the size, status and national orientation of 'Germanized Poles'. The process of relaxation resulted in mainstream Polish society being confronted with the fact that in the early 1990s anything up to 500,000 Germans lived in Poland, and not the officially estimated figure of around 2,500. For many Poles, such figures were scarcely believable. Moreover, the re-appearance of the minority opened up old wounds, and generated the belief that Poland's German minority was largely made up of two equally odious groups. Respectively, these groups were taken as being Germans who, as such, should have emigrated long ago, and opportunists who were taking advantage of some vague ancestral connection with Germany in order to seek financial gain. Ironically enough, in Germany, most of the population viewed (and views) Poland's German minority in exactly the same way.

In the late 1980s, some of the attitudes articulated by German activists in Poland had only served to complicate the process of German–Polish rapprochement. Through calls for a revision of the border, and of the status of Silesia (no matter how ill-defined), as well as at least one instance even for the re-introduction of the *Volksliste*,[2] many members of Poland's

German minority demonstrated the extent to which they had been cut-off from political realities. The view that somehow the border could once again be re-defined, contrasted sharply with the views of the Bishop of Opole, later Archbishop, Alfons Nossol. He believed that the 'multi-cultural nature' of society in (Opole) Silesia demonstrated that, when left to their own devices, people of differing backgrounds could live alongside one another, and that over-arching tensions between Germany and Poland could be subsumed through the extension of the EU in an eastward direction (Wichard 1998: 34ff.). A final factor in promoting (limited) hostility was the fact that in the 1991 treaty no analogous provision was made for recognition of Germany's Polish minority. Rather, the treaty accords analogous rights to 'German citizens of Polish descent or persons who identify with Polish language, culture or tradition'. The German side rejected formal recognition of these people as a minority on the grounds that there is no indigenous Polish community in Germany.[3]

The deal that was nevertheless done between the two governments can, at the broadest level, be expressed thus: in return for recognizing that Poland hosted a (much larger than previously acknowledged) German minority, the German government would act as Poland's ambassador to the EU. It would also support Polish accession to other North Atlantic and (West) European institutions (Meckel 2004). In the short term, the treaty facilitated a massive growth in cross-border trade, increased German investment in Poland and provided the gateway for Poland to partake in EC/EU programmes such as PHARE (Ingram and Ingram 2002: 53ff.).

From the Polish perspective, as indeed from the (West) German view, the gathering rapprochement bade well for both sides. The losers were of course the SED, and anyone who in the GDR believed that the communist German state had some kind of a future. The Mazowiecki government formed in the summer of 1989 made it clear that they respected the German right to self-determination. Their concern was that the unification process not be misused to call the position of Poland's western border into question. As we have seen, Poland became locked into the 2+4 process, and despite various wrangles and the occasional misunderstanding, the issue of Poland's western border was finally and forever laid to rest, at least among serious political actors. It is also important to note that during these negotiations neither the Poles, nor more informally Prague, sought to obtain prior assurances from the BdV that with unification, they would cease making claims against either state (Vollmer 1997). What was a significant concession by both governments, and one which could have engaged the BdV in constructive dialogue, was ignored. Instead, the BdV sought to pursue various peculiar and risky initiatives aimed at securing further geopolitical change in Europe (see Chapters 6 and 7).

Despite disagreements concerning the size and nature of Poland's German minority, this issue, unlike that of property restitution and compensation, has never got in the way of what some have called the 'German–Polish community of interests' (Reiter 2004). Yet, the activities and ideas of the BdV continue to have a greater capacity to disturb inter-state relations as Erika Steinbach's September 2003 speech to the Polish parliament showed. On the other hand, even here the capacity for damage is somewhat limited. As Hajnicz correctly points out, in 1990, for the first time since the foundation of the Second Reich in 1871, Germany was not surrounded by (largely) hostile neighbours (Hajnicz 1995: 16). If nothing else, the situation promotes greater inner security in Germany, which in turn facilitates greater peace of mind among Germany's former antagonists. The climate for enhanced co-operation is correspondingly more benign. Moreover, anyone in Germany who had the remotest interest in politics was keenly aware that German unification was in fact the by-product of Poland's long struggle with 'really existing socialism'. In other words, the actions of the Poles helped to create a reservoir of goodwill towards them among Germans. Similarly, the actions of (West) Germans in providing aid to Poland during the period of martial law were instrumental in creating a more positive view among Poles of Germans (Reiter 2004). This is of crucial importance, and helps to differentiate the Polish case from that of its Czechoslovak counterpart. Not only did the 'Velvet Revolution' begin after Poland's transition from communism was well underway, it actually post-dated the *Wende* in the GDR.

It would be as well to pause at this juncture and consider the state of civil society in Czechoslovakia and Poland in the early 1990s, for it was by no means identical. If we understand this basic fact, we can better understand why contemporary Czech insecurities regarding the *Landsmannschaften* are greater than they are in Poland. Both were subject to authoritarian/totalitarian rule and foreign occupation, in Poland's case between 1926 and 1989, and in Czechoslovakia between 1938 and 1945 and then again in the years 1948 to 1989. Yet, despite the absence of formal liberal democracy, the roots of post-communist civil society in Poland go back to at least 1956. Within the context of our study it is important to note that as early as 1965 Polish clergy acknowledged the injustice that had been done to innocent German civilians after the Second World War (Meckel 2004). Moreover, in the 1970s and especially during the 1980s, political alternatives to the official ideology were obvious, ever present and discussed even within the state-run educational sector. This state of affairs simply has no parallel in Czech(oslovak) society. The Prague Spring was led by reformists from within the communist party who sought the renewal of its ideology and not its overthrow. The actions of Charter 77 are not to be denigrated, but neither should their impact be over-stated. With regard to residual issues stemming from the Second World War, the upshot is equally clear. Politically engaged Poles, and indeed 'ordinary' Poles, who together have experienced expulsion, and mass murder at the hands of various parties, were emotionally much more ready to discuss matters in a less inhibited manner than were their Czech counterparts (Meckel 2004).

In a similar vein, in the wake of the collapse of communism, the restructuring of economy and society in Poland was pursued in a more thorough and radical manner than was the case in Czechoslovakia/the Czech Republic. This restructuring itself has contributed to increased engagement with Germany, and at a more prosaic level the calling into question of old taboos. Nor has any politician in Poland of the stature and status of Václav Klaus either called into question the principle of EU entry, or uttered analogous public statements with regard to the expellees.

The Polish–German experience, can therefore serve only in a limited way as a role model for German–Czech(oslovak) relations. This is not to deny that progress was and continues to be made. As Antje Vollmer acknowledges, the debris of the past had first to be cleared out of the way. She also correctly points out that in every respect the Czech Republic is smaller than Poland, and this fact, coupled with the memory of previous German aggression, cannot be ignored (Vollmer 1997). In 1992, a treaty modelled upon its 1991 Polish equivalent was signed between the Czech Republic and Germany. Aforementioned differences notwithstanding, Poland and the Czech Republic in some ways did start from a similar base when it came to Germany. For example, for both sides the treaties with Germany finally closed the border question and afforded the growth of inner security among the wider population (Lintzel 2004).

Yet overall, relations between Germany and the Czech Republic did not develop as smoothly as they did between Germany and Poland. Despite the signing of the Treaty on Good Neighbourly and Friendly Relations in 1992, a variety of issues remained unresolved and continued to complicate bilateral relations. A renewed attempt to overcome the difficulties was made with the German–Czech Declaration of 1997. Signed on 21 January after years of negotiations, it highlighted that the two governments could only agree on very little in relation to the two most critical issues: the role of the Sudeten Germans in the break-up of Czechoslovakia in 1938 and their collective victimization and expulsion after the end of the Second World War. Berlin accepted German responsibility in the developments leading up to the Munich Agreement and the destruction of Czechoslovakia, expressed its deep sorrow over the suffering of Czechs during the Nazi occupation of their country and acknowledged that it was these two issues that had prepared the ground for the post-war treatment and expulsion of members of the German minority in Czechoslovakia. In turn, the Czech government recorded its regret for the treatment of ethnic Germans in the closing stages and in the aftermath of the war. Both governments agreed that the remaining members of the German minority in the Czech Republic and the expellees and their descendants could play an important role in the future relationship of the two countries and that the support of the German minority in the Czech Republic was a matter of mutual interest. It also acknowledged and legitimized certain long-standing demands pursued by all expellee organizations. The Declaration recognized the fact of the expulsions but it also implied an acceptance of its injustice and of the victimization of innocent people. This would become a major issue in the years after 1997 when the notion of victimhood would regain its post-war prominence in a different context. However, many of the expelled Sudeten Germans and their descendants remained sceptical about the value of the Declaration. A survey in Bavaria, where most of the Sudeten German expellees and their descendants live, showed that only half of all respondents who had heard of the declaration considered it as contributing to an improvement of relations with the Czech Republic. Only one-fifth felt that the interests of the Sudeten Germans were adequately reflected in the declaration. However, the same survey is also very telling from a different point of view. Only a little more than half of those of Sudeten German origin, or with a family member of Sudeten German origin, included in the survey had actually heard of the declaration (Köcher 1997: 53f.).

Nevertheless, the German–Czech Declaration of 1997 and various initiatives flowing from it, including another similar declaration in 2003, have had a positive impact on German–Czech relations. However, they have not been able to resolve all outstanding issues. Many expellees remain disappointed at the refusal of the Czech government to rescind the so-called Beneš Decrees of 1945 and 1946 that legalized the collective victimization of the Sudeten Germans and gave amnesty to anyone who committed a crime in the course of their expulsion. More recently, in the Czech Republic initiatives have begun that seek to address unresolved issues at the local level. This has been welcomed, but the situation has not yet fundamentally improved, and it is unlikely that this will occur as long as hardliners on both sides give one another the pretext to sabotage a comprehensive process of reconciliation.

Leaving these treaties and declarations aside for the moment, there is, however, another dimension in which the two cases share similarities. In both countries the communists assumed the garb of pre-war nationalists and drew sharp caricatures of centuries of Germanic-Slav contact (Sakson 2004). By way of paradox, the protagonists of a 'progressive', 'enlightened' and 'scientific' ideology drew heavily from the past. From the end of the nineteenth century onwards, Roman Dmowski had portrayed German–Polish relations as little more than a perpetual struggle between good and evil, and in the nineteenth century, František Palacký had similarly distorted the historic pattern of Czech–German relations. Neither should we forget that during that same century, German intellectuals as diverse as Engels, Mommsen and Nietzsche were not beyond denigrating Slavs in general as being less civilized than their German neighbours (Mezihorák 1998: 39). In other words, the reproduction of negative stereotypes was common to all societies and by no means the province of the political right only. In the wake of the collapse of 'really existing socialism', the problem was one of how best to overcome decades of negative stereotyping.

Limited periods of reform to one side, in both Czechoslovakia and Poland, no public discussion of the exact nature of inter-societal contact prior to the rise of the Nazis was allowed, even within the narrow confines of communist ideology. This conspiracy of silent distortion was aided and abetted by the behaviour of the SED in the GDR, who in public seemed to wish to wipe centuries of history from the map. They sought to do this by way of their policy of referring to former German districts, cities and towns solely by their Polish and Czechoslovak equivalent names (Rossmanith 2004). The level of engagement with Polish society on the part of East Germans was also quite limited, and throughout the 1980s affected by negative stereotyping on the part of the SED. The GDR's opposition movement sought to counter this picture, but the level of contact with their Polish counterparts was not great, and until the spring of 1989, their impact upon GDR society was negligible (Meckel: 2004). On the other hand, Czechoslovakia was a prime holiday destination for East Germans, and inter-personal contacts were greater, so knowledge of the 'Other' was somewhat enhanced. The consequences of these and similar engagements are by no means clear-cut. Different sources offer distinct assessments on the nature and extent of knowledge held by the German general public concerning either country. What is clear, however, is that despite elite and economic rapprochement, the majority of Germans is not particularly engaged with either Poland or the Czech Republic.

Unresolved questions

Whereas a cross-section of observers today characterizes contemporary German–Polish relations as being without major problems, the 'Sudetenland issue' continues to vex Czech–German relations (Rossmanith 2004). Many Czech commentators evince a certain degree of unease concerning the issue, and the SdL's attitude and expectations. To an extent this can be explained by simply glancing at a map. The Czech Republic is smaller than some German Länder. Correspondingly, fears of German intentions are bound to be greater than in Poland. Not only that, with the dissolution of Czechoslovakia, the original geopolitical disparity between Poland and the newly founded Czech Republic with regard to Germany was enhanced (Křen 2004). Whereas all commentators recognize that the Sudetenland is an issue in bilateral German–Czech relations, the extent to which it interferes with day-to-day business or indeed high politics is a matter of ideological disposition. Despite the fact that no serious political force in Germany views this issue as being in any way open, it has the ability to stir the emotions in both countries. In terms of solutions the metaphorical and literal passing of the wartime generations may facilitate a resolution. From the Czech side, the presentation of a more balanced view of history might perhaps reduce the ability of both the left and right to manipulate anti-German sentiment (Handl 2004). Similarly, Germans could be more cognizant of how their economic power and the disparity of size between the two states create and keep alive fears in the minds of many Czechs (Mezihorák 1998: 39).

In sum, bilateral relations between Berlin and Prague continue to be slightly more fraught than are those between Warsaw and Berlin, although unlike in the Polish case, the status of the Czech Republic's German minority barely registers, even at the local level. The core of disagreement concerns the former Sudeten Germans, and the hard-headed attitude of elements of their leadership towards the very country of which they apparently want to be citizens. The 1992 Czech–German treaty forms the foundation stone upon which contemporary Czech–German relations are based (Houžvička 2004). Yet the results could have been greater than they so far have been. Not only that, the joint Czech–German declaration of 1997, which took two years of painstaking negotiation (Houžvička 2004), provoked an unexpected debate in the Czech Republic. In Article 2 of the declaration, the German side apologized for German maltreatment of Czechoslovakia and Czechs in the wake of the Munich Agreement of September 1938. Naturally enough, this caused little fuss in Germany itself, and in Article 2 the Germans had done what Czech public opinion expected them so to do. However, huge sections of Czech society were furious over the Czech government's expressions of regret in Article 3 for the 'harm and injustice' caused and for the collective nature of the expulsions (*Dialog*, 62/63: 2003: 31). Some Czech commentators allege that in so doing, the Czech side simply did not adequately represent Czech national interests. For example, it is pointed out that the declaration makes no explicit mention of the expulsion of ethnic Czechs from the Sudetenland following its annexation by Germany in the wake of Munich (Kovanic 2004).

Such reactions highlight how the Sudetenland issue and the post-war expulsions continue to complicate Czech–German relations, which is, of course, precisely why in a sense the issue is constantly being swept under the carpet. In 1990, with the establishment of liberal democracy in Czechoslovakia and German unification, old taboos were bound to re-appear on the agenda (Kunštát 2004). What is surprising is the continued capacity of the Sudetenland to cause elements of Czech and German society to act in stereotypical fashion. The fact that the 1997 declaration also led to the establishment of the Czech–German future fund is sometimes lost in the debate concerning events of which no-one under the age of seventy has any memory (Kafka 2004). For all its faults, German–Polish reconciliation could serve as a role model for relations between Prague and Berlin. Especially as Germany's relationship with Poland is not completely without problems either, elements on both sides of the Polish–German border need to deal with the hubris that surrounds residual matters left over from the Second World War and its aftermath. Doing this in a constructive and future-orientated manner could provide a model and give momentum to similar steps in German–Czech relations, thereby repeating the pattern of engagement in the early 1970s and 1990s.

Interestingly enough, both Czechs and more especially Poles, did not let these residual issues influence them unduly during the EU accession referenda of 2003. Of course, as negotiations became more detailed and national sensitivities came to be exposed, there were difficulties (Stadtmüller 2004). Yet, the laborious years of negotiation and partial integration into the West European alliance system brought rich dividends. This is another theme to which we shall return later in the volume. In the short and medium term in order to deepen our analysis there is first a need to address the attitudes of several key actors on the German political scene, and it is to them we shall now turn.

5 Foreign policy and its domestic consumption
The German political parties and Ostpolitik

The purpose of this chapter is to account for the changing attitudes and different positions of the major German parties in terms of Germany's relations with the Czech Republic and Poland. We will assess the position of each party individually, but as and where appropriate we will also consider issues on a comparative basis. Rather than adopt a thematic narrative, we shall assess each party in turn, according to a left–right spectrum. In so doing we will be able to highlight differences between the various actors in a way that clarifies the differences in opinion that exist between the main German parties.

The Party of Democratic Socialism

As the successor to the old governing party of the GDR, the SED, the *Partei des Demokratischen Sozialismus* (Party of Democratic Socialism/ PDS), represents a thread of German politics that considers itself to be particularly sympathetic to the needs and experiences of its eastern neighbours. To this end, it condemns actions and policies that it deems to be revisionist or insensitive towards the Czech Republic and Poland. Whether or not in either country the PDS receives much credit for this stance is an entirely different matter. As the successor party to the SED, the PDS is hampered on a number of counts. Whereas it has sought to distance itself as far as possible from the more insalubrious dimensions of the SED's rule, it is handicapped by the fact that the SED was vociferous in its condemnation of all efforts at reform in the Czech Republic and Poland. We have seen how Walter Ulbricht, as First Secretary of the SED, was particularly concerned to ensure the Prague Spring was crushed in 1968, lest its influence in any way percolate through to the GDR. During the 1980s, his successor, Erich Honecker, was no more tolerant of the Polish reform movement. In fact, there are persistent rumours that at the time Honecker was an advocate of joint GDR–Soviet military intervention in Poland, and that he even advocated (in private), the 'correction of anomalies' in the border between the GDR and Poland. These stories, even if untrue, do at least further demonstrate the friction that often existed between the SED and its allies concerning ideology, détente and how to deal with dissent (Görgey 1972: 93ff.).

Of course, during the period of SED rule, relations between the GDR and the fraternal Polish state were correct. Despite prior reservations, the SED recognized Poland's post-war border as early as 1950 with the signing of the Görlitz Treaty. Interestingly enough, from 1956, the GDR assumed responsibility, along with Poland, for the latter's ever shrinking 'designated German minority', comprised primarily of former *Reichsdeutsche* from Lower Silesia (see Chapter 7). In terms of inter-state relations, during this period the GDR and Poland indulged in the stiff formulaic rituals that passed for 'fraternal socialist relations'. Party delegations regularly trooped across the border in both directions. These missions were supplemented by trade union and youth delegations and visits by others active in the various mass organizations on both sides. At the unofficial level, such formal contacts were complemented in a number of ways. These included labour mobility, whereby Germans worked in Poland, and in the 1980s in particular, Poles were employed in the GDR, predominantly in construction. There were also numerous family ties across the border. From the early 1950s, both sides permitted divided families to visit one another, and in the 1970s a simplified visa system was in play until the rise of *Solidarność* led to a tightening of border controls. On the other hand, the GDR press repeated the official nonsense that in essence there were no Germans in Poland, so family contacts actually served to highlight the contradiction within the SED's own position.

During the 1980s, a clear and obvious gulf appeared between the two sides. Poland was to become wracked by political dissent and economic chaos. On top of re-introducing stricter border controls, in the 1980s articles appeared in the GDR press that not only were critical of *Solidarność*, but also revived German stereotypes of orderly, sober and disciplined Germans, who of course were portrayed as being the polar opposites of disorderly, drunk and undisciplined Poles.

Once the GDR's citizens' movement and *Ausreiswelle* got underway, ordinary Polish people, together with *Solidarność* activists, the Catholic Church and the Red Cross stood shoulder to shoulder with their counterparts in the GDR. Above all they offered hospitality and emotional support to those seeking to flee the country. This, however, does not imply that a majority of Poles welcomed the prospect of German unification. On the contrary, it worried them. For most Poles, the problem was that as the Cold War alliances unravelled, what was there to stop as newly united Germany from seeking further to expand its territory?

Today, the PDS is in fact rather handicapped by this very mixed legacy. It has no serious counterpart in Poland, and as such it lacks either a natural partner, or any degree of influence in Polish domestic affairs. Moreover, the presence of a neo-Leninist wing in the party simply serves to revive Polish wariness of German-style state-centred socialism. The fact that the PDS takes a harder line on the *Landsmannschaften* than do main-stream Polish parties creates something of a paradox. It actually places the PDS in the same political space as the Polish nationalist right on this issue, which in turn has a blanket dislike/distrust of all things German. No amount of politically correct posturing on the part of the PDS, with regard to matters such as whether to refer to former German cities by their German or their Polish names, can make up for that fact. This situation, when taken together with the PDS's roots, and coupled with its lukewarm attitude towards the EU, and more especially NATO, make it an unattractive prospect to almost the entire political spectrum in Poland.

What applies for Poland and the PDS also applies to the Czech Republic. If we return briefly to relations between the GDR and Czechoslovakia, with the exception of 1968, we find they broadly follow the pattern set by the relationship between Poland and the GDR. In signing the Prague Agreement of 1950, the SED signalled its acceptance of the expulsion process and the absolute invalidity of the Munich Agreement. The GDR subsequently admitted relatively small numbers of German migrants from Czechoslovakia, and had a slight degree of involvement in the preservation of German culture among the residual German community in Czechoslovakia. As we mentioned earlier, in 1968 the SED was a prime instigator of the invasion of Czechoslovakia. In so doing, the sight of the *Nationale Volksarmee* (National People's Army/NVA) in Czechoslovakia simply served to re-enforce memories of Munich and its aftermath. As with Poland, no amount of stiff speeches and official programmes of exchange could do much to break down the barriers of hostility between the two populations. On the other hand, everyday contacts did help to reduce the replication of stereotypes (Meckel 2004). In 1989/1990, the activities of emergent civil society in Czechoslovakia also did a great deal temporarily to break down barriers, but the objective here was not to legitimize any reformist trend within the SED. Paradoxically, today the PDS's closest ideological bedfellow is the only partially re-constructed *Komunistická Strana Čech a Moravy* (Communist Party of Bohemia and Moravia/KSČM), which itself is by no means averse to playing the anti-German card. Naturally enough, this makes co-operation difficult even for the PDS, which likes to present itself as a party that is in tune with the post-modern, post-national world.

In sum, the attitudes and positions of the PDS with regard to Poland and the Czech Republic have not had, and do not have particular relevance for German foreign policy and bilateral relations with either Poland or the Czech Republic. First of all, there is no realistic prospect of the PDS ever being asked to enter into government in Germany. Second, for the reasons outlined in the previous paragraphs, neither is it in a position to act as a broker between the two sides. Its legacy as successor party to the SED, and its aforementioned attitude towards NATO and European integration (as currently conceived), make that task difficult. In particular, the more positive views held of NATO in the Czech Republic and especially Poland, combined with the PDS' lack of a natural partner in either country render such a task all but impossible. Finally, the PDS needs to rid itself of the view that the *Landsmannschaften* can be crudely equated with the extreme right. Some members of the *Landsmannschaften* may indeed be stuck in a historical and emotional time warp. Then again, the same could be said of some PDS activists. To be sure, as a member of coalitions in some of the eastern German Länder, the party plays a part in functional cross-border co-operation with Poland. However, if the PDS ever wishes to play a positive role in changing the mind-set of the expellee organizations, it must simultaneously alter its own.

The Social Democratic Party of Germany

The immediate post-war stance of the SPD towards Poland and Czechoslovakia was governed by a number of factors. The first of these was the fact that the majority of SPD politicians and activists felt little if any personal responsibility for the actions of the Third Reich. After all, they had been among the first to fall victim to the Nazis. Second, they took the view that as they were not responsible for this catastrophe, and represented a democratic Germany, why should they assent to territorial losses incurred as the result of actions undertaken by their mortal enemies? Third, many SPD activists and voters came from territories lost to the Soviet Union and Poland, or from Czechoslovakia. Naturally enough most were aggrieved at the treatment meted out to them. Finally, up until the early 1960s many refugees and expellees who were active in the *Landsmannschaften* also supported the SPD. Such people wielded enormous influence within the party, and as such acted as a brake upon innovative thinking. Perhaps the prime example was Wenzel Jaksch, a veteran leader of the pre-war German social democratic movement in Czechoslovakia. Although an active force for restraint and co-operation prior to and immediately after the Munich Agreement, relations between German Social Democrats and their former Czech counterparts soured during the early 1940s. The reasons for this state of affairs are immediate and obvious. As Beneš and other Czech politicians took an ever-harder line on the future of the Sudeten Germans, so at elite level mutual alienation grew. During the War, Jaksch, unlike other German social democrats had refused to entertain any of Beneš's schemes for population transfer and territorial exchange. Instead, he advocated autonomy for the Sudetenland, and even more worryingly from the Czechoslovak side, refused to agree to the position that, as the Prague authorities had been subject to duress, the Munich Agreement was invalid from the start (*Historikerkommission* 1996: 63). After the War, Jaksch and others continued to pursue a hard line with regard to Czechoslovakia. This even included staging a theatrical walkout from the party conference in 1956 in protest at the presence of a representative of the exiled Czechoslovak social democrats (Rouček 1990: 27). This incident demonstrates two things. First, some members of the SPD were already seeking to break the post-war impasse as early as the 1950s, thereby foreshadowing the sea-change that was to occur a decade later. Second, it also indicates that such attempts were bound to provoke a counter-reaction. Although some SPD politicians did actually visit Czechoslovakia in the 1950s, it was only with Jaksch's death in 1966 (he actually became head of the BdV in 1961), that Willy Brandt and his allies were able to effect a more flexible attitude towards Czechoslovakia, and embed German–Czechoslovak issues firmly within the wider Ostpolitik. Indeed during the period of re-evaluation that took place in the wake of the building of the Berlin Wall, others within the party also recognized that the SPD could not formally write off the former *Ostgebiete*. If it had advocated a policy of reconciliation and rapprochement, in response a large slice of its electorate would have deserted it. Indeed, this is precisely what happened later in the 1960s when the SPD openly moderated its stance.

During the 1950s, the SPD had pursued a policy of quasi-neutrality that was shaped by the party's first post-War leader, Kurt Schumacher. With regard to Poland, Schumacher and his advisers seem to have believed that a 'neutral' Germany under SPD leadership could be the state to which Poland might be prepared to cede territory. As for Czechoslovakia, although the party accepted that the Munich Agreement had no validity, it still pressed for the right of return, the restoration of Czechoslovak citizenship to, and compensation for, refugees and expellees.

Such ideas found no echo in either Warsaw or Prague. In fact there is no reason to believe that Polish and Czechoslovak public opinion, had it been allowed to express itself, would have shown any enthusiasm either. Indeed, the SPD's European and security policies, which were often confusing in nature, held no particular appeal to the West German electorate any more than did other of the party's policies during the period. It was only with the coming to power of a younger generation of activists such as Willy Brandt and Egon Bahr that change became discernible. This new generation of leaders sought to modernize the SPD, and to change it into a 'catch-all' party of the left. In addition to changes in domestic policy, this entailed the modernization of foreign policy. Thoughts of 'neutrality' in exchange for 're-unification' were abandoned. The SPD accepted the Federal Republic's role as a key member of the West European and North Atlantic alliances, and sought to develop a strategy of détente that would complement and supplement the endeavours of the superpowers. Gradually, in its most radical and innovative form, the idea that borders could be transcended through the creation of some kind of European Peace Order began to take shape (Brandt 1967a: 733). Brandt, Bahr and others were aided in this venture by two of the older generation, Fritz Erler and the highly controversial Herbert Wehner. As members of the old guard who favoured reform, they were able to persuade many scep-tics of the value of the project. Ironically, the building of the Berlin Wall on 13 August 1961 helped them as it proved that in the short and medium terms the GDR was there to stay. In short, the shock of the Wall demon-strated that Adenauer's strategy had out-lived its usefulness and paved the way for new initiatives. Persuading large sections of German society of this was not going to be easy. Then again, persuading the party itself had not been easy either (Brandt 1993: 138ff.). However, for Brandt, who had been Mayor of (West) Berlin in August 1961, the matter was imper-ative, and adherence to entrenched Cold War positions had to come to an end (Bender 1986: 56ff.).

Throughout the 1960s and into the early 1970s, the SPD pursued a series of policies that were aimed, above all, at promoting reconciliation between Germany and its eastern neighbours. In so doing, the SPD played a crucial role in breaking down stereotypes, although among the German minority in Poland Brandt was and to some extent remains a figure of disdain for his apparent 'concessions' to his Polish counterparts (Franzen 2001: 307). From the mid 1970s, as the wider détente process began to crumble, a change in relationships became apparent. First, Ostpolitik had run out of steam without having promoted any real systemic change in East-Central Europe. Second, many in the SPD took a rather dim view of *Solidarność* in Poland, which they saw as a factor destabilizing the balance of power. From the Polish perspective, the SPD's argument seemed to consist of: 'reform yes, but of a nature we find acceptable and at a time of our choosing.' Third, in the 1980s, the limited rapprochement between the SPD and SED that led to the production of a joint declaration did nothing to endear the SPD to the Polish population at large.

These points are important. By pursuing its strategy of elite co-operation and encouraging gradual reform from above, the SPD threw away a lot of the goodwill it had built up during the 1970s. Helmut Schmidt's passivity in the face of Jaruzelski's coup, and Wehner's declaration in February 1982 that *Solidarność* was finished were particularly vivid examples of the SPD's irritation with the former organization (Hajnicz 1995: 26). The problem was further compounded by episodes in 1985 such as the publication of an article in the German magazine *Die Neue Gesellschaft*, by Horst Ehmke, who was extremely close to Willy Brandt, in which he urged caution when dealing with *Solidarność*, and warned against sup-porting initiatives that might disturb the European balance of power (Hajnicz 1995: 18). For its part, *Solidarność* suspected that the fact that the SPD's Ostpolitik was not predicated on undoing the territorial changes of Yalta and Potsdam also meant that for the foreseeable future it accepted the Soviet domination of Central and Eastern Europe and merely advocated a more humane division of Europe.

With regard to Czechoslovakia, the situation was somewhat different. For a start there was no mass opposition movement within that country.

Charter 77, which actually sought as best it could to work with the SPD, consisted of a few hundred overwhelmingly intelligentsia activists. The majority of the population seemed to have come grudgingly to terms with 'normalization', and the comparative material benefits it had brought. As for the Czechoslovak government itself, it was a keen supporter of the SPD's 'new realism' with regard to the Soviet bloc, and supported the West German peace movement with even greater enthusiasm.

Of course, between 1988 and 1989, as 'really existing socialism' began to collapse, the Polish opposition transformed itself into the government. In a sense it was fortunate that the SPD was out of office during this period. They had no natural negotiating partner in Poland any more than they did in the Czech Republic. In a time of such rapid change, the rising Polish political class was in no mood to listen to sermons on the paramount need to maintain global stability and to support the Gorbachev regime. In effect, the stance the SPD had taken in the 1980s meant that, rather like the Greens, they were faced with a series of events that had been omitted from their particular script. In reality, they had come to accept the division of Germany, and sought to overcome the situation through means other than the re-creation of a German nation-state.

Having said that, once it became clear that the train was underway and that nothing could stop it, the SPD proved to be a useful ally to the CDU/CSU in tying up the loose ends with regard to unification and residual matters arising from the Second World War. This to one side, the years 1982–1998 may be characterized as having been 'wilderness years' for the SPD. Nevertheless, the party quickly came to terms with the changed situation in the former Soviet block. At the general election of 1998, after sixteen years in opposition, the SPD was returned to power in coalition with the Greens. Since its return to office the SPD cannot be said to have been particularly bold in its initiatives towards either Poland or the Czech Republic. Neither can relations with its Czech and Polish equivalents be described as being close (Sułek 2004). With regard to the Czech Republic, it is fair to say that all but residual historical bilateral questions have been solved. On the other hand, when it comes to German–Czech relations, statements such as those made in Israel by the former Czech Prime Minister Miloš Zeman, himself a social democrat, in which he portrayed comparatively both Sudeten Germans and Palestinians in lurid negative terms did nothing to enhance the Czech Republic's status throughout Europe and the Middle East, any more than they did in Germany (Handl 2004). The furore in Germany was so great that Chancellor Schröder was forced to cancel a visit to Prague. It was only in summer 2003, after Zeman's resignations as party leader in the spring 2002 and as prime minister in summer 2002, that the German and Czech governments were at last able to hammer out an agreement that built on the earlier Czech–German declaration of January 1997. His replacement in both posts, Vladimír Špidla, showed himself to be more flexible on the issue. In the July 2003 agreement both sides condemned the expulsions employing a formula of words that allowed Prague further to distance itself from what had occurred in such a way that did not contradict the fundamentals upon which the state is built.

Thus the SPD–Green coalition has sought to consolidate the programmes initiated by the previous government, and during the EU accession negotiations it consistently promoted the Polish and Czech causes. In so doing, for the first time since the mid-1960s, the SPD has engaged in a meaningful dialogue with the BdV (Meckel 2004). The fact that the SPD was back in power forced the two sides to develop a pragmatic relationship with one another. Regardless of its relationship with the BdV, the German government is genuinely committed to the creation of better relations between the governments and populations of all three countries. It is, however, hamstrung by the parlous state of the German economy and a certain cooling off in German–Polish rapprochement that was so prevalent in the early 1990s.

In addition, the SPD has found itself at the helm at a particularly delicate time. As EU accession loomed, old questions re-emerged. They concerned the post-war expulsions of Germans, on the one hand, and wartime treatment of forced labour by the Germans, on the other. If we deal with the latter issue first, we need to note the extent to which bitterness rose in Poland and the Czech Republic over the tardiness of the response by German industry to the compensation claims (Handl 2004). Indeed, Chancellor Schröder had to intervene personally in order to ensure that obligations were met. With regard to the expulsions, it is fair to say that Poland and Germany have come to a modus vivendi on the issue. The SPD-led government backs neither claims for compensation nor the collective right of return of ethnic Germans to their former areas of residence in Poland. In return, the Polish government recognizes that once the transition periods are completed, Germans, regardless of their place of birth, will have the same rights as any other EU citizen to live, work and own real estate in Poland. Any domestic legislation that contradicts this stance will simply be regarded as incompatible with EU law.

Just as some in Germany regard this stance as a sell-out of German interests, so many in Poland regard such concessions as a completely unacceptable capitulation to Germany. Yet, the subtle progress made by Poland and Germany is still not mirrored with regard to the Czech Republic, where sensitivities regarding the Sudeten Germans are even more of an issue (Handl 2004). It is not appropriate for us here to repeat arguments made elsewhere in the book. All we really need to note is that until recently the current SPD-led coalition government has made scarcely more headway on this issue than did its CDU-led predecessor. There is near unanimity across the political spectrum in the Czech Republic that the expulsions were wholly justified, and that there can be no (collective) right to return. The collective restoration of Czech citizenship that is sometimes demanded by the SdL on behalf of its professed constituency is rejected out of hand by the SPD and all Czech parties (Handl 2004). The dialogue of the deaf over these issues creates all kinds of difficulties that both German and Czech governments find difficult to deal with. Regardless of degrees of difficulty, the conundrum remains. The Czech Republic wishes to participate within the EU as a full member, but Czech society is still wary of the SdL. Given that there is widespread cross-party consensus on this matter throughout the Czech Republic, progress is bound to be slow. What compounds the problem is that the SdL is equally adamant in its demands for some form of compensation and the collective right of return. The fact that since the early 1990s, Germans as individuals can live and work in the Czech Republic irrespective of where they were born is sometimes buried beneath the rhetoric (Handl 2004). This situation contrasts quite vividly with that which exists between the Polish government and a majority of the various 'Polish' *Landsmannschaften*, where, occasional posturing to one side, both accept that compensation is out of the question, as is (hypothetical) discrimination against particular groups of Germans once the accession process is completed. For the SPD, the result is that it has to perform a difficult balancing act.

The Greens

Unlike the remainder of their parliamentary competitors and partners, the political origins of *Die Grünen* (The Greens) cannot be traced, except in the most nebulous form, back to the nineteenth century. They are a decidedly post-industrial phenomenon, Romantic German affinities with nature to one side. Given their late appearance on the political scene in the 1970s, they do not carry the complex legacies and burdens that other German parties do. Moreover, whilst in opposition, like the PDS, they were emphatic in their rejection of nostalgia for the former *Deutsche Ostgebiete* and for anything they thought smacked of 'revanchism' or might offend Czech and Polish sensibilities. Since entering government in 1998, there are definite signs that, while they have not changed their overall attitude towards the issue of potential 'revanchism', there is recognition that the *Landsmannschaften* (could) have a role to play in the process of reconciliation.

   In Joschka Fischer they have a charismatic figure, who happens also to be the foreign minister of Germany.[1] However, the personal charisma that Fischer uses to such good effect in Germany and parts of Western Europe does not necessarily carry the same weight in the Czech Republic or Poland. As the third Gulf War showed, both at elite and mass level, neither Czechs, nor more especially Poles showed the kind of reserve with regard to military action that was so widespread in Germany (Schwall-Düren 2003). In fact, many Poles welcomed aspects of the rift that developed between Berlin and Washington. Rumours that America might signal its displeasure with the German government by re-deploying forces based in Germany to Poland were greeted with widespread enthusiasm. Many felt that such a move would be of benefit to the Polish economy and act as a further guarantor against acts of aggression from Russia, or even at some point in the future, Germany itself. As this example shows, Green misgivings about NATO are, as we have already noted in connection with the PDS, not widely shared by either of Germany's immediate eastern neighbours.

The Greens have an additional problem, one that they share with the SPD. Except at the most abstract of levels, the Greens accepted the post-war division of Europe. The Soviet Union was accepted as a legitimate, albeit unnecessarily authoritarian, partner. The territorial losses of 1945 were recognized as the price that had to be paid for Nazi atrocities, and the division of Germany was similarly rationalized in this manner. With regard to Poland in the 1980s, and the very material concerns of *Solidarność*, ritualistic gesture to one side, there was, as much as anything else, mutual miscomprehension. The interests of the Polish peasantry and industrial working class were not those of the new German middle class. As a result of this misconstruction, the Greens were completely unprepared for the coming to power of the decidedly pre-post-modern *Solidarność* government, just as they were wrong-footed by the direction that the *Wende* in the GDR eventually took. Only since 1998, when the Greens entered government in coalition with the SPD, have both parties had a genuine opportunity to overcome this unfortunate legacy.

It would therefore be wholly inaccurate to dismiss the Greens out of hand. In the early 1990s, Antje Vollmer became the first prominent Green to attempt to open a dialogue with the BdV (Linztel 2004). In so doing she had a number of objectives. First, she wished to end the estrangement that existed between the Greens, and indeed the left in general, and the expellees. To this end she explicitly rejected the notion of collective guilt (Vollmer n.d.). Second, she wished to draw the expellees into a constructive dialogue with Poland and the Czech Republic. Third, she hoped that as a result of such an engagement the expellees would move away from the 'prison of history' and their maximalist positions (Lintzel 2004).

Despite these endeavours, the initiative continues to meet with only limited success. The majority of BdV activists have little comprehension of post-modernist politics, which is hardly surprising given their own rather antiquated mindsets. Also, whereas Vollmer extended the hand of friendship, she has also reminded the SdL of some necessary, if uncomfortable, truths. These include the fact that the *Heimat* to which it aspires no longer exists, and as such they cannot 'return' to it (Vollmer 1997). Unfortunately, with regard to the Czech Republic and more especially Poland, as with the PDS, the Greens continue to lack viable partners. The Czech Greens are unrepresented at national level. By way of 'compensation', their German counterparts are active within various Czech–German NGOs, such as the German–Czech Future Fund (Larischová 2004). In addition, Czech candidates appeared on the joint European Green list in the European elections of 2004 (Lintzel 2004).

In Poland the pattern is slightly different in as much as the Polish Greens are not only absent from parliament, but in some parts of the country they have ties to the populist *Samoobrona* (Self-Defence) movement. So, albeit for slightly different reasons, like all German parties, they have found it difficult to enter into sustained high-profile engagements with political parties in either country. A wide emotional gulf exists between the Greens and those who are still wedded to the territorial nation-state. In particular, the sensitivities of many Czechs towards the 'issue' of the Sudetenland illustrates the breadth and depth of this gulf.

The Free Democratic Party

The Free Democratic Party was formed from the remnants of a number of pre-war 'liberal' political formations. Rather like the CDU/CSU, the creation of a single liberal party was meant to limit the catastrophic effects of political-religious sectarianism that had, in part, facilitated the rise of the Nazis. The FDP represented the first successful attempt by German liberals to create a party that could appeal to Catholics, Protestants and secularists on the basis of a shared affinity to liberal principles. The party was also supposed to provide a common home for both 'classical' and 'new' liberals, but to this day, tensions between the two schools of thought are sometimes apparent.

In other words, the FDP has always been prone to division on issues of church and state, and more especially concerning the relationship between state and society. Up until the early 1970s, such divisions were also mani-fest in the attitudes towards Poland and Czechoslovakia. For example, in the 1950s, FDP politicians, together with their counterparts from the SPD, visited Czechoslovakia, despite their membership in the Adenauer-led coalition. To some extent, these visits reflected a generational struggle within the party, but they also reflected the pre-war divisions within the liberal camp, and a northeast–southwest divide within the politics of the Federal Republic.

The extent of these divisions becomes apparent from the fact that, while in the 1950s, some FDP politicians were prepared to talk to the Czech government, the majority of FDP activists were among the most steadfast backers of Adenauer's uncompromising attitude towards Poland and the Czech Republic. However, as the *Politik der Stärke* failed to bring results, a minority of essentially southern 'new' liberals began to advocate the pursuit of a more flexible line. The final straw came on 13 August 1961, with the building of the Berlin Wall. FDP politicians such as Walter Scheel, were gradually able to out-manoeuvre more conservative elements led by such figures as Erich Mende, and, together with more flexible members of the CDU/CSU, sponsor the *Politik der Bewegung*. Although this policy did not actually produce very much in terms of tangible outputs, it did, however, represent an important first step away from entrenched positions and did at least achieve a slight softening of the fronts between Poland and the Federal Republic through the establishment of bilateral trade missions. Given the inability of the CDU/CSU to go that extra mile, the failure of its Ostpolitik further strengthened the basis for co-operation between the increasingly left-leaning FDP, which shared a more pronounced interest in détente with the increasingly centrist SPD. Once the grand coalition of 1966–1969 had achieved its purpose in the domestic sphere, without having accomplished any decisive breakthrough in the realm of Ostpolitik, electoral arithmetic and shared goals meant that an SPD/FDP coalition became possible.

The basis of the coalition was above all a determination to break the impasse that existed between the Federal Republic and its eastern neighbours. Moreover, both parties sought to embed their Ostpolitik within the wider European context, with western integration acting as an anchor of reassurance for Germany's former enemies. Although the FDP was at one with the government, and supplied the foreign minister and vice-chancellor in Walter Scheel, the FDP's path to rapprochement had not been easy. During the late 1960s and into the early 1970s, bitter debates wracked the party with regard to its evolving strategy. The party's former leader Erich Mende and others resigned the parliamentary whip in 1970 in protest at what they perceived to be far too conciliatory a line that in fact promised very little in return. In part, the struggle was generational, but it also reflected the aforementioned fissure between classical and new liberalism within the party, and indeed between those born in the former *Deutsche Ostgebiete* and those who were not.

It could be argued with some justification, that, during the years of the Brandt chancellorship, Walter Scheel and the FDP were sometimes side-lined in foreign policy as a result of Brandt's close personal relationship with Egon Bahr and the role the latter played in formulating and implementing the coalition's Ostpolitik. Either way, Brandt's government quickly abandoned the non-negotiable positions of the Adenauer years, and the new flexibility did at first pay dividends. Having said that, the party's experiences between 1969 and 1974 served it well during the Schmidt years of 1974–1982 and more importantly during the Kohl chancellorship of 1982–1998. Of particular importance here was the role of the vice-chancellor, and long-time foreign minister Hans-Dietrich Genscher.

Genscher may well be a figure who still excites controversy, if nothing else because of the way he engineered the FDP's change of coalition partners in 1982 and because of his sudden resignation as foreign minister in 1992. Yet, there can be little doubt that the continuity in office as foreign minister he provided was of great importance when it came to the diplomacy that led to German unification and the creation of a more settled relationship with Poland and Czechoslovakia/the Czech Republic.

While Genscher's role with regard to the Allies and German unification was absolutely pivotal, it was less so with regard to Poland and the Czech Republic. There are two reasons for this. In the case of Poland, Genscher's marginalization was as much as anything else due to the close personal relations that Kohl struck with several prominent Polish politicians. In the case of the Czech Republic, once again we find something of a vacuum, which no-one was willing to fill. With Genscher pre-occupied with negotiating the external aspects of German unification, and Kohl similarly engaged with Poland, it would perhaps have been useful if another senior politician from within the ranks of the government had reached out in a similarly decisive manner with regard to the Czech Republic. However, it was not to be, and a slight window of opportunity quickly closed.

Since losing office in 1998, the FDP has become somewhat marginal with regard to the policy communities and publics of Poland and the Czech Republic. By the same token, the party is pre-occupied with trying to re-define a role for itself and in staving off the threat of electoral oblivion. Small wonder that relations with the Czech Republic and Poland are not its highest priority. Nevertheless, like all main-stream German political parties it supported Czech and Polish accession to the EU, but unlike its erstwhile coalition partners, it does not suffer from the same constituency pressures as does the CDU/CSU.

The Christian Democratic Union/Christian Social Union

What is often thought to be a single party is in fact comprised of two distinct parties that sit in effective permanent coalition at national level. Both parties are Christian democratic in nature, but the CSU is somewhat more socially conservative than its non-Bavarian cousin. In addition, as we shall see, Bavaria has a distinctive electorate, a large element of which has set views on the Czech Republic.

As we have noted elsewhere, Konrad Adenauer had little doubt that the territory 'under provisional Polish administration' and ceded to the Soviet Union had gone forever. Indeed in 1955, Adenauer actually visited Moscow and established diplomatic relations with the Soviet Union. He did so ostensibly in the hope that a 'real' German presence in Moscow would encourage flexibility on the part of Moscow. Adenauer was, however, aware that in the 1950s, any public admission that the *Ostgebiete* had gone forever would be tantamount to electoral suicide, and could in fact badly destabilize the infant Federal Republic. Apart from Bavaria, up until the early 1960s, the refugee vote was fairly evenly distributed among the major political parties. However, as the SPD began to move away from entrenched positions, so the refugee vote began to consolidate around the CDU/CSU.

This put the leadership of the CDU in a tricky position. Many of the older generation were themselves expellees and refugees (Ther 2001: 61). In 1961, the refugees had abandoned their own political party and in effect submerged it within the CDU/CSU. Also during the early and mid-1960s, as the SPD moved towards a strategy of détente and rapprochement with Central and Eastern Europe, so the CDU/CSU became the 'natural' political home of refugees and expellees. In order to keep them on side, the CDU found that its room for manoeuvre in the field of Ostpolitik was heavily constrained. In effect, CDU politicians were forced to continue to mouth platitudes concerning the non-finality of the post-war borders and the inalienable right of ethnic Germans to return to their former homes. Increasing numbers of CDU politicians knew that this was never going to happen. The problem was convincing the refugees of this fact, without simultaneously alienating them.

Towards the end of his term, Adenauer was, however, forced to concede to more adventurous colleagues that a new strategy should be tried. As a consequence, a slight shift in policy came with the accession of Gerhard Schröder to the post of foreign minister in 1963. In an effort to bring about some movement, an offer to establish diplomatic relations with Warsaw and Prague (among others) was made. The aforementioned *Politik der Bewegung* came into effect, but for various reasons it did not differ greatly from the previous course and apart from the establishment of trading missions in various Soviet bloc capitals, little came of this initiative. The central problem was that hardliners within the CDU/CSU connived to hamstring the initiative from the moment of its inception. Although they did not manage to veto the change in policy, they forced Schröder to incorporate the so-called *Geburtsfehler* theory. This inspired piece of nonsense essentially posited the idea that diplomatic relations could after all be established between Bonn, Prague and Warsaw, because the circumstances of regime birth in East-Central Europe, namely the midwifery of Stalin, meant that such governments had had no choice but to recognize the GDR. While there is little doubt that the governments in Warsaw and Prague would have welcomed greater freedom of movement vis-à-vis the Soviet Union, there is equally no doubt that they had no intention of taking up this rather ungenerous offer. Indeed, it actually played into the hands of hardliners in Prague and East Berlin who, for different reasons, were both petrified at the prospect of Bonn and Moscow reaching out to one another to the detriment of the interests of 'the wider socialist bloc'.

In effect, during the 1960s and into the late 1980s, no opportunity structure existed that the CDU's leadership could utilize in order to move away from positions that had been prepared in the 1950s. This is not to say that the party sought to imitate the SPD, but it is to say that their rhetoric on these issues was more for domestic consumption than anything else. There was also the thorny issue of the CSU's leader, Franz-Josef Strauß, who dominated the party from 1961 when he became chairman, until his unexpected death in 1988. Strauß was a larger-than-life figure, who some accused of having a cavalier attitude towards the law and of sometimes being led by his heart as opposed to his mind. With regard to Poland and the Czech Republic he acted as brake on any initiatives aimed at reconciliation. Naturally enough, he did put forward his own alternatives, which were dismissed out of hand by Warsaw, Prague and of course Moscow. This was hardly a surprise. Strauß was no revisionist, but his immoderate use of language and his (public) lack of understanding for the concerns of ordinary Poles, Czechs and Slovaks resulted in him becoming something of a figure of fear and hatred in both countries.

Apart from anything else, Strauß had his own distinctive electorate to deal with. Bavaria has integrated by far the largest number of Sudeten Germans. They are linguistically and culturally close to indigenous Bavarians, 'solidaristic' and as a social group comparatively wealthy. Then as now, their *Landsmannschaft* reflects these characteristics and pursues a particularly hard line with regard to the right of return, the restoration of citizenship and the demand for compensation (Handl 2004). The CSU is also overwhelmingly the Sudeten German party of choice. The fact that probably a majority of these self-confessed Sudeten Germans have never in fact lived in their ascribed *Heimat* is immaterial. The reality is that many of them regard themselves as having been dispossessed and have acted as a brake upon the CSU and more especially the CDU, which has long been more flexible in these matters.

At this point we shall pause to examine in some depth how the rather narrow parochialism of the CSU is still at work today. In order to do so, we need to step back to the late 1980s. Strauß died in 1988, on the eve of the *Wende*. The new leadership, first under Max Streibl, then under Theo Waigel and finally under its current incumbent Edmund Stoiber, was uncertain of its position and the extent to which support for the CSU would wane without its long-time chief. To compound the situation, in the wake of the *Wende*, the CSU faced a decline in both its electoral importance and weight within the newly united Germany. In order to increase support, various strategies were employed. Aside from pointing to the continued Bavarian economic miracle, and the special nature of Bavarian society as personified by the CSU, successive CSU leaders sought to shore up votes in another direction. By publicly endorsing the claims of the SdL, they hoped and managed to further solidify support from among the ranks of the *Sudetendeutsche* (Meckel 2004). Interestingly, Meckel's views are echoed by the former Czech deputy foreign minister Otto Pick, who in so doing demonstrates a rare and acute understanding of the internal dynamics of politics in Bavaria (Pick 2004).

What works in Bavaria, however, doesn't necessarily work in the rest of Germany. Prior to the general election of 2002, as chancellor candidate, Stoiber became involved in a nasty dispute with several Czech public figures, and it must be said Czech public opinion in general over the Sudetenland issue. In fact, even Chancellor Schröder cancelled a planned visit to Prague in the wake of rising anti-German invective, and an apparent failure on the part of many Czechs to realize that (Sudeten) Germans could not be permanently excluded en masse from residence in any part of the EU. Just as there seemed to be an absence of cool heads in Prague, in Munich, Stoiber voiced not only support for his constituents, but exacerbated the situation by demanding that Poland repeal its version of the Beneš Decrees, the so-called Bierut Decrees. This was a controversial statement on at least two counts. The first is that although in the aftermath of the War various laws were passed that discriminated against Germans, there was no single package of legislation as in Czechoslovakia, nor was any such package created ex post facto. Second, Polish commentators were quick to point out, that any such (vaguely) analogous legislation had already been repealed and that Polish law places no legal restrictions upon German citizens irrespective of place of birth with regard to their legal rights in contemporary Poland (*Dialog* 2002: 19/20). Having said that, Stoiber's pronouncements caused consternation in Poland. Unsurprisingly, the subtleties of Bavarian politics are not widely known in the Polish public. However, Polish observers sometimes evince a tendency to over-estimate the extent to which such issues play a role in national German politics, and the extent to which the expellee vote is of importance in German federal elections. For example, it is simply not true to state that one fifth of the German electorate is comprised of expellees and their descendants and then to imply that, in terms of voting behaviour, this group acts as a coherent whole (Sakson 2004). If nothing else, it ignores the real pattern of voting behaviour in Germany, the passage of time, inter-marriage and change of interest, if not attitude. In effect, such views are little more than the contemporary reproduction of a Cold War stereotype.

With regard to the right of Germans to settle in Poland until the EU transition periods expire, restrictions of various sorts that affect former *Reichs-* and *Volksdeutsche* do actually exist, even if they are not explicitly spelled out in current legislation. Within this context it is important to consider Polish citizenship and nationality law. First, the law of 1950 effectively confirmed the expulsions and accorded Polish nationality upon all (former) Germans bar the designated German minority. Under the terms of further legislation in 1962, remaining members of the designated German minority were also offered Polish nationality. Today, in Polish law, the status of those who fled or were expelled to Germany prior to 1950, or emigrated to Germany between 1950 and 1962, and wish to move to Poland is still in need of clarification. In recent years, money and rank have usually proven to be important factors in overcoming (hypothetical) legal obstacles. This even includes the restoration of Polish citizenship on a case by case basis. Either way, today the situation with regard to the Czech Republic is not directly comparable, precisely because there was no set of constitutional or other laws that in part set out the criteria either for expulsion or of acceptance.

It is worth pausing at this juncture to illustrate how the affiliation between the CSU and the Sudeten Germans in effect prevents the CSU entering into constructive and public discourse with Czech society and its political representatives (Handl 2004). In the spring of 2003, the ten CSU representatives to the European Parliament (EP) voted against Czech accession to the EU. In a press release of 9 April 2003, Bernd Posselt, the foreign policy speaker of the CSU delegation to the EP, and more importantly the federal chairman of the SdL, explained his and the actions of his colleagues in the following manner. Whereas they welcomed Czech accession to the EU, it was felt necessary to register a protest at the continued refusal of successive Czech governments to repeal those of the Beneš Decrees that dealt with expropriation and expulsion of Czechoslovakia's German minority. Posselt couched his language within the overall discourse of human rights, and denied he and other CSU MEPs were attempting to relativize the crimes of the Nazis (Posselt 2003). Despite the fact that Posselt has a reasonably positive image in the Czech Republic, such intellectual sophistry cuts little ice in that country, where the CSU's 'No' vote was taken at face value.

Given these and other constraints, the CSU is unlikely in the near future to become a major force for new thinking in this area. This can only come about when and if the party and its constituency together with elements of Czech society affect a move away from a culture built around mutual recrimination and one-sided interpretations of the past. As long as the CSU is so intimately bound with the SdL, this is unlikely to happen. On the Czech side, until such a move takes place, in essence the party will simply be seen by many as anti-Czech (Kovanic 2004). Again, the contrast with Poland is clear, when during the late 1980s and early 1990s, despite various protestations, the CSU was unable to put a stop to Helmut Kohl's unlikely but blossoming friendship with Poland.

As we noted earlier, prior to becoming chancellor, Poland had not been one of Kohl's main priorities. In fact, he didn't pay it much attention before the summer of 1988. Having said that, in the early 1980s *Solidarność* did enter into a tentative rapprochement with elements of the CDU. It came about as a result of the Polish trade union's disappointment with the SPD with regard to martial law, and the gradual realization on the part of the CDU that many *Solidarność* activists were in effect Christian democratic in orientation. The Polish opposition was also reassured to learn through an oblique answer to a planted parliamentary question, that the CDU/CSU accepted Poland's western border (Hajnicz 1995: 28ff.). It was one less thing for them to worry about, and dealt a blow to the anti-German propaganda that formed one of various shaky props that the Jaruzelski regime relied on in legitimating itself.

Returning to Kohl himself, we find that between 1988 and 1990, he helped effect a sea change in attitudes towards Poland on the part of the CDU. Like the CSU, in the 1970s and early 1980s the CDU had endlessly repeated old shibboleths with regard to the Czech Republic and Poland. However, with the rise to power of *Solidarność* in the summer of 1989, Kohl seized the opportunity to re-cast relationships with Poland. In truth, he was probably aided by Strauß's untimely death, and the need of his successors – Streibel, Waigel and ultimately Stoiber – to bed down and consolidate their authority within the CSU. From whichever way it is viewed, with regard to Poland, Kohl once again showed himself to be a consummate foreign policy maker.

Kohl was also aided by the fact that the majority of his negotiating partners in Poland were either liberal intellectuals or de facto Christian democrats. This was important. Given that the two sides shared a basic worldview, it was relatively easy for rapport to be achieved. There was ideological affinity, coupled with willingness on both sides to start from scratch and not on the basis of what had happened between 1939 and 1950. In effect, the German government managed to find natural allies in Poland with whom business could be done. Given the subsequent re-alignment within the Polish centre-right, it was somewhat fortuitous that this opportunity was not wasted. The prospects of a speedy consensus being reached with the post-*Solidarność* centre-right would have been much more uncertain.

Kohl and his advisers quickly realized that, in order to secure German unity, there would have to be full recognition of the territorial status quo between Poland and Germany and that the refugees would have to renounce any right to return outside of a united Europe. The question was more of timing and the exact formula of words to be used. In order to facilitate the creation of such a Europe, Kohl was prepared to offer Germany's services as Poland's de facto ambassador to Brussels. The treaties of 1990 and 1991 in effect cemented this deal.

The *Landsmannschaften* were divided in terms of how to respond to the changed situation. The older generation looked upon Kohl's actions as a betrayal. The younger generation, on the other hand, recognized political realities and the fact that what was now Polish territory could not be 're-Germanicized' in any shape or form. In 1989 and 1990, Kohl faced down his own hardliners and presented them with a choice: either you want unification with the GDR or you do not. He made it clear that, in the light of historical and political realities, no other form of unification was possible, any more than were special administrative arrangements for former German territories beyond the existing boundaries of the two German states.

By acknowledging these facts, the Kohl government laid the groundwork for a decade of co-operation between Poland and Germany that resulted in bilateral relations improving beyond recognition. There was also an increase in trade and in inter-personal contacts, including between German refugees and Poles, who themselves often were refugees and understood the

German sense of loss. This is not to say that problems do not remain. The aforementioned gaffe (with regard to the 'Bierut Decrees') by Stoiber is a case in point. Furthermore, as EU accession beckoned, the voluble Polish right sought with some degree of success to play upon traditional fears of Germany. Nevertheless, the situation that exists between Poland and Germany can be contrasted favourably with that between the Czech Republic and Germany. The question we must now address is why was the CDU unable to replicate its success with Poland in terms of relations with the Czech Republic?

The reservoir of goodwill that existed towards Poland does not and did not exist to the same extent with regard the Czech Republic. This is despite the fact that in the 1980s, a new point of departure became apparent with the *Wende*, and the hospitality offered in Prague to GDR refugees in transit to the Federal Republic (*Historikerkommission* 1995: 79). Apart from the fact that Germany accords the Czech Republic less geopolitical weight than it does Poland (Handl 2004), a number of factors account for this differentiated state of affairs. First, we have the aforementioned non-negotiable positions that occupy both the CSU and elements of the Czech polity. Second, although Kohl personally showed great interest in, and great enthusiasm for, Polish–German reconciliation, he was unable to affect the same strategy with regard to the Czech Republic. Neither was any other German or indeed Czech politician able to step in to fill the breach. In fact, when President Havel tried, he found himself isolated from the majority of Czech society (Handl 2004). German politicians with an interest in the wider region were pre-occupied with Poland, and in the early 1990s Czech politicians became pre-occupied with the 'Velvet Divorce'. The result was that both sides took their eyes off the ball. Third, Christian Democratic parties, such as the *Křest'anská a demokratické unie* (Christian and Democratic Union/KDU), exist in the Czech Republic. So in theory at least, the CDU (if not the CSU), does have natural partners with which to build relationships. The problem is that, although limited co-operation on the basis of ideological correspondence is possible, historical baggage and a refusal to move from long entrenched positions means that the possibilities for co-operation are limited. This applies equally to Czech Christian Democratic parties as it does to the CSU. The CDU is less handicapped in this respect precisely because its links to the *Landsmannschaften* are not as intimate as they are with respect to its sister party (Handl 2004). In turn, this state of affairs exists due to the final factor we must consider, namely the psychological inheritance that burdens relations between the two countries, with which we will deal in more depth later.

At the time of writing, Edmund Stoiber continues to be the joint chancellor candidate for both parties. Given the unhappy experience of the 2002 general election, it remains open to question whether under his leadership the CDU/CSU can affect a further quantum leap towards the Czech Republic analogous to that taken in the 1990s by the CDU with regard to Poland. Having said that, in order for such a step to be accomplished, many Czech politicians, including President Václav Klaus, will have to re-assess their own position on various issues linked to Germany and the Germans. The hostile reception dealt to former President Havel in 1990 by many of his fellow citizens concerning his personal apology with regard to the post-war expulsions does not bode well.

6 Domestic constituencies and foreign audiences

The *Landsmannschaften* and their impact on German–Polish and German–Czech relations

Between 1945 and 1949, large numbers of ethnic Germans were expelled from their homelands in Central and Eastern Europe. The bulk of these expulsions occurred in Poland and Czechoslovakia. Since then about another 4 million ethnic Germans (together with non-German family members) have left Central and Eastern Europe and settled in the Federal Republic. In the early post-war years their political organization was prohibited by the Allies, but the foundation of the Federal Republic in 1949 offered the opportunity for expellees and refugees to organize themselves politically and socially. Initially a powerful political actor, since the mid-1960s, their influence on German domestic and foreign policy has declined. Yet, the ferocity with which their claims are still sometimes made has kindled the impression among sections of the wider Polish and Czech populations, strategically facilitated by some elements within both countries' political establishment, that their influence on, if not dominance of, German Ostpolitik continues unabated.

In this chapter we will outline the major developments in the formation, ascent and marginalization of expellee organizations in the Federal Republic and contextualize expellee policies towards Poland and the Czech Republic and the remaining ethnic Germans in both countries within a broader German domestic policy discourse. We will focus our attention particularly on the changed situation after the collapse of communism and the end of the Cold War and analyse the new opportunities that have since arisen for a sustained process of constructive reconciliation between Germany and its two eastern neighbours. The obvious legacy of the past in this context, in different and selective ways, has been, and is being, dealt with in all three countries. This is a factor that has retained its significance with regard to relations between Germany and Poland, and Germany and the Czech Republic.

Coping with expulsion and loss, 1945–1955

The major problem facing German policy-makers after the First World War had been the territorial truncation of German territory and the level of reparations to be paid by Germany. A completely new challenge presented itself after 1945. Ethnic Germans, in particular from Central and East European countries, were either expelled or fled from their traditional areas of settlement. During and after the expulsion process Germans were subjected to systematic popular and state discrimination as a result of the atrocious occupation policies of the Nazis during the war, in which many of them had actively participated. Although this wave of expulsion had ended by 1950, repression did not, and full citizenship rights were restored only gradually. Unsurprisingly, the West German goverment deemed this situation to be unsatisfactory. In part this was partly because ethnic Germans in countries such as Poland suffered all the 'usual' disadvantages of life under communism, and partly because residual bitterness from the German occupation left them vulnerable to continued discrimination.

In the early years of its existence, the Federal Republic was preoccupied with other issues both domestically and in its external relations. Domestically, the rebuilding of social and economic life, including the integration of over 8 million refugees and expellees took priority.[1] On the international stage, Chancellor Adenauer had set a foreign policy agenda whose foremost aim was to ensure the integration of the country into the Western alliance.

This process of western integration, which provided a path to political security, economic recovery and gradually also to social prosperity, was the preferred option of the overwhelming majority of the population and politicians. Yet, at the same time, as a symbol of post-war developments the Western alliance signalled, at least temporarily, an acceptance of the status quo, which, given the German borders in 1949, found significantly less public support. While it was generally accepted that neither Alsace and Lorraine nor the Sudetenland could be rightfully claimed by Germany, the establishment of the German–Polish border along the Oder–Neiße line was publicly denounced by West German politicians from across the political spectrum. Simultaneously, however, it was equally clear that the federal government was in no position to offer a credible political approach as to how to revise the German–Polish border. Not only was this contrary to the interests of the Four Powers, West Germany itself lacked a common border with Poland. Despite the claim of the Federal Republic to be the sole representative of the German people, it was a matter of political reality that in July 1950 the East German state, in violation of the Potsdam Agreement, had officially recognized the new border in a treaty with Poland. On top of that, the SED denied it had any refugees or expellees on its territory. According to the official terminology they were dealing with *Umsiedler* or re-settlers. No form of *Umsiedler* self-expression was tolerated, even within the confines of communist front organizations. On the contrary, the SED argued that the existence of such organizations simply served to slow the integration of new arrivals within the host-society.

Therefore, there was no point in permitting the establishment of such organizations even as affiliates of the ruling party.

This unfavourable position, however, did not prevent political activists among the expellees from keeping the issue of expulsions and of the territorial losses Germany had incurred after 1945 on the domestic political agenda of the Federal Republic. Expellees and refugees had not only suffered the trauma of being forced from their ancestral homelands, but of being transported to underdeveloped areas of rural Bavaria, Lower Saxony and Schleswig Holstein. Despite the popular mythology cultivated by the political authorities of the newly emergent Federal Republic, the indigenous population did not necessarily welcome the incomers with open arms (Hoffman 1996: 77). Their customs and dialects were different. In some cases, as with arrivals from Russia and Romania, the incomers spoke varieties of German that had long since disappeared in Germany itself. Others, for instance Kashubes and Masurians, often spoke little or no German. In general, the refugees were viewed as being a further unwelcome burden on the available scarce resources. In fact, opinion surveys in 1949 found that as much as 61 per cent of the indigenous population viewed the expellees and refugees as unwelcome intruders (Franzen 2001: 224).

The Western Allies faced something of a conundrum when dealing with the expellees and refugees. In part they were in the western zones as a result of decisions taken at Yalta and Potsdam. Germany had not only been defeated it had been destroyed. With regard to the expellees and refugees the question was how to integrate them before they developed a special refugee group identity (Franzen 2001: 231). Eventually it was decided to reverse an earlier ban on the formation of expellee organizations in the hope that such societies could in fact aid rather than hinder the integration process. Particularly after the Prague coup of 1948, the Allies recognized that the refugees constituted a staunch anti-communist reservoir of support. The danger was that if they remained outside the fabric of the emergent Federal Republic they might fall prey to National Socialist remnants. Thus, although an official ban on expellee organizations in place in all three western occupation zones existed until 1949, refugees and expellees began to organize themselves at the local level as early as July 1945 and often in close association with the churches (Franzen 2001: 257). Following the rescinding of the ban on the formation of statewide organizations competing structures arose. The *Zentralverband der vertriebenen Deutschen* (Central Association of Expelled Germans/ZvD) (from 1951 the *Bund vertriebener Deutscher*/Federation of Expelled Germans/BvD) concerned itself primarily with social and economic issues of integration and compensation, while the individual *Landsmannschaften* focused on the preservation of the expellees' distinct geographic identities, including their traditions, customs and culture. In August 1949, nine of those organized at the federal level, or in the process of so doing, formed the *Vereinigung der ostdeutschen Landsmannschaften* (Union of

Eastern German Regional-Cultural Associations/VoL). In 1951 four of the *Landsmannschaften* joined the BvD, whilst simultaneously retaining membership in the VoL. Later in 1951, the first attempt to overcome this duality failed. The VoL pursued its own organizational consolidation, and admitted further regional-cultural associations of expellees from Southeastern Europe. In August 1952 it changed its name to the *Verband der Landsmannschaften* (League of Regional-Cultural Associations/VdL), and began to establish branches throughout West Germany.

The political agenda of the various expellee organizations had been laid down in the 1950 Charter of the German Expellees. This document has guided expellee demands and policies ever since and is a vivid expression of the identity of expellees as a particular group in West German post-war society united by their collective experiences of suffering and their desire to correct the wrongs of expulsion. In the Charter, the expellees proclaimed their willingness to forgo revenge and retribution, to support the creation of a united and free Europe, and to contribute to the reconstruction of Germany and Europe. On this basis, they demanded complete equality in West Germany: that the entire population share the financial burdens brought about by flight and expulsion; the integration of all occupational groups in the German economy, and the inclusion of the expellees in the European reconstruction effort. Despite their demands being focused on integration in West Germany, the expellees insisted on their right to return to their particular *Heimat* and demanded that this be recognized as a fundamental human right.[2] Recognition of this identification with the *Heimat* provides the key to understanding what united people from the most diverse geographical, professional, social and political backgrounds:

> To separate human beings with force from their homeland means to kill their spirit. We have suffered and experienced this fate. Therefore, we feel called upon to demand that the right to homeland be recognised and implemented as a God-given basic right of all humankind.
>
> (Charta 1950)

The expellees' articulation of a common suffering and loss of homeland did initially not result in the creation of a common political platform. Between 1948/1949 and 1952 two wings within the broad spectrum of expellee and refugee organizations fought for political leadership. One wing focused on the so-called 'national principle' and made the recovery of the lost homeland its political priority. Oriented towards the political far right, it did not manage to generate sufficient electoral support. In contrast, the *Bund der Heimatvertriebenen und Entrechteten* (Union of Expellees and DisDisenfranchized/BHE), after November 1952, the *Gesamtdeutscher Block/Bund der Heimatvertriebenen und Entrechteten* (All-German Bloc/Union of Expellees and Disenfranchized/GB/BHE) raised its profile. It gained spectacular electoral support by addressing the specific social and economic interests of the expellees in the Federal Republic. Electoral successes, however, resulted in a gradual decline of the party. The greater the social and economic integration of the expellees, the less this population group felt the need for a distinct political party. The BHE's failure to form a permanent and stable coalition with other smaller right-of-centre parties led it to fall below the 5 per cent threshold in the federal elections in 1957 and again in 1961 after it had been subsumed within the *Gesamtdeutsche Partei* (All-German Party/GdP). Despite its short existence, the BHE played an important part in the contribution the German refugees and expellees made to a post-war West German history characterized by the successful development of democracy and rule of law, and the peaceful realization of German unification.[3] The road was to prove to be a long one, and the shared loss of homeland and feelings of suffering continued to be essential components of the expellees' identity in the Federal Republic. These experiences shaped expellee organizations in West German civil society, as they began to develop a foreign policy agenda of their own.

Maintaining memory and identity, 1955–1990

By the mid-1950s, it had become clear to activists in both the BvD and the VdL that the representation of expellee interests could become more efficient if a single organization would be created within which the thus far separate entities would pool their resources. This process was completed in October 1957, and the *Bund der Vertriebenen–Vereinigte Landsmann-schaften und Landesverbände* (Union of Expellees–United Regional-Cultural Associations and State Organizations/BdV) came into being. It consisted of twenty regional-cultural associations,[4] eleven state organizations (one in each of the federal states as of 1949, with five new ones being founded after German unification in 1990), and seven special-interest groups.[5] The organization's main publication, the *Deutscher Ostdienst* (German Eastern Service/DOD), published a statement by the first president of the BdV, Hans Krüger, in which he defined the mission of his organization as one of mediation between east and west. Krüger (1999[1958]: 3) went on to say:

> In the spirit of a humanist-Christian worldview, in the spirit of the best eastern German cultural traditions, in the spirit of Leibniz, Kant, Herder and Lessing, the expellees not only forgo revenge and retribution, but they seek reconciliation of the seemingly irreconcilable in order to prepare the ground for a peace of law and justice. This noble attitude gives them the right to demand justice for themselves and for all expellees and refugees in the world.

As does the Charter of the German Expellees itself, Krüger (ibid.) also emphasized the right of the expellees to their homeland and to self-determination and their claim to contribute to the peaceful coexistence of all peoples in freedom. The fact that the fulfilment of these wishes would have had an obvious and clearly detrimental affect on the post-war inhabitants in former German areas of settlement seems to have been lost upon such authors. No matter the genuine sentiment that lay behind such statements, the reality of the situation is that in order to facilitate return others would be at best subject to even greater insecurity, and at worst, renewed dislocation.

By the mid-1950s, when Germany's integration into the western world had sufficiently progressed through membership in NATO and the precursor institutions of today's European Union, the country's leadership could turn eastwards more confidently. As a result of public pressure and political lobbying by the various expellee organizations, the Federal Republic committed itself to a foreign policy vis-à-vis the communist countries in Central and Eastern Europe that, while avoiding an official recognition of established borders, for the time being implicitly accepted the status quo. This policy shift included humanitarian efforts to improve the situation of ethnic Germans in these countries. The possibilities of direct involvement, however, were extremely limited throughout this period until 1989 so that the major instrument of German external minority policy was the negotiation of agreements with the host-states that facilitated the migration of ethnic Germans Germany.[6] A precondition for this was the establishment of diplomatic relations with the relevant states in the eastern bloc, a necessity also recognized by the expellee organizations. In his 1958 contribution to the first issue of DOD, Krüger (1998 [1958]: 4) noted that an

> isolated German *Ostpolitik* and with it the realization of the political goals of the expellees with respect to their homeland are impossible. Both depend on the correct analysis of the geopolitical situation and they have to be executed in consideration of the policy of the western bloc. [...] Geopolitically, they depend on political détente between east and west.

The first step in this direction taken by the federal government was the Soviet–German Treaty of 1955, followed by a verbal agreement between the two sides in 1958 according to which all those persons of ethnic German origin who had been German citizens before 21 June 1941 were entitled to repatriation.[7] Treaties with Poland (1970) and Czechoslovakia (1973), both of which were rejected by the apposite *Landsmannschaften*, followed, specifically addressing the sensitive issue of borders and confirming that the German government of the day respected the territorial status quo. In both treaties, the signatory states assured one another of respect for each other's territorial integrity and affirmed that neither had territorial claims against the other (*Bulletin der Bundesregierung* 1970:

1815 and 1973: 1631). Nonetheless, rulings of the German Constitutional Court in 1973, 1975 and 1987, rejected any suggestion that the treaties with Moscow and Warsaw violated fundamental assertions of Germany's Basic Law. In other words, in the absence of a peace treaty, Germany still continued in law to exist within its borders of 1937. While this interpretation pleased the BdV, it did not have a practical impact on the foreign policy of the federal government. Nor did it improve the opportunity structure for the BdV to become more actively involved in foreign policy matters.

Throughout the 1970s, the BdV lost influence, at first with the left, and then also with the CDU. The shrill nature of its rejection of Willy Brandt's Ostpolitik carried echoes of both the language of the 1930s and the Federal Republic's Neo-Nazi movement. Only the BdV leadership and activists failed to see how they helped to bring others to this conclusion. Having said that, the extra-parliamentary left, which in turn helped later to spawn the Greens, was itself keen to portray those who rejected Ostpolitik as potential neo-Nazis. As we noted in the previous chapter, it was only in the late 1980s, when the rhetoric between the BdV and the left had moderated, that both sides were once again able to view the other as legitimate (Meckel 2004). As for the BdV's relationship with the CDU, it was to be sorely disappointed when that party returned to government in 1982.

The insistence of leading BdV officials up until the late 1980s that the border question was still open led to serious disagreement with the CDU-led governments of Helmut Kohl. The political impotence of the expellee organizations became strikingly obvious in 1985, when, after a personal intervention by Chancellor Kohl, the motto for the annual convention of the Silesian expellees had to be changed from '40 Years of Expulsion – Silesia Remains Ours' to '40 Years of Expulsion – Silesia Remains Our Future in the Europe of Free Peoples'. The marginality of the *Landsmannschaften* was further illustrated in 1987 when Herbert Hupka, the chairman of the *Landsmannschaft Schlesien*, lost his safe seat on the CDU list for the forthcoming federal elections.

From the late 1980s, the lack of expellee political power was offset by a growing interest on their part in social and cultural issues in the expellees' countries of origin, particularly at the local level. Activists, including many who had been born in the Federal Republic, took advantage of the crumbling of the Soviet block. They began to commit more time and funds to helping ethnic German resettlers from Central and Eastern Europe (*Aussiedler*) integrate in German society, to preserving their own cultural heritage and traditions, and to developing and increasing cross-border human contacts with Czechoslovakia and Poland and other host-states of ethnic German minorities in Central and Eastern Europe.

As we saw in Chapters 3 and 4, the period between 1955 and 1989/1990 was characterized by the priority of promoting co-existence between East and West against the background of the political realities of the Cold War.

This did not leave the West German government any option other than to facilitate the emigration of ethnic Germans from Central and Eastern Europe to the Federal Republic. By the mid 1980s, the BdV and its associated organizations had backed themselves into a rather dank and unpleasant corner. Almost without influence within the SPD, the FDP and especially the Greens, they were rapidly losing sympathy among the hierarchy of the CDU and could only find a hearing within the CSU. For much of German society at large, at best they were an embarrassment, and at worst suspiciously nationalistic in terms of their demands. Quite unexpectedly however, in the late 1980s when fortunes were at their lowest, a surprising twist of fate came to pass that had the effect of reviving general German interest in East-Central Europe and beyond.

The expellee organizations and the challenge of the post-Cold War environment

The transition to democracy in Central and Eastern Europe provided an entirely different framework of new and enlarged opportunities for Germany's external minority policy. On the one hand, democratization meant the granting of such basic rights and liberties as the freedoms of speech, association and political participation. As a result, ethnic Germans in their host-countries were allowed to form their own parties, stand for election and actively advocate the interests of their group. On the other hand, it also meant that there were no longer any restrictions on emigration, and given the experience of the past, many ethnic Germans, particularly in Poland, Romania and the Soviet Union and its successor states seized this opportunity and migrated to Germany. Both developments required a measured and carefully considered policy response. This was necessary domestically because of the enormous influx of resettlers, and internationally in order to assure Germany's neighbours in Central and Eastern Europe of the inviolability of the post-war borders, while simultaneously supporting German minorities at qualitatively and quantitatively new levels and ensuring their protection as national minorities. All this had to take place within the framework of general German foreign policy premises, such as the support for the transition to democracy and a market economy, the creation of a new collective security order embracing all states in Europe and respect for international law and human rights.

Following the collapse of the Soviet bloc, the most important law passed in response to the vast increase in ethnic Germans[8] leaving their host-states in order to migrate to Germany was the 1993 War Consequences Conciliation Act. Entitlement to German citizenship, formerly automatic, was revoked. In order to qualify for migration ethnic Germans now had to provide evidence of discrimination in their host-states and a long-standing affinity with German culture, language and traditions. They also had to demonstrate that they were of German descent. Furthermore, the annual intake of ethnic Germans was limited to the average of the years 1991 and 1992 within a 10 per cent margin, i.e. an annual maximum of about 250,000 people. Before this piece of legislation was passed, a bill was approved that required ethnic Germans to apply for admission to Germany in their host-states. Restricting migration to the specified quotas could therefore be made easier. In 1996, authorities introduced a language test as a way of ensuring applicants' affinity to German language and culture. These new regulations have considerably reduced the influx of ethnic Germans into Germany. From a number of around 220,000 each year between 1993 and 1995, the immigration figures dropped to 178,000 in 1996 and 134,000 in 1997. In 1998, just over 100,000 ethnic Germans migrated to Germany. In 1999 their number was marginally up to 104,916. By 2000 the number of ethnic Germans migrating to the Federal Republic was below 100,000 for the first time in more than a decade.[9]

Realizing that the changed conditions also required a fundamentally different foreign policy approach, the German government embedded its external minority policy into the wider framework of its efforts to promote democracy, prosperity and security in Central and Eastern Europe. Given the ethnopolitical demography of the region with its many national minorities, latent border disputes and inter-ethnic tensions, it was obvious that the role of minorities would be crucial. The ultimate test of successful democratization would have to include an assessment of whether or not members of national minorities, individually and collectively, were entitled to full equality and the right to preserve, express and develop their distinct identities in their host-states. Furthermore, it would not be possible to operate a viable collective security system without settling existing ethnic and territorial conflicts and establishing frameworks within which future disputes could be resolved peacefully. Taking these assumptions as a starting point, the German government concluded that national minorities could play a crucial part in bringing about results in these two inter-related processes as they were in a position to bridge existing cultural gaps (*Bundestagsdrucksache* 13/10845; *BMI-Pressemitteilung* 18 May 1999; and *BMI-Pressemitteilung* 14 June 1999). The federal government sought to create partnerships with the Central and East European host-states and the German minorities living there that, on the basis of international treaties and bilateral agreements,[10] would promote the government's 'overall foreign policy concept of a European peace policy of reconciliation, understanding and co-operation' (*Bundestagsdrucksache* 13/3195). Importantly, they sought to draw the *Landsmannschaften* into this process. In so doing the government hoped that constructive engagement on the part of the *Landsmannschaften* would steer them away from their old obsessions and simultaneously demonstrate to Czechs and Poles that the *Landsmannschaften* were not armed to the teeth and ready to invade (Rossmanith 2004).

It was held that resultant cultural, social and economic measures to support German minorities, although primarily 'aimed at an improvement of the living conditions of ethnic Germans in their host-countries', would benefit whole regions and their populations independent of their ethnic origin. Inter-ethnic harmony and economic prosperity would be promoted while the emerging democratic political structures would be strengthened *(Bundestagsdrucksache* 13/3428 and *Bundestagsdrucksache* 13/1116). By creating favourable conditions for the integration of ethnic Germans in the societies of their host-states as citizens with equal rights, the German government hoped to provide an alternative to emigration *(Bundestags-drucksache* 13/3428).

Not all of the subsequent projects have been successful. In the early stages, there was a general lack of co-ordination because a comprehensive concept of external minority policy was still in the process of being formulated and adapted to the new conditions. Millions of Deutschmark were pumped into large-scale schemes. Yet, once the money had been allocated, there was often little or no control of the progress of a given project and outcomes in terms of increasing the willingness of ethnic Germans to remain in their host-countries. Even closer to home, the *Verein für das Deutschtum im Ausland* (Association for German Culture Overseas/ VdA) was involved in a financial scandal about the misuse of 22 million Deutschmark of support funds allocated to it by the Federal Ministry of the Interior.

It came as no surprise when, soon after it came to power in 1998, the new Red–Green coalition government began to re-conceptualize German external minority policy. In 1999, it decided to abandon all large-scale investment plans as they did not have any measurable positive effect on the decision of ethnic Germans whether to emigrate to Germany or not. Instead, various small-scale strategies were drawn up, and a number of them have since come to fruition. These seek to concentrate resources on projects to facilitate self-help, in particular through providing start-up funding for small and medium-size businesses, to improve the services offered by the meeting centres for ethnic Germans abroad *(Begegnungs-stätten)*, to increase training and qualification programmes, to provide more German classes, to fund initiatives by communal partnerships, and to intensify social work with young ethnic Germans. Furthermore, the government decided to focus these efforts primarily on Russia and Poland *(BMI-Pressemitteilung* 1 September 1999; and *BMI-Pressemitteilung* 10 August 1999). Aid programmes for German minorities in other countries, such as Romania or the Baltic Republics, were not phased out. Rather, they were scaled down and re-focused upon social work, as the new federal government came to realize that these programmes were an important instrument of a foreign policy aimed at 'the peaceful and tolerant coexistence of various national groups' in states that host German minorities *(BMI-Pressemitteilung* 2 July 1999; and *BMI-Pressemitteilung* 21 October 1999).

Today, the restructuring and partial re-conceptualization of Germany's external minority policy is, on the one hand, driven by the desire for greater effectiveness, and, on the other, also by the need to decrease spending in all areas in order to consolidate the federal budget. For the period from 2000 to 2003, annual cuts of 26 million Deutschmark were proposed with regard to 'Measures in Support of German Minorities in Their Host Countries'.[11]

While expellee organizations generally acknowledge the need for structures that are more efficient and accept that spending cuts in the area of external minority policy cannot be completely avoided, they have particularly criticized the new concept for the promotion of the 'German Culture of Eastern Europe'.[12] The main criticisms have not been directed at the proposed budget cuts, but at the plans for restructuring the entire network of organizations and institutions involved in the preservation of expellee culture and cross-border cultural co-operation with the former homelands. The new concept proposes the centralization of the network through the grouping of various organizations and institutions on a 'broad regional basis' – north-eastern Europe (Pomerania, East and West Prussia, parts of the former Soviet Union, and Baltic Republics), Silesia, the *Sudetenland* and south-eastern Europe. Despite the fact that there were numerous inconsistencies in the previous scheme of administering the cultural work of expellee organizations, including the costly duality of institutions at many levels, the proposed centralization is more likely to undermine the basis of this cultural work, most of which has been carried out by expellees and *(Spät)Aussiedler*. The government justifies these changes by claiming that expellee organizations have not fully come to terms with the post-1989 geopolitical changes. Moreover, the policy presumes that on the grounds of old age alone, the expellees of 1945–1950 could and should no longer be the main activists of cultural exchange (cf. Rossmann 1999 and Müller 1999). These developments are uncomfortable reminders of past ideological battles and cast a shadow of doubt at the commitment of the current federal government to continue the co-operation with expellees in the process of reconciliation.

Unreconstructed irredentism or reconciliation?
A new opportunity for the expellees

The collapse of communism came as unexpectedly for the expellee organizations as it did for the German government. Yet between the two, the perception of the opportunities arising from the dramatic events in 1989/1990 was rather different. Government policy, which was aimed at achieving unification, at the price of abandoning all territorial claims and formally guaranteeing the borders of the GDR as those of the united Germany was seen as unacceptable and treacherous by many in the leadership of the BdV. Instead, activists proposed that a referendum be held in

(Polish) Silesia under the motto *Frieden durch freie Abstimmung* (Peace through Free Choice). This strange initiative raised completely unrealistic hopes among many members of the German minority in Poland, particularly in rural Upper Silesia where the response to the signature campaign in support of the referendum had been strong. These hopes were dashed when Chancellor Kohl declared at an event celebrating the fortieth anniversary of the Charter of the German Expellees in 1990 that the recognition of the Oder–Neiße line as Germany's eastern frontier was the price that had to be paid for the reunification with East Germany.[13]

Even though a border question similar to that between Germany and Poland never existed in the relationship between the Federal Republic and Czechoslovakia/the Czech Republic, the rhetoric of expellee activists has, if anything, been more aggressive on the Sudeten German issue. This became particularly obvious in a 1991 collection of essays written by leading figures of the Sudeten German community on the obligation of the Sudeten Germans vis-à-vis their homeland (Eibicht 1991). In one of the essays, Harry Hochfelder (1991: 58), a member of the Sudeten German Council and the Sudeten German Academy of Sciences and Arts, demanded that the:

> restitution [of property] has to be handled in a way that the ethnic group [of Sudeten Germans] can exercise unlimited sovereignty in its homeland. Certainly there will be emigration of the non-German population currently living in the area, for which incentives have to be made available, but which must not be forced.

Roland Schnürch, Vice President of Federal Assembly of the *Sudetendeutsche Landsmannschaft*, stated the claims of some Sudeten Germans to Czech territory even more forcefully. He 'decisively' rejected the 'belonging of the *Sudetenland* to any Czechoslovak state'. From this, he concluded that 'the border question has not yet been solved' (Schnürch 1991: 83). Another contributor, Willi Wanka (1991: 75), a member of the advisory committee on foreign affairs of the Sudeten German Council, insisted that 'without the return of the Sudeten areas to the Sudeten Germans, there will be no resolution of the Sudeten German question'.

In order better to understand the attitude of the *Sudetendeutsche Landsmannschaft*, it would be just as well to pause at this juncture, and consider the nature of Sudeten 'expellee' society in Germany. Of all the various expellee groups, they are the most cohesive, and have been the most adept at maintaining a collective identity (Hahn 2001: 254). They not only maintain an interest in the folklore and history of the region from where the elder generation came, they also maintain an active political interest in that region. This is not to say that other *Landsmannschaften* are politically disinterested in their regions of origin. It is to say, however, that protestations to the contrary to one side, contemporary politics is very often secondary to the purpose of re-creating the *Heimat* in Germany and organizing *Nostalgiereisen* to the *Heimat* itself.

Since 1956, the *Sudetendeutsche* community in Bavaria has been officially recognized as constituting the fourth tribe of Bavaria alongside the Franks, Swabians and Old Bavarians. This cultural identity is complemented by their collective political identity that, as we have seen, articulates a strident message towards the Czech Republic. In fact, the way in which the *Sudetendeutsche* have embedded themselves within Bavarian society is seen by some Czech observers as a hindrance to the cause of Czech–German reconciliation (Larischová 2004). It is argued that as a result they exercise a disproportionate influence in internal Bavarian politics, at the federal level in Berlin and most of all in Germany's relations with the Czech Republic (Žák 2004).

Given the time that has elapsed since the Munich Agreement and its aftermath, what is particularly curious is the fact that politically active members of the SdL are grouped around the ancestral political tendencies that dominated *Sudetendeutsche* politics prior to Munich. So to this day Christian Democratic, Social Democratic and National Conservative trends, all of whom have their roots in pre-1938 Czechoslovak politics are observable within the political statements of the SdL (Hahn 2001: 255ff.). Once again, some Czech observers of the scene cite this lack of intellectual modernization as hindering progress between the two sides (Žák 2004). Others go so far as to label it a 'disaster' (Křen 2004).

Certain observers acknowledge that in recent years the SdL appears to have moderated its stance. They question, however, the extent to which this is a tactical move as opposed to genuine change (Kunštát 2004). Nevertheless, some Czech commentators point to distinct differences between the three strands that manifest themselves in terms of varying degrees of flexibility towards their erstwhile co-citizens (Handl 2004). Despite these ideological differences, the SdL leadership is united in its collective refusal to compromise with the Czech authorities on the issues of citizenship and the Beneš Decrees. The SdL's close relationship with the Bavarian CSU also affords it a national political profile that supplements its activities in Bavaria. The SdL can rightly point to the fact that Sudeten Germans and their descendants have played a full part in the transformation of Bavaria from being a rural backwater into an economic power house. Ultimately however, what guarantees the SdL the prominence it has is in fact wider societal apathy and disinterest with regards to the expellees.

As a result of the disinterest that the wider general public in Germany displays towards the whole issue, the SdL has the field to itself. In the Czech Republic it can therefore present itself as being the sole and authentic voice of Sudeten German society (Handl 2004). Large sections of German society have only the vaguest of notions about where the Sudetenland is (or was), a fact that is not apparent to wider sections of society in the

Czech Republic (Pick 2004). Naturally enough, they focus upon those elements of German society who show an interest in the Czech Republic. In effect the SdL is allowed to present itself as something that it is not. The fact is that membership lists are constantly shrinking, and have continued to do so ever since the early 1960s (Rouček 1990: 37).[14] Moreover, the *Landsmannschaft* and its wider purported constituency demonstrate some peculiar features. First, fewer than 10 per cent express any desire to live in the former Czechoslovakia. Yet, particularly in Bavaria, where they are largely concentrated, the older generation still largely feels itself to be not fully integrated into a society they have been a successful part of for over fifty years (Franzen 2001: 255). Unfortunately, such paradoxes are not necessarily apparent to a majority of Czechs. In the absence of alternative sources of information, and in the light of over-exposure in the Czech media, the SdL is viewed as being the authoritative and influential voice of (all) Sudeten Germans and their descendants. Czech media broadcasts of the SdL's annual Whitsun convention simply serve further to cause anxieties among wider sections of Czech society (Larischová 2004). This is not to say that the whole of Czech society shares such concerns. In fact some acknowledge the fact that the SdL should be differentiated from the majority of Sudetenlanders who simply feel themselves to be German and not members of some dispossessed tribe (Křen 2004). The problem is one of conveying that message to wider Czech society.

The struggle to be heard

The fact that most Germans have no interest in re-fighting the battles of over sixty years ago is to some extent lost upon the target audience of the SdL and other *Landsmannschaften*. Increasingly, that audience is not German, but rather Czech or Polish. What, for most Germans, are archaic and odd institutions can present themselves in the Czech Republic and Poland as the authentic voice of the dispossessed. What facilitates this venture in the Czech Republic in particular, is the maintenance and prevalence of stereotypical ideas of Germany and the Germans that permeate wide sections of society. In part this is a generational factor that is held in common with Poland. That more should in theory be done to combat such stereotypes is beyond dispute (Schwall-Düren 2003). Given the legacy of history, the extent to which that is possible is open to question. Indeed, some Czech commentators go as far to claim that, as an organization, the SdL's role in German–Czech relations is quite simply counter-productive. From this perspective, the SdL represents a mindset which is unable to get past September 1938 (Brod 2004). What is of particular interest here is the fact the SdL does not appear to (want to) acknowledge the extent to which this sentiment permeates Czech society, or that its attitudes could possibly be part of the problem.

Unsurprisingly, the sort of maximalist demands proffered by the SdL and other immoderates are not popular with either the German or the Czech (and Polish) governments. In recent years, however, the tone of the rhetoric has softened and more reconciliatory approaches have been made. As early as 1993, the leadership of the BdV, at that time still dominated by the 'old guard' around Herbert Hupka and Herbert Czaja, acknowledged the positive steps taken by the Polish government to improve the situation of ethnic Germans in Poland (Dobrosielski 1992: 144). In 1999, Erika Steinbach (the chairperson of the BdV since May 1998) stated in a speech delivered to students at Charles University, Prague, that five decades after the end of the Second World War 'coming to terms with the past cannot be about guilt and retribution. We have to face the history of this century together in order to build a peaceful and prosperous future.' She even accepted the critique of the Czech ambassador to Germany that it was painful for Czechs to hear her use the term 'expulsion states' (*Vertreiber-staaten*). She emphasized that today's Czech Republic was a democracy that had not expelled any Germans. Yet she insisted that both the Czech Republic and Germany, had to accept the legacy of the past. More importantly for the particularly sensitive relationship with the Czech Republic, Steinbach reassured her listeners that although the expellees loved their ancestral homelands, 'they respect the dignity of the people living there now. And they do not want . . . that other people will ever be expelled'. The SPD–Green coalition has also recognized this shift towards moderation. In her address on the occasion of the twenty-fifth anniversary of the Cultural Foundation of the German Expellees, the chairperson of the Culture and Media Committee of the Bundestag, Elke Leonhard (1999) of the SPD, emphasized that nobody had the right to 'discredit as revanchism the legitimate interests of the expellees in the preservation of their culture and the public acknowledgement of their fate: territorial questions that could affect national rights are no longer an issue . . .'.

However, two issues, although not directly contradicting these statements, continue to influence German–Polish and German–Czech relations: restitution of property or adequate compensation thereof, and the right of expellees to settle in their former homelands. Both issues have strong political implications. During the summer of 1999, the demand for property restitution (or compensation) entered a new phase. First, the SdL decided to support the filing of a collective court case in the US against the Czech Republic. Second, ethnic German resettlers from Poland who had left the country between the 1950s and 1970s brought their case for restitution or compensation to the Polish Supreme Court.[15] At the same time, on several occasions the BdV and the SdL demanded that accession to the EU be made dependant upon the restitution of property to expellees, or alternatively that they be adequately compensated. This stance did not go unnoticed in the Czech Republic (Brod 2004). In March 1999 Chancellor Schröder made it clear that he would not support Sudeten

German property claims and that his government did not intend to make any claims itself (*BK Pressemitteilung* 9 March 1999). Expellee organizations nevertheless persisted in their demand to link EU accession to a satisfactory resolution of the property question, often pointing to the examples of Hungary and Estonia, who had introduced legislation to this effect. The BdV was unsuccessful in its objective. In neither the Czech nor the Polish case has such a link been established. The German government refuses to support such claims, and for the Polish and Czech governments the matter is closed, having been regulated in international law by various wartime and post-war agreements (Handl 2004). Instead what is implicit in the accession agreements is the fact that all Germans have the same rights as any other EU citizens who wish to purchase property or reside in either state. That said, this issue still raises concerns among huge sections of Polish society that the BdV will encourage some kind of German 'land grab' of Polish territory (Sakson 2004).

One side effect of the expellees' overall approach has been that the remaining German minorities in Poland and the Czech Republic find themselves in an increasingly awkward position in their host-countries. In this context, in October 1999 one of the leading activists of the German minority in Poland, Heinrich Kroll, a member of the Polish *Sejm* (lower house of parliament), asked Erika Steinbach publicly to drop the demand to make restitution/compensation for the expellees a condition of EU accession. Analogous appeals have been made by ethnic German activists in the Czech Republic.

As we have seen, the most controversial and potentially most explosive issue in German–Czech relations is that of the Beneš Decrees, which form the political-legal foundations of the current Czech Republic. They also, in part, dealt with the confiscation of German (and Hungarian) property in Czechoslovakia and citizenship issues in relation to members of the two ethnic groups. In recent years, the matter has re-surfaced at a number of levels, some of which have been exploited by expellee activists. In April 1999, a resolution was passed by the European Parliament in which its members called 'on the Czech Government, in the same spirit of reconciliatory statements made by President Havel, to repeal the surviving laws and decrees from 1945 and 1946, insofar as they concern the expulsion of individual ethnic groups in the former Czechoslovakia'. Prior to this resolution, the US House of Representatives passed an analogous resolution on 13 October 1998. In it its members called upon the formerly communist countries in Central and Eastern Europe to 'return wrongfully expropriated properties to their rightful owners or, when actual return is not possible, to pay prompt, just and effective compensation, in accordance with principles of justice and in a manner that is just, transparent and fair'. In 2000, in another resolution of the European Parliament on the status of negotiations on the Czech Republic's membership application, the European Parliament stated that it 'welcomes the Czech government's willingness to scrutinize the laws and decrees of the Beneš Government dating from 1945 and 1946 and still on the statute books to ascertain whether they run counter to the EU law in force and the Copenhagen criteria'.

In Germany, the European Parliament resolution was immediately seized upon by a group of CDU/CSU parliamentarians. They proposed a motion, co-sponsored by the CDU/CSU parliamentary party, in which the federal government was asked 'to take appropriate action in the spirit of the [resolution of the European Parliament] . . . on its own and in collaboration with the other EU member states and the institutions of the EU'. In October 1999, government MPs introduced a counter-motion. Here the Bundestag was asked to welcome the statement by Chancellor Schröder and Czech Prime Minister Miloš Zeman of 8 March 1999, that 'neither government will re-introduce property issues [into their bilateral relationship] either today or in the future'. This motion received a majority vote both at committee stage and after a parliamentary debate in June 2000, while that of the CDU/CSU parliamentarians was rejected.

German dismemberment and occupation of Czechoslovakia, which cannot be separated from the subsequent expulsions, has been dealt with in the 1992 German–Czechoslovak treaty, the 1997 and 2003 German–Czech Declarations, and in a number of other official statements by both governments. Yet, comments by Czech Prime Minister Zeman on the Sudeten Germans being 'traitors' and 'Hitler's fifth column' considerably soured relations between the Czech and German governments. The German Interior Minister's contribution to the debate has also been controversial. In his address to the Sudeten German Day in May 2002, Otto Schily of the SPD called on the Czech Republic to eliminate the Beneš Decrees from its legal order, but also reiterated his government's policy that none of this implied a demand for compensation or restitution of property. Further, in 2002 CSU leader Edmund Stoiber declared that his party insisted on a repeal of the Beneš Decrees prior to the Czech Republic's EU accession because their continued existence contravened the Copenhagen criteria for EU membership. In contrast to the current government, Stoiber continued, a government led by him would seek a resolution of past issues rather than simply ignore them. The astonishing capacity that the expulsion of the Sudeten Germans has to affect Czech–German relations is thus not only a matter of bilateral and international relations, but also plays a part in domestic politics. Just as government and opposition in Germany traded blows over the issue in the run-up to the federal election of September 2002, it has also been a topic for Czech domestic pre-election politics. On the same day that Edmund Stoiber demanded the strict application of the Copenhagen criteria (then) Czech Prime Minister Zeman declared during a memorial act at the former concentration camp of Theresienstadt/ Terezín that, as they had supported the idea of '*Heim ins Reich*', the expulsion had in fact fulfilled the *Sudetendeutsche* desire to live in Germany. Czech Interior Minister Stanislav Gross, then Vice Premier Vladimír Špidla (now the Czech Prime Minister) and leading opposition politicians further justified the post-war expulsions as having contributed to European peace and stability after 1945. Both have since toned down their rhetoric, and the Joint Declaration of July 2003 can be taken as an attempt by the Czech side to take into account German sensitivities.

In contrast to the thus rather stormy relationship between Germany and the Czech Republic, relations between the latter and the EU seem more stable. In April 2002, EU Enlargement Commissioner Günter Verheugen and Prime Minister Zeman issued a joint statement. They acknowledged that 'there has been much public discussion on some of the Czechoslovak Presidential Decrees of 1945 and on some of the ensuing Czechoslovak legislation of the immediate post-war period'. They went on to insist that 'as was the case with measures taken by other European countries at that time, some of these Acts would not pass muster today if judged by current standards – but they belong to history'. This policy is widely supported by governments across Europe, in particular because a ruling by the Czech constitutional court noted that Presidential Decree No. 108/45 (on the confiscation of property) was a unique act which 'for more than four decades has established no legal relations and thus no longer has a constitutive character' in the Czech legal system. In other words it is not valid or applicable in the contemporary Czech Republic. However, what is also, and perhaps more interesting from our constructivist perspective is the fact that the same court ruling stated that the decree 'was not only a legal but also a legitimate act', thus effectively justifying the collective victimization of ethnic Germans and ethnic Hungarians in retrospect, and, at least indirectly, supporting contemporary arguments about the legitimacy of the entire expulsion process, of which this decree was part and parcel.

In February 1999, the Czech government stated in its Foreign Policy Concept that the decrees were 'extinct', a view that was subsequently adopted by the Czech parliament. Officials at all levels have thus managed to find ways out of the dilemma created by the high aspirations that the EU has in terms of human rights and acts committed after the Second World War that contradict these norms. For obvious reasons, such a difficult balancing act is unlikely to please everyone involved, but the commitment of all governments and the EU Commission to leave the past behind and move on to a common future is in the general spirit of post-1990 developments of reconciliation rather than confrontation.

Likewise, the issue of a right for expellees to settle in their former homelands also regained prominence in the political debate about the accession of Poland and the Czech Republic to the European Union. The expected extension of EU principles, including the right of residence in both countries, caused considerable unease in Poland and the Czech Republic. This issue played a role in both the Czech and Polish EU assession referendums. In Poland in particular the question of land ownership was, and continues to be instrumentalized by national conservative circles as a means of evoking fears of a sell-out to returning Germans (Schwall-Düren 2003). Although scarcely reported by West European media, Polish nationalist and populist political parties have made great play of the 'German threat' on whose behalf the EU is allegedly acting. The overwhelming majorities with which accession was endorsed in both countries serves as an indication that these arguments carry progressively less weight in either country. Having said that, the referendum results mask the continued anxiety that exists towards Germany, particularly among older and less well-educated members of society.

The extent to which refugees and expellees, or indeed, increasingly their descendants would actually wish to move to either Poland or the Czech Republic is open to question. Since the early 1960s opinion polls have consistently shown that the desire to return wanes with the passing of the years. In fact what seems to be articulated is not so much the desire to return to either an unknown *Heimat* or to one that has changed out of all recognition, but rather an aspiration to the right of free residence within the EU. Problems result from the factors cited towards the end of the previous paragraph and the sheer stridency of the BdV's message coupled with their reluctance to contextualize the expulsions within a wider framework.

In the context of the relationship between expellee organizations and their former host-states, it is also noteworthy that the issue of expulsions is treated rather differently in Poland and the Czech Republic. Poland has long pursued a more open policy, including the engagement of expellees and their representatives in a process of reconciliation and increased cross-border co-operation. This strategy has been particularly successful with the *Landsmannschaft Schlesien*. Although similar strategies are being employed within the Czech Republic, the issues of occupation, dismemberment and expulsion, are still far too political in the Czech Republic and have occasionally soured relationships at inter-governmental level.

There are a number of reasons for the continued existence of this state of affairs. First, while all anti-German legislation in Poland has been annulled, the offending elements of the Beneš Decrees are merely regarded as having no contemporary legal validity (Schwall-Düren 2003). Second, the blunt fact of the matter is that from the Czech perspective, for a variety of reasons Germany accords greater weight to its relations with Warsaw than it does with Prague. It is perceived to have spent more time mending fences with Poland than it has with the Czech Republic. Whereas the bilateral German–Polish relationship may well be rational in terms of the relative economic weight of the two (the Czech Republic and Poland), the situation does little to ease Czech sensibilities on the matter (Žák 2004). In addition, there is the rather negative perception of the SdL. The *Ostpreußische Landsmannschaft* to one side, its 'Polish' counterparts are not as intransigent in their public posturing as is their 'Czech' equivalent.

Finally, according to some the fact that Poles experienced expulsion at first hand on the part of the Soviet authorities and Ukrainian nationalists as well as the Germans, allows them to take a more understanding approach towards the *Landsmannschaften* and their positions (Rossmanith 2004).

Finally, we must recognize the fact that in neither Poland nor the Czech Republic are there many votes to be gained on a ticket that could be perceived as bowing to German demands (Žák 2004). Lest we paint too gloomy picture, however, we should not lose sight of the fact that we are dealing with the realm of politics here, and on occasion politicians will embark upon various opportunistic strategies in order to shore up their majorities and to glean votes. In this instance, what applies to Poland and the Czech Republic applies in equal measure in Germany.

The *Landsmannschaften* and the post-communist transition

For reasons that are now hopefully clear, the precise nature of the relationship between the various *Landsmannschaften* and Czech and Polish society is difficult to ascertain. Sometimes it seems as if different commentators, politicians and others engaged in the field simply wish to airbrush out aspects of reality with which they are uncomfortable. This applies equally to Czechs, Poles and Germans, and cuts across the ideological spectrum. Moreover, the *Landsmannschaften* do not constitute a uniform whole. Within the Polish context, for example, the much more conciliatory approach adopted since the mid-1990s by the *Landsmannschaft Schlesien*, must be contrasted with that of its more consistently hardline East Prussian counterpart. Polish observers are just as aware of these differences as are their German counterparts (Reiter 2004). The extent to which any relaxation of attitudes permeates wider Polish society is a matter of conjecture. The BdV itself likes to portray a rosy picture. Indeed, German commentators are in general more sanguine on this issue than are their Polish equivalents. Despite public assurances to the contrary, some well-placed Polish observers, like Czech commentators, still harbour an instinctive distrust of the BdV and insist that their public statements mask an undying desire to re-annex former German territory. They claim that just as they cannot voice their fears of the BdV in public, nor does that organization dare openly to state its real agenda (Anon. 2004a). While making a definitive judgement on whether such an assessment holds water is beyond the scope of this volume, there is a case for distinguishing the attitude of the *Apparat* from that of the ordinary members. Worryingly, there are signs that the younger generation of BdV activists, who did not experience expulsion themselves are less flexible than the older generation (Byrt 2004).

All sides acknowledge that when people actually engage in face-to-face co-operation, relations are good. Expellees and the current inhabitants find that their shared interest in a given locality binds them together with one another (Reiter 2004). However, with regard to the *Landsmannschaften* as organizations, there is in fact little common agreement. German observers claim that the relationship is generally positive (Rossmanith 2004). Czech observers in particular, claim the opposite to be true (Žák 2004). Similarly, some German observers point out that in light of EU expansion, the time is right for the BdV to amend its Stuttgart Charter, which after all dates back to 1950, and address the question of *Recht auf Heimat*, which is within this context no longer relevant (Lintzel 2004).

In the Czech case, no responsible Czech political forces today would describe what happened anymore as 'population transfer', nor do they deny the death and misery that occurred in the process of expelling about 3 million ethnic Germans. Neither does the SdL uniformly demand anything other than unspecified symbolic compensation. Czech membership of the EU and all that it implies is also seen as providing an answer to the citizenship issue. To the outside observer it sometimes appears that official positions are maintained for the sake of face, and little else, because in reality, even when it comes to the Beneš Decrees, the argument is as much about the exact formula of words to be used as it is a dispute as to whether they can be regarded as having involved a violation of human rights.

The earlier observation that once people directly engage with one another the aforementioned reservations and issues of high politics are placed firmly on the back-burner applies as much to members of the *Landsmannschaften* themselves as it does to ordinary Germans, Czechs and Poles. Examples of co-operation include partnerships between towns in the Federal Republic and in the former homelands of expellees, especially in former East Prussia, Upper Silesia and the Czech Republic. Such activities include the restoration of churches, theatres, cemeteries and monuments, the creation of small *Heimat* museums and so forth (Larischová 2004). Increasingly, the various expellee organizations have made efforts to foster dialogue with their former host-states at various levels. Joint workshops have taken place in Germany, Poland and the Czech Republic that bring together officials and activists from both sides and explore the past and, even more importantly, ways of how to build the future. Nevertheless, in the Czech Republic in particular these contacts can easily awaken old fears and re-ignite similarly aged controversies (Brod 2004). On the other hand, information trips (*Informationsreisen*) to the former hometowns and villages of expellees are designed to assess the specific needs of these regions and initiate aid programmes. Even less formally, many expellees and their children and grandchildren have become involved individually in projects that facilitate the reconstruction of their former homelands after decades of communism, most of them without any intention of resettlement, promoting border revisions, or the like. Expellees from East Prussia have started an initiative for the preservation of cultural monuments in their former homeland, while Sudeten German expellees have contributed to the reconstruction of many churches in the Czech Republic and have initiated exchange projects with their former homeland communities. From this perspective, since 1990 the work of the refugees, expellees and their descendants has made a significant and positive contribution to Germany's external minority policy. It has fostered reconciliation and is part and parcel of the efforts to improve the living conditions of German minorities in their host-countries. In particular the former of these two claims is still a matter of debate even within Germany. Representatives of the BdV certainly present a positive picture (Koschyk 2003). However, some Czech and indeed Polish observers are keen to differentiate between the successes of ordinary members of the various *Landsmannschaften* and the organizations themselves. For example, for Otto Pick, no matter how hard it tries, the SdL as an organization does not play a positive role in Czech–German relations. From this perspective the answer as to why this is the case is obvious: Adolf Hitler and a refusal on the part of the SdL fully to acknowledge the complicity of many sections of Sudeten German society in the destruction of Czechoslovakia (Pick 2004). Others have observed that instead of facing up to the reality of complicity, the SdL presents itself as the organization of some of the first Germans to have been duped by Hitler, who are therefore to be counted among his earliest victims (Kovanic 2004).

In the Polish case, Andrzej Sakson points to how elements of the Polish right use Erika Steinbach as an example of how wider German society and the BDV in particular 'remain unreconciled' to the territorial status quo (Sakson 2004). Apart from her obvious enthusiasm for the European project and the increasing permeability of inter-sate borders between EU member states, there is no evidence to support claims that Mrs Steinbach covets Polish territory. Yet, this message is lost on large sections of Polish society, who similarly see the BdV's plan to build a memorial centre to the expelled *of Europe* in Berlin as further evidence of that organization's plans to reverse by stealth the results of the Second World War. Indeed, tentative cross-party agreement in Germany on the appropriateness of such plans is taken by some in Poland as evidence of German 'hypocrisy' on the wider issue of the expulsions (Sakson 2004).

On a more positive note, other Polish commentators take a more nuanced view of the BdV. Although pointing to the fact that there are real differences of opinion and over the interpretation of fact between the two sides, the BdV is not dismissed out of hand as a nationalist organization (Góralski 2004). Rather, an attempt to understand the BdV is made by assessing its view of the legal consequences of the expulsions and by taking into the account that the Cold War was in part constructed upon the constant reproduction of negative stereotypes. This is not to say that the BdV receives an unconditional vindication of its stance. On the contrary its demands for both the unilateral granting of *Recht auf Heimat* and compensation for material damage and loss are refuted as being incompatible with international law (Góralski 2004). Nevertheless, understanding of their position and a readiness to enter into dialogue are two entirely different matters that do not easily sit side by side.

Such views contrast with the situation within Germany itself. Here there seems to be growing consensus that the involvement of expellees has, especially since 1989/1990, complemented the reconciliation policy of German governments. 'Contrary to frequent prejudice, the ethnic German expellees have, in their overwhelming majority, actively partici- pated in the process of reconciliation between the European nations, and they continue to do so today' (Schily 1999).

Conclusion

The democratization of the formerly communist societies in Central and Eastern Europe opened new opportunities for Germany's external minority policy. These included new possibilities of supporting the German minori- ties in their host-states and the need to do so in order to halt the mass exodus of ethnic Germans. There is also the commitment of the German expellees to become involved in this process, and a genuine interest on the part of former communist countries in improving their relationship with Germany, which was seen as an important stepping stone towards accession to the European Union and NATO. Yet a certain schizophrenia exists, as illustrated by the aforementioned actions of CSU MEPs. These actions did nothing to ease fears in Czech society with regard to Germany, despite the protestations of those very MEPs that they did not wish to sour bilateral German–Czech relations. Similarly, the attempt by elements within the BdV to enmesh bilateral Polish–German and bilateral Czech– German issues within the wider integration process did not go down well in either state. In fact, it could be argued that in the early 1990s, the BdV missed a golden opportunity to engage fully with Czech (and Polish) society but rather than engage, the BdV saw Czech and Polish desires to join the EU as the perfect opportunity to wring concessions concerning the expulsions and their aftermath (Žák 2004).

Germany's stated desire to bridge the gap between cultures and across history can only be fulfilled through reconciliation and mutual under- standing. Part of this process was the eventual unconditional recognition of the borders with Poland and Czechoslovakia. This process of creating a common future for Germany and its eastern neighbours cannot be secured without addressing the situation of the German minorities in these countries and the suffering of the post-war refugees and expellees. On the basis of numerous treaties and within the framework set out by the 1990 Copenhagen Declaration of the Conference on Security and Co-operation in Europe (CSCE), Germany and Poland, and Germany and the Czech Republic have developed relationships that allow to tackle the issue of minority protection and external support for ethnic Germans and that include representatives of the minorities and the expellee organizations in this process. Yet, for historical as well as contemporary reasons, this has remained a very sensitive problem. German external minority policy, therefore, has always been only one part of a more comprehensive foreign policy approach towards its eastern neighbours. Since the beginning of the transformation process in Central and Eastern Europe, German foreign policy has aimed at stabilizing democracy and creating a market economy in its eastern neighbour countries as the wider social framework within which harmonious inter-ethnic and cross-border relationships can develop that will inevitably also benefit the remaining German minorities.

The integration of expellee organizations in this process has been vital despite the difficulties it has sometimes caused. In order for reconciliation to continue, it is essential that the human dimension in the relationship between Germany and its neighbours in the east is not ignored. Only the collective effort of all the governments and populations concerned, together with the ethnic German minorities and the expellees, will provide a framework within which old wounds will not be re-opened.

7 The role of the minority populations

The purpose of this chapter is to assess the ways in which the residual post-1949 German minorities in Czechoslovakia/Czech Republic and Poland have influenced the (West) German government in its dealings with its two neighbours in East Central Europe. Reference to the GDR will be made as and where appropriate. This latter aspect of post-1945 Polish–German relations is often ignored, and it is assumed that the two sides blithely agreed to put differences to one side for the sake of bloc solidarity. As we shall see, tensions simmered between the SED and the PZPR, and in reality relations between the two sides were poor (Czapliński 2004). For example, the two dominant figures between the late 1940s and early 1970s, Walter Ulbricht and Władysław Gomułka, had a poor personal relationship. Not only that, Ulbricht's request to Gomulka after the latter's return to power in 1956 for the return of the Baltic ports of Szczecin and Świnoujście, simply served to strengthen Gomułka's belief that in reality Germans and Poles could never have anything more than relations that were formally correct (Fiszer 2004). Similarly, Erich Honecker's offer of troops to help 'restore order' in Poland in 1981, is seen by some as a reminder of 'true' German intentions (Byrt 2004).

Wartime German occupation and the post-war expulsions cast a giant shadow over bilateral and inter-ethnic relations. Moreover, these very real memories and experiences, coupled with the political manipulation of those events, contributed to the often deliberate production of negative stereotypes and to ensuring that old wounds remained unhealed. In the Federal Republic, crude anti-communism and the memory of flight and expulsion were sometimes used as a legitimizing device by CDU-led governments. This was even more the case in Czechoslovakia and Poland, where until the late 1960s anti-German sentiment formed an essential element of governing ideology and served as a rallying point for large sections of the population.

As for the minority populations themselves, in many ways, the situation of Germans in Czechoslovakia and Poland between 1945 and the late 1980s was very similar. Both groups suffered as ethnic minorities in states whose ideological premises purportedly placed notions of class above those

of ethnic identification. In addition they suffered as Germans as a consequence of the crimes committed by the Nazis during the Second World
War against Poles, Czechs and Slovaks.

The most significant difference between the two countries is that the
remaining German minority in Poland is much larger than in the Czech
Republic, both in absolute and percentage terms. This was already the
case after the end of the expulsions, and subsequent emigration of those
who were spared from forced migration between 1945 and 1950, although
it was, in absolute numerical terms, much larger from Poland, did nothing
to change this state of affairs.

In Europe, compulsory and if necessary forcible population transfer had
been first established as a legitimate means of creating ethnically homogenous states as early as the late nineteenth century. By 1922/1923, such criteria
were accepted and employed as a means of helping to settle the long-standing
Greek–Turkish conflict (Lemberg 2001: 192). We should also note that
instances of what we now call 'ethnic cleansing' occurred during the Balkan
Wars during the early part of the twentieth century, prior to the final collapse
of the Ottoman Empire. The latter example has in fact been offered as a
legal precedent by at least one Czech commentator (Houžvička 2004). Legal
niceties to one side, throughout the twentieth century, ethnic cleansing in
the form of forced (cross-border) population transfers and (internal) deportations, was endemic throughout Central and Eastern Europe, the Balkans,
Turkey and the Soviet Union and we should never lose sight of that fact.
What happened to German civilians between 1945 and 1950, although
unique in its scale, was by no means a singular German experience, and
was in no small part the direct consequence of the implementation of Nazi
racial theory by means of genocide.

Since 1937, initially with respect to South Tyrol, the Nazis had pursued
a resettlement programme of ethnic Germans living outside of the borders
of the hypothesized *Großdeutsches Reich*, which gathered pace during the
course of the Second World War and was part of a much wider strategic
plan of the Nazis – the *Generalplan Ost*. This strategy linked to the
so-called *Lebensraum* question, itself a central element of Nazi ideology
claiming that the German Volk needed, and was in fact entitled to, a far
larger area of contiguous territory for the realization of its full potential.
Yet, the *Lebensraum* question was not only a territorial issue, it also
required large-scale resettlement of ethnic Germans from outside the designated territories of Greater Germany – Germany proper, Austria, the Czech
lands, Alsace and Lorraine and large parts of western Poland occupied in
1939 and incorporated into the Reich. This, in turn, 'necessitated' the
deportation or otherwise elimination of most of the non-German population from these areas. Heinrich Himmler, the head of the SS was put
in charge of this *Heim ins Reich* policy and pursued all elements of it
with a combination of vigour and venom. With few exceptions in the case
of South Tyrol, Luxembourg and Alsace and Lorraine, the resettlement

programme affected almost exclusively the ethnic Germans of Southern and Eastern Europe. It was selective in that not all German minority groups were 'eligible' for resettlement – those which could serve valuable purposes in projecting the image of the superior German and in strengthening relations with Hitler's allies in the region were to remain in their traditional settlement areas. Others that could become a potential source of tension, for example with Italy in the case of South Tyrol or with the Soviet Union in the case of the Baltic Germans, were resettled to the Reich. However, resettlement also depended on racial suitability according to the criteria established by the *Volkslisten*, which distinguished between four groups: racially above average, racially average, racially below average and racially unsuitable. Ethnic Germans in the first two categories were deemed useful for colonizing the new *Lebensraum*, in exceptional cases, some from the third category were also included in this group. Germans in the last two categories and non-Germans in categories one and two were to undergo Germanization in parts of the so-called old Reich (i.e. Germany in the borders of 1938), while non-Germans found to be racially below average or even unsuitable were simply excluded from the resettlement programme or, if they had somehow slipped through the net of the initial screening, sent back to where they came from.

On the surface, Hitler's announcement of the resettlement programme on 6 October 1939 marked a departure from what had appeared to be his policy towards ethnic German minorities at least in Central and Eastern Europe, namely their incorporation into the Reich by way of territorial aggrandizement. Yet this interpretation of events overlooks the primarily instrumental role Hitler had assigned to them at this stage. With further acquisitions and conquests temporarily ruled out for strategic reasons after the victory over Poland, resettlement served two purposes: the elimination of minorities as potential threats to friendly relations with Germany's allies at the time (in particular Mussolini and Stalin) and the beginning of the building of a new racially pure nation in Germany's enlarged *Lebensraum*.

A first wave of resettlement affected, apart from South Tyrol, the three Baltic republics and Eastern Poland, all of which had become part of the Soviet zone of influence according to the August 1939 Molotov–Ribbentrop Pact and its amendment at the end of September. Some 135,000 ethnic Germans were re-settled in the Reich from Volhynia and Galicia in Eastern Poland, followed in the summer of 1940 by about 30,000 ethnic Germans from those areas of Central Poland that had not been annexed to the Reich, i.e. the so-called *Generalgouvernement*. In contrast to the latter, which was the first unilateral resettlement action taken by the Nazis, the former resembled very much earlier Balkan cases, such as the Bulgarian–Turkish population exchange of 1919 and the Greco-Turkish exchange of 1923, in that it was based on the principle of reciprocity. According to a German–Soviet Treaty of November 1939, Germans from Eastern Poland were to be 'exchanged' against Russians, Ukrainians and

Belorussans from those parts of Poland that had been assigned to the German zone of influence. At this time, further population transfers were conducted by the Soviet Union and Poland with regard to the Baltic states.

A second wave of resettlement began in the autumn of 1940 and mainly affected the Romanian territories of Bessarabia and northern Bukovina. Other resettlement operations in Eastern Europe and the Balkans were primarily determined by the course of the war. Ethnic Germans were removed from Yugoslavia, Bulgaria, Greece and the Soviet Union. In the latter case, Stalin reacted by deporting almost all ethnic Germans from the European part of the Soviet Union, including those from the centuries-old Volga Republic, to Siberia and Central Asia.

Resettlement was only one element in the Nazis' strategy for solving the German question their way. One day after his announcement of the resettlement programme to the German Reichstag in October 1939, Hitler signed a formal decree with far wider implications, namely not just to resettle ethnic Germans to the Reich, but also to remove all racially or otherwise undesirable elements from the German nation and its *Lebensraum* and to colonize those of the occupied territories assigned for resettlement. The latter two policies affected initially above all Jews and Poles, but later on also most other peoples living under German occupation. Polish losses amount to almost one-quarter of the entire pre-war population – 6 million people, half of them Jews. Their elimination was part of a deliberate strategy – the so-called *Generalplan Ost* drafted in 1941 – to create a large contiguous area suitable for the building of a racially pure German nation in its exclusive *Lebensraum*. While Jews, Poles and other *fremdvölkische* (alien) elements were deemed racially unsuitable by the Nazis to share the same living space with Germans, the Nazis had considerably fewer problems with these people serving as forced labourers in German industry and agriculture. By 1944, about 8 million civilian workers and prisoners of war, more than half of them from Poland and the Soviet Union, were condemned to contribute to the German war effort. As many of them were literally worked to death, the use of slave labour fits well into the Nazis' extermination strategy.

Having so established the context within which the subsequent expulsion of Germans took place, it should come as no surprise that many have pointed to these Nazi policies as a means of rationalizing the post-war expulsions. We also need to consider the views of the Allies who, from 1942 onwards, became enamoured of compulsory population transfer as a potential solution to the problem of rendering nation and state co-terminous, in particular with regard to Germany and the Germans.

Germans in post-war Czechoslovakia

In the case of Czechoslovakia, no major revisions to its borders were contemplated by the allies in their post-war planning at Yalta in early 1945.

In essence, the state was restored within its pre-Munich borders, although the Soviet Union did help itself to the heavily Ruthene-populated eastern tip of the country. The policy of rendering states more congruent with nations that the Allies adopted as one of their 'lessons' from the inter-war period was predicated upon ridding the country of as many non-Czechs and non-Slovaks as possible. This necessitated the removal of all but a relatively small number of Germans, including in some instances surviving German-speaking Jews, to Germany. It also meant a forced population exchange with Hungary, affecting some 75,000 Hungarians and Slovaks. This hypernationalism also caused renewed tension with Poland. Neither country had been satisfied with the post-First World War demarcation of their common border in Upper Silesia. Warsaw had eventually annexed disputed Czechoslovak territory in 1938. Prague had re-occupied it in 1945, and subsequently both sides engaged in sabre rattling and tit-for-tat expulsions of several tens of thousands of people. The territorial status quo was affirmed only in 1947 in the wake of sustained Soviet pressure.

After the completion of the expulsion of ethnic Germans in 1948, the strategy with regard to remaining non-Czechs and non-Slovaks was to assimilate as far as possible all remaining elements within society into a single Czechoslovak nation, within which the Czechs would constitute the *Leitkultur*. Although according to the Košice Programme of April 1945, Slovaks were recognized as constituting an ethnically distinct nation (Auer 2000: 251), this policy of homogenization was applied to them as well as to Hungarians, Germans, Ruthenes and those who designated themselves as Silesians, Poles or Moravians. It was carried out with the full support of the communists, but it is important to note that they did not instigate it. Rather, it was initiated by returning non-communist government politicians, most notably Beneš and the younger Masaryk and their immediate allies. Their experience of inter-war Czechoslovakia had convinced them that the first Czechoslovak state had failed because large numbers of its (former) citizens did not in fact have any loyalty to the state. We most commonly identify Edvard Beneš with the post-war expulsion of Germans. In fairness to Beneš, he was, to some extent, clearly guided by circumstances that had long created a climate in which forced migration was seen as a legitimate tool of conflict prevention and management.

We should also take into account the sharp radicalization that occurred within the Czechoslovak population following Munich, and how it was exacerbated by the German occupation regime (Lemberg 2001: 195ff.). In fact, even after war broke out, Beneš was still prepared to cede territory to Germany, and envisaged that a slightly truncated Czechoslovakia could still accommodate up to 800,000 Germans. As we noted earlier in this volume, it was not until 1942/1943 that Beneš finally swung round to the increasingly popular option that the vast majority of Germans be expelled (Lemberg 2001: 200). The solution eventually decided upon was that since these people had not been loyal to the Czechoslovak state they should be deported to whichever state they had been loyal to, whether it be Germany or Austria, and in the case of Hungarians and Poles, to their respective homelands. The issue at stake here was dual, and is disputed to this day. On the one hand, a decision was taken to render Czechoslovakia ethnically homogenous by all means necessary. On the other hand, the Beneš Decrees were part and parcel of a necessary de-Nazification process (Houžvička 2004). What separates to this day many Czechs from those Germans who have an interest in this subject is disagreement concerning the extent to which de-Nazification was used as a pretext for straightforward ethnic cleansing. Some Czech commentators advance the argument that in promulgating the Decrees the Beneš government actually prevented massacres from occurring (Kovanic 2004). While that argument does not square with the massacres that took place, both in and outside of the camp system, the fate of ethnic Germans in the then Soviet Union, who were deported to inhospitable locations in Central Asia or to labour camps in Siberia as early as 1941, indicates that in a general sense far worse could have happened.

As is usual in these circumstances, the principle of national self-determination was applied above all by the victors. This is not to say that Czechoslovak politicians were incorrect in their assessment of with which state(s) the loyalties of Sudeten Germans lay. Having said that, the circumstances under which Czechoslovakia had been created were unusual, and in the absence of genuine power-sharing mechanisms in this period, a consensual political culture and a stable political and economic environment were unlikely to emerge. The Sudeten Germans in effect signed their own deportation papers, and in some cases death warrants, by allying themselves with the Hitler regime. While this should not be taken as endorsing the principle of collective guilt and the punishment of almost an entire population group without anything even remotely akin to due legal process, the events across Central and Eastern Europe in the decade from 1938 onwards provide much of the context in which the expulsions were implemented.

The circumstances under which ethnic Germans were permitted to stay in Czechoslovakia were strictly defined. In total, around 660,000 Germans are estimated either to have fled, or to have been expelled through unofficial means. A further 2,336,000 were 'officially expelled'. By the time the process was completed in 1948, a little over 200,000 Germans remained in Czechoslovakia. Of those, some were considered to be loyal Czech citizens. Others were denied permission to leave as they were classified as essential workers whose skills were necessary in aiding economic recovery. There were also some who remained in Czechoslovakia because the Americans had simply refused to admit them into their zone of occupation on the grounds that there was nowhere to put them (Myant 1981: 64). It should also be noted that the number of those killed among the 3 million, who were either expelled or fled, is disputed to this day. Estimates range from

30,000 to approximately 250,000 having perished through ill health associated with the conditions in which they found themselves or directly at the hands of vengeful erstwhile compatriots. The higher figure comes from the BdV and associated organizations. As much as anything else it appears to be based upon an estimate of the Sudeten German population as of September 1939, and a comparison of that same population at some indeterminate point after the end of the war. It is somewhat vague to say the least. On the other hand, the lower, more recent figure from the Czech–German Historical Commission was determined through means of an incredibly exact definition under which a German can be considered to have been the victim of revenge attacks. It is based primarily on death certificates issued by the Czech authorities in concentration camps and elsewhere (Kučera 2001b: 231ff.). In addition, no definitive wartime population records are available. The civilian population was increasingly transient as the war drew to a close, and there is little common agreement concerning who ought to be counted among the ranks of the *Sudetendeutsche* and therefore among the number of *Sudetendeutsche* refugees and dead. Neither are various pre-war Czechoslovak and German censuses of much help as criteria of national classification varied from census to census and between the two countries. As Kučera points out, this whole exercise may be rather meaningless. The Czech records on the episode have not been accessed in full, and trying to determine how an individual died is fraught with some rather macabre methodological issues. How, for example, can you be sure what the motivation for suicide was? Is someone who died at the hands of bandits a victim of the expulsions? (Kučera 2001b: 241ff.). The questions are legion: and at the end of the day one is forced to ask to what extent this debate is of any practical use to anyone, or whether it acts primarily as some kind of psychological prop to elements of both societies. Inevitably, the truth regarding the number of deaths lies somewhere between the two extremes. Whatever the final death toll, the expulsion process was brutal and involved random as well as organized acts of terror against the remaining civilian German population.

By the time the communists had assumed sole power in February 1948, the expulsions were all but complete. Of the approximately 3.2 million Germans living in the country in 1945, the aforementioned 200,000 remained, about 10 per cent of whom lived in the Slovak part of the country. Precise details with regard to their composition are not readily available. However, we can make some observations. Around 20,000 were proven German anti-fascists. A further 60,000 were classified as essential labour. Some 15,000 German women married to Czechs were exempted from expulsion, as were approximately 30,000 German men who also had a Czechoslovak spouse. Their children were similarly spared, and presumably count for the bulk of the remainder. Incidentally, professed Germans from the Český Těšín and Hlučín areas were unilaterally re-classified as Czechs (Staněk 2001: 225).

By 1950, the ethnic German element of the population was down to 165,000. In other words, within less than two decades, the (official) German population had fallen from 23.6 per cent in 1930, to 1.3 per cent. Ethnic Germans constituted more than 10 per cent of the population only in three small areas of the country (Rouček 1990: 201). This further reduction was partly due to migration, but also because of identity switching as the communist policy of cultural assimilation over time proved to be fairly successful. The internal deportations in the late 1940s and early 1950s all but destroyed the last remnants of the historical settlement structures of the German population. Ethnic Germans were removed from their traditional areas of settlement and re-settled in areas where it was believed they would be of greatest economic benefit, such as in uranium and coal mining centres (Hoffman 1996: 91). German schools and the teaching of German as a native language were banned, and the fear of discrimination by authorities and majority population initiated a trend towards 'voluntary' assimilation among the younger generations.

Yet, in a seemingly contradictory way, the communist authorities also allowed some degree of expression of German culture, and restrictions upon remaining Germans were gradually eased. Under the terms of Decrees 33/45 of 2 August 1945, all ethnic Germans (designated exceptions aside) had been stripped of their Czechoslovak citizenship, which in effect none them had had since, and most had rejected in 1938. In 1948 they were allowed permanent residence, and the possibility of (individually) applying for the return of citizenship. Citizenship was restored en masse by means of the Nationality Law of April 1953 (Rouček 1990: 202/3). Having said that, the feeling persisted that under the communists, the Prague Spring to one side, ethnic Germans were always considered to be second-class citizens.

In 1951, with support from the GDR, a German-language newspaper was published and the first cultural groups were formed. In the summer of 1953, parts of the country were hit by a wave of strikes in which ethnic Germans were prominent. Rather than use these events as a pretext to further restrict ethnic Germans, the government reacted by easing remaining restrictions and encouraging German political participation in the (official) political life of the country. For example, ethnic Germans were permitted to stand for election as trade union officials, and in 1954 three Germans were actually elected to the (admittedly insipid) parliament. In the same year, German-language radio broadcasts re-commenced for the first time in almost ten years (Rouček 1990: 202f.).

At the beginning of the 1960s, this policy was abandoned, as it seemed to be counter-productive to the official efforts at total assimilation (Müller 1993: 22) and so the few opportunities for preserving German culture that were available in the 1950s were gradually rescinded. In the years that followed, the Czechoslovak communist authorities were largely successful in their attempt to assimilate the remaining Germans. By 1983, after fairly sustained migration during the years 1966 to 1969, the total German population had dropped to an estimated 56,000. By this time the death/emigration rates had begun to exceed the birth rate, thus setting into motion the post-expulsion decline of the German population that continues to this day.

Policy change occurred once more when a more minority-friendly policy was introduced in the wake of the Prague Spring. The German minority was officially recognized as such in January 1969 (Uhl 2004). In law, mother-tongue education was now guaranteed, along with various other rights such as the right not to be (culturally) assimilated, and to a mother-tongue press. A minority organization called *Kulturbund der Bürger deutscher Nationalität* (Cultural Assembly of Citizens of German Nationality/KdBdN) was established (Auer 2000: 257). Even by the standards of the day, this organization seems to have been particularly inactive. It proclaimed that it had around sixty branches with between 7,000 and 10,000 members, and appears to have produced little of any substance. The KdBdN, published its own official paper the *Prager Volkszeitung* (*Prague People's Paper*). Like the two smaller German-language press organs, the *Neue Prager Presse* (*New Prague Press*) and *Tschechoslowakisches Leben* (*Czechoslovak Life*), it did little other than repeat what could be read in the Czechoslovak press (Kotzian 1998: 21). The extent to which the communists merely tolerated as opposed to supported the KdBdN is unclear. No German-language education was provided on the grounds that the German minority was too small and scattered. Yet, in the 1970s the numerically smaller, albeit territorially concentrated Ukrainian/Ruthene minority was provided with 7 grammar and Secondary schools, 59 middle schools, and over 250 primary schools (Rouček 1990: 211).

Thus, while the older generation had some limited opportunities to preserve their cultural heritage, including their language, traditions and customs, the persistent absence of a public commitment to preserve a German cultural tradition across the generations meant that the assimilatory pressure on the younger members of the minority continued unabated (Löffler 1997: 95). This and the increasing opportunities to migrate to Germany resulted in an almost 80 per cent decrease in the number of Germans in just four decades. According to the first post-communist census, by 1991 just over 50,000 citizens in Czechoslovakia registered as German. The census of 2001 showed a further decline, although there is some suggestion that in both censuses many ethnic Germans have failed to reveal the nature of their 'true' identity for fear of reprisal (Larischová 2004). Whatever the real figure, given that the majority of Germans in the Czech Republic have reached retirement age, the minority seems destined for oblivion.

What then of the relationship between Germany and the German minority in the Czech Republic during the period of communist rule? We have already seen how early on the GDR played a small role in disseminating German culture. The position of the Federal Republic was complicated by the fact that Bonn and Prague initially had no formal diplomatic contacts. As a result, Bonn was unable to play any kind of meaningful role with regard to the German minority. The only exception came during the Brandt years, when, as part of the process of rapprochement between the two governments, there was an increase in the number of Germans who were allowed to emigrate to the Federal Republic.

Prior to the establishment of full diplomatic relations in 1973, consular support was heavily circumscribed, as was material assistance from Bonn. Contacts between Czechoslovak Germans and West Germans were maintained mainly as a result of the efforts of the Red Cross, occasional family visits and the international postal services. The fact that the East German state had established formal diplomatic relations with Czechoslovakia as early as 1949 and maintained an embassy in Prague as well as several consulates was of little consolation to ethnic Germans in the country, as they barely figured on the agenda of the SED.

With the overthrow of the Dubček government in 1969, any possibility of anything but incremental changes to the position of the German minority ceased. Once the anti-German hue and cry that accompanied the invasion of 1968 subsided, the German minority did not find itself subjected to any special restrictions. In fact, it simply continued to decline in numbers as a consequence of death, migration and assimilation.

Ethnic Germans in the Czech Republic today

Naturally enough, the relationship between the Czech Republic's German minority and wider Czech society, is, in part, governed by the wider pattern of relations between the two peoples during the twentieth century (Kafka 2004). Yet, despite the difficulties mentioned elsewhere in the text, the situation of the German minority in today's Czech Republic is much changed. Since 1995, the Czech Republic has been a signatory to the Framework Convention for the Protection of National Minorities. The German minority is catered for under the terms of this and other international agreements that are given force of law by the Czech constitution and domestic Czech legislation. Funding to minority organizations is distributed through the ministry of culture. The Council of National Minorities is charged with the function of co-ordinating minority related activity. The legislative framework for national minorities[1] in the Czech Republic is very liberal, and at least the equal of Poland's. There is little evidence, if any, to support claims that as a consequence of its ethnic provenance the minority is discriminated against at the official level (Kovanic 2004).

Yet, the minority's small size and the fact that it lives scattered throughout the country account in part for the fact that the situation of ethnic Germans is more difficult than official statements would admit. Germans have virtually no chance of achieving collective political representation at any level. The only exception to this lack of political representation occurred when the Prague Citizens Forum in the first post-communist elections in June 1990 elected the Deputy Chairman of the Association of Germans, Walter Piverka, as a candidate (Löffler 1997: 97). Part of the problem is also that ethnic Germans in the Czech Republic do not have a common platform. Their cultural organizations are deeply divided between the *Verein der Deutschen in Böhmen, Mähren und Schlesien* (Association of Germans in Bohemia, Moravia, and Silesia/VdBMS), itself an umbrella organization for various regional groups, and the various successor organizations of the KdBdN (Kotzian 1998: 26). By 1999, 39 civic organizations within the German minority existed in the Czech Republic (Report 1999).

In the 2001 census, the number of those registering as German dropped to 39,000. Interestingly enough, the census also reveals the existence of a total of 11,000 declared Silesians, some of whom have an affinity with German language and culture and could fairly easily effect an identity shift. A German minority presence remains in the larger cities and some parts of the Sudetenland, but even there they have minimal political significance because of their small numbers and the fact that the consciously German element of the population is overwhelmingly elderly. The German associations that have been established since 1990 are as much social clubs and advice centres as anything else. These associations are extremely introverted, to the extent that not only do they shy away from engagement with Czech society, they keep contacts with the SdL to an absolute necessary minimum (Uhl 2004). The reasons for this are complex, but three main causes can be identified. First, there is the memory of the expulsions and their aftermath. Second, we have to acknowledge the fact that the majority of ethnic Germans who stayed behind regarded themselves as loyal Czechoslovak citizens. Third, the SdL whether it likes it or not, is in effect the modern day representative of those ethnic Germans whose loyalty towards Czechoslovakia was at best ambiguous.

Moreover, anti-German attitudes still persist in the Czech Republic, and they do so both at popular and official levels. They manifest themselves, for example, in the law on property restitution which excludes Czech citizens of German descent from either the restitution of property confiscated under the terms of the Beneš Decrees, or receiving compensation for such property. Ethnic Germans with proven anti-fascist records have still not received the same levels of compensation from the Czech government as have their ethnic Czech compatriots (Žák 2004). This is despite the fact that in August 2003, the foreign minister announced that the Czech government was in principle prepared to pay up to 1.5 million Euros in compensation to up to 1,500 surviving ethnic German Czech citizens who had suffered as a result of the policies of post-war Czech governments (*Süddeutsche Zeitung* 2003).

Existing popular prejudice against Germans and Germany has forced successive Czech governments to take a tough stance on such matters and in bilateral negotiations with Germany. A 1996 public opinion poll revealed that 86 per cent of those Czechs surveyed would not vote for a party that supported an apology to the Sudeten Germans for the expulsions in the post-war period. Negative images of Germany as a neighbouring state were also uncovered in this survey with about half of all interviewees believing Germany to be an economic threat, 39 per cent seeing it as a political threat and 25 per cent as a military threat. Such views are understandable among those who actually experienced the dismemberment of Czechoslovakia after the Munich Agreement of 1938 and the subsequent German occupation and atrocities committed against the civilian population. It is, however, rather surprising that such thoughts are fairly widespread among the younger generation. One explanation of this phenomenon may lie in the fact that, despite a decade of democratization, Czech schoolbooks still portray the nation's history as one of continuous struggle between an ethnically defined Czech nation and the German arch-enemy (Report 1999).[2] Through their consistent and disproportionate coverage of hardline activists of the Sudeten German expellees, Czech media have also contributed to the persistence of anti-German sentiment. Such sentiments, both real and imagined, have been a factor in the German minority's decision to keep its distance from the SdL. In the early 1990s its previously close identification with the latter organization, resulted in many Czechs coming to regard the remaining German minority as being little different in attitude from the SdL itself. Some Czech commentators claim that the more cautious approach on the part of the German minority in the Czech Republic has served to throw them into a more positive light at home (Handl 2004).

Despite these difficulties, considerable progress has been achieved since 1989. The Czech state budget subsidizes two weekly papers of the German minority with an average of 4 million Czech Crowns annually, and has not objected to financial aid from Germany channelled into the creation of, thus far, twelve community centres. Having said that, some with an interest in the field claim that the German government by no means does all that it could to aid the remaining German minority (Stemke 2003).

Czech Radio has an independent German minority department, alongside similar departments for the Polish, Slovak and Roma minorities, and regularly broadcasts programmes aimed at the minority. More recently, the VdBMS has opened a school in Prague that provides German-language education to it students who come primarily from the German minority but also include members of other ethnic groups. The state budget covers all operational costs of the school, and additional funds are provided by contributions from private associations in Germany and the Czech Republic. Otherwise, a German-language educational system is rather underdeveloped for two reasons. On the one hand, numbers of Germans are often so small that German schools, or even German classes, cannot be opened. This situation is also not helped by the fact that the Czech government does not promote the establishment of bilingual Czech–German schools. On the other hand, it must be recognized that cultural and linguistic assimilation among the younger generation of the German minority has progressed so far that many families do not speak German even at home (Uhl 2004). Neither do they register their children as German at school and are not particularly interested in professing German culture and traditions, partly because of fears of being disadvantaged if they do.

The German minority in the Czech Republic seems destined to go a different path than its counterpart in Poland. From the point of view of cultural diversity, the gradual disappearance of the German minority might be seen as unfortunate by some and regrettable. However, it should also be welcomed as a development that coincides with the apparent wishes of those few Czech citizens of German extraction who still remain and does not hold any dangers for ethnic peace in the Czech Republic. Consequently, despite the sometimes-strained relations that exist between the two sides over former Czechoslovak citizens of German ethnicity, there are few real problems between Prague and Berlin with regard to the ethnic Germans who remain in the Czech Republic. They are too small as a group to be considered to be any kind of a threat to the internal political stability of the state. Similarly, they are far too few in number to act as a so-called bridge between the two states and societies. Germans in general and minority activists in particular are almost invisible, alienated from wider Czech society and overwhelmingly elderly (Born 2000: 182–185). The demographic imbalance is neatly illustrated by the fact that the German population has fallen by over a quarter since the census of 1991.

The German minority in communist Poland

The process of post-war expulsion of ethnic Germans from Poland differed from the process in Czechoslovakia in a number of ways. It was less comprehensive, with the exception of those who had been entered into the first category of the *Deutsche Volksliste*.[3] Skilled workers (usually *Reichsdeutsche*) in the mining and metallurgical industries were often considered essential for the country's economic recovery and therefore allowed to stay, at least until the late 1950s when Poles were available in sufficient numbers to take over. In addition, from the autumn of 1945 onwards, those pre-war Polish citizens (*Volksdeutsche*) who had undergone 'rehabilitation' in forced labour camps and spoke Polish were increasingly offered their Polish citizenship back (depending upon where they had stood on the *Volksliste*). Finally, after the expulsion process was completed in 1950, the Polish authorities claimed that the overwhelming majority of (former) Germans, both *Reichsdeutsche* and *Volksdeutsche* who had not been expelled, were merely 'Germanicized Poles', who were being offered the opportunity to re-discover their true, i.e. Polish, identity.

In some respects, the means by which the expulsions were effected, however, also parallelled the Czechoslovak experience. In both cases, mass expulsion occurred prior to the Potsdam Conference, and 'it is an open secret' that on occasion the actions of those carrying out the expulsions were clearly criminal in nature (Czapliński 2004). Concentration camps were quickly re-opened and filled with Germans. The remaining German population was divided into various categories. The first consisted of *Reichsdeutsche* who did not fulfil the necessary criteria for the 'verification' process and were expelled. The second consisted of *Reichsdeutsche* who fulfilled the criteria for expulsion but who, by virtue of their expertise, were forced to stay. The third consisted of *Reichsdeutsche* who were considered to be 'Germanicized Poles'. The fourth category was formed by the *Volksdeutsche* who underwent a 'rehabilitation' process, at the end of which they were either expelled or offered return of their Polish citizenship, which unsurprisingly most of them rejected in favour of expulsion. These processes of 'verification' and 'rehabilitation' were in fact simple programmes of incarceration and slave labour. The end result was that individuals would either be served with expulsion papers or be offered (the restitution of) Polish citizenship. As with post-war Czechoslovakia, there is no consensus with regard to how many Germans died during this time, any more than there is with regard to ultimate responsibility for the deaths. Recent research that tries to steer away from both extreme body counts and nit-picking detail indicates that around 400,000 Germans died as a direct consequence of the expulsion process. This figure includes those who died while in flight, either directly or indirectly at the hands of Polish civilians, various Polish armed forces or the Soviet army. About half the number is comprised of those who died in Polish/Soviet concentration camps (Eberhardt 2003: 173). It is also interesting to note that, in contrast to the Czechoslovak case, neither the Polish nor German government feels it necessary to establish a commission to determine the 'exact' number of deaths.

From 1947 in particular, if an individual was considered to be sufficiently well disposed towards Poland they were offered (the restoration of) Polish citizenship. Otherwise, skilled workers aside, they were thrown out. Here as in so many other walks of life, theory and practice often diverged. In reality, the process was messy, rules were constantly changed and local officials had a large measure of discretion. In fact, the situation was so confused that around 120,000 people who either fled or were expelled to post-war Germany were later allowed to return (Kulczycki 2001).

Examination of the Polish census of 1950 indicates that around 1.1 million residents had possessed German citizenship prior to 1945 (Franzen 2001: 305). Of this number approximately 900,000 were resident in either Upper Silesia or Masuria. Polish officials continued to make a distinction between the autochthonous or 'Germanicized Poles' primarily of Upper Silesia, southern Masuria and eastern Pomerania and the much smaller 'designated German minority' that resided primarily in Lower Silesia.[4] The former group was treated as having been originally of Polish or Slavic origin. It was argued that due to centuries of Germanicization, their true Polishness had become submerged beneath a German veneer. A policy of re-Polonization was pursued throughout the country. This included banning any use of German in public and in religious services, destroying as many physical traces of the (former) German presence as possible, and generally attempting to re-orient people towards Poland.

The religious issue played a far greater role in southern Masuria than it did in Upper Silesia. Although church and state were at loggerheads on most issues, in the late 1940s they were united in the belief that re-Polonization of certain groups of people was the correct strategy. In southern Masuria the situation was particularly acute for the locals. Not only was their loyalty to the state open to question, they were overwhelmingly Protestant. The religious cleavage re-enforced the effective ethnic cleavage between the overwhelming majority of (Polish-speaking) Masurians and the incoming Polish authorities. The fact that the policy of re-Polonization met with only limited success, particularly among the Masurians, can be measured in rates of emigration to Germany between the early 1950s and 1990s. With regard to linguistic restrictions the evidence is patchy. Certainly, there were numerous instances, particularly in the late 1940s and early 1950s of people being fined or imprisoned for speaking German, whether at home or in a public place. Then again, some 'Germanicized Poles' could not in fact speak Polish (in 1945) at any rate, thereby creating something of a conundrum for the authorities.

As for the small 'designated German minority' restrictions placed upon them were gradually eased, so that by 1956 they enjoyed the same rights as all other minorities indigenous to Poland. Thus, in 1951 the Germans of Lower Silesia were recognized as a national minority. With the support of the GDR a German-language weekly, *Die Arbeiterstimme* (Workers' Voice) and several German primary schools were established. A number of libraries with German-language books existed in the area as well. In April 1957, a German Social-Cultural Association was established in Wrocław, which had around 7,000 members (Neubach 1998: 26). Having said that, as in Czechoslovakia, the majority of Germans eligible to join such organizations stayed well away, and preferred either inner or physical emigration.

The GDR played a prominent, if low-key role with regard to the 'designated German minority', and recently available archival material demonstrates that rarely acknowledged tensions between Warsaw and East Berlin existed concerning their fate. Above all what governed (official) Polish attitudes towards this minority was fear of Germany. As such, they were wary of a new fifth column and initially, at any rate sought to eject them from Poland just as soon as they could be replaced with newly trained Polish labour (Ihme-Tuchel 1997: 12). For its part, the SED was not particularly keen on encouraging emigration to the GDR, on the part of people who, according to SED propaganda, did not actually exist. Another difficulty that faced the SED was the inability of their Polish counterparts to supply them with exact numbers. Put simply, Polish estimates varied from year to year, and in such a way that cannot be accounted for either in terms of birth and death rates or by emigration to (West) Germany. The main explanation seems to lie in the fact that individuals were subject to continuous administrative re-classification as Poles or 'Germanicized Poles', and that the Polish authorities either could not or would not supply any data concerning children under the age of 15 (Ihme-Tuchel 1997: 15ff.). Moreover, the Polish Citizenship Law of 1951 arbitrarily imposed Polish citizenship upon tens of thousands of Germans who had previously survived deportation and had also refused to take out Polish papers. Remarkably, it was not until 1956 that the last of the recalcitrants actually complied and acknowledged receipt of their new citizenship.

With the onset of de-Stalinization, the GDR and Polish authorities sought once and for all to resolve the issue. A joint commission was established in order to determine how many people in Poland could prove their entitlement to German citizenship.[5] Once again the results were incomplete, as the commission was not allowed to operate in areas in which large numbers of 'Germanicized Poles' lived. Despite that, over 40,000 individuals were found to be Germanicized under German law (Ihme-Tuchel 1997: 42ff.). The question was one of how they should be dealt with. The SED, keen to preserve the obvious fiction (disproved by constant migration) that there were no Germans left in Poland seems to have favoured a policy of socialization into Polish socialist society. For the Poles, migration was the favoured option. By the early 1960s, the large majority of ethnic Germans had left, allowing the rest to be assimilated into wider Polish society and the issue was regarded as closed. Despite rhetorical adherence to the principles of socialist internationalism, atavistic sentiments are clear as is witnessed in this statement by a prominent Polish politician made in July 1963 that '[n]o socialist country is interested in a large number of its citizens permanently residing abroad, or in hosting foreigners' (quoted in Ihme-Tuchel 1997: 15).

Finally, after 1957 the GDR played an active but discreet role in aiding in the education of 'designated German' children and in the establishment of various German cultural societies. At one level, these served as meeting points for the ever-dwindling numbers of 'designated Germans', at another they performed a classic transmission belt function common to all 'mass organizations' in totalitarian regimes.

The SED and PZPR did not see eye to eye on the issue of the 'Germanicized Poles' any more than they did with regard to the 'designated Germans'. The problem for the SED was that it had no more room for freedom of expression on this matter than did this group of persons itself. For many 'Germanicized Poles', a form of passive resistance became the norm. In the early years this took the shape of non-co-operation with the authorities in such matters as refusing formally to apply for Polish papers following the promulgation of the 1951 Nationality Law. The most obvious and safest form of resistance for these communities was in fact simply to cut themselves off as far as possible from the wider world. In 1956, we do, however, see a manifestation of their political presence. Some individuals sought to use the brief thaw to obtain official recognition from the courts for the establishment of German societies, but to no avail. Throughout the 1960s, Polonization continued. The net result of this process was that today it is common to speak of a 'lost generation' among the Germans of Poland. Both the elderly and their grandchildren have a better knowledge of Germany and the Germans than does the generation in between.

Emigration to Germany always remained on the agenda in one form or another, and the overwhelming majority of Germans who became eligible to leave in the late 1950s, after Red Cross mediation between Poland and West Germany, did so. The fact that about 55,000 Germans from Lower Silesia left, virtually destroyed the basis of the cultural life of the German-speaking population there. In addition to them, approximately 120,000 Germans from Upper Silesia also emigrated. As a consequence, the assimilation pressure on the remaining Germans in both areas grew, again resulting in an even greater rate of emigration, so that, as a result of several inter-governmental agreements between Poland and the Federal Republic, by 1990 about 1.1 million people of German descent had left Poland.[6] With almost all of the 'designated' Germans having emigrated, until 1989 Polish assimilationists could comfortably deny the existence of a German minority. In areas of German residence what this meant was that until the 1970s German was not offered in the education system at any level, not even in institutes of higher education. There was also discrimination against members of the minority in terms of public sector employment. On the other hand, from the mid-1950s people were unlikely to be discriminated against for things as trivial as owning kitchen appliances with German labels on them (Strobel 1997: 29). At the political level, organizations of the German minority, which gradually emerged from the early 1980s, were denied official recognition, and their members were subjected to various forms of discrimination (Rogall 1993: 33ff.).

In essence, the (re-)Polonization campaign involved the Polish authorities in an attempt not only to change the everyday orientations of these people by rendering Germany redundant and by imposing sanctions upon recalcitrants but also to alter the physical landscape and re-inventing the past. By the 1970s Polish had become the lingua franca throughout all parts of Upper Silesia and the education system was the means by which the younger generation was inducted into the wider Polish nation. Having said that, the educational achievements on the part of the children of 'Germanicized Poles' remained poor in comparison to those of the wider population.

The policy of (re-)Polonization did meet with limited success. However, as mentioned earlier it was an overall failure. This was particularly the case in southern Masuria where by the late 1960s almost all of those who had been exempted from the expulsions by the late 1960s had emigrated. For the most part, despite the absence of any real links with Germany, the levels of identification with Germany on the part of 'Germanicized Poles' seems to have grown. This phenomenon is doubly curious given the way that in Germany these groups had often been considered to be less than fully German, and in fact had often been Polish-speaking, bilingual or indeed simply the speakers of Germanic-Polish dialects. The poor economic performance of Poland in comparison to that of either German state was certainly a factor, but the causes of this growing identification with Germany can also be very firmly located in the nature of, and reaction to Polish governmental policies towards the group itself.

With regard to the wider role of the German governments in this area, although the GDR authorities assumed responsibility for the designated German minority, it remained silent with regard to the 'Germanicized Poles'. For its part, the Federal Republic was powerless to act. Until the early 1960s, it lacked even a trading mission in Poland, and diplomatic relations were not established until 1970. In the intervening years, all that West German politicians could do was berate their Polish counterparts over the treatment of the minority, and lobby the Red Cross and other charitable agencies. There were also those who stimulated wishful thinking on the part of their constituents concerning the possibility that Poland's western border might be subject to future change. This 'belief' seems to have also influenced the actions of many ethnic Germans still living in Poland as became apparent in the late 1980s.

Contact with Germany was maintained through family visits, usually from west to east, and migration that invariably followed the reverse route. When Brandt travelled to Warsaw in 1970, it was felt that, unless it was dealt with in a sufficiently sensitive manner, the issue of the German minority was seen as likely to interfere with the greater prize of establishing diplomatic relations. Having said that, the issue was discreetly discussed and following the establishment of diplomatic relations, the Polish government did permit an increase in emigration to the Federal Republic on the basis of 'family re-unification'. Indeed, the 1970s did see a steady rise in ethnic German emigration from Poland; and in connection with West German loans, money was sometimes explicitly linked to the issue of emigration.

The situation began to alter somewhat in the late 1970s as BdV activists began to penetrate Poland under the guise of regular tourism or as visitors to family and friends. They took advantage of the deteriorating political and economic situation to disseminate knowledge about Germany, and to encourage Germans to create embryonic organizational structures. These efforts bore fruit in 1990, when the courts in Katowice finally allowed a delegation of German activists to register their society as such. This action in turn led to an explosion of political and other activity on the part of 'Germanicized Poles' and their descendants, and a nation-wide network of *Deutsche Freundschaftskreise* (German Friendship Circles/DFKs) was established.

Of particular interest here is the response of the (West) German government to this burst of activity. Given the relative isolation on the part of Upper Silesian (and other Polish) ethnic Germans from the Federal Republic, and the rather limited means through which the image of West Germany could be mediated, the demands of the activists and their constituents were somewhat unrealistic (Sakson 2004). Some, fuelled by conservative elements within the *Landsmannschaften* hoped for the achievement of a special administrative status for part of Silesia. Even more bizarre was the belief that the collapse of the GDR and 'really existing socialism' would lead to a revision of the Polish–German border. The fact that ethnic Germans living outside of Germany could entertain such hopes, and also believe that the German government shared them, points to significant disconnect that existed between the two sides.

Needless to say, it was made clear to the German minority that the German government was not about to act as their champion with regard to either scheme. What Bonn/Berlin did offer was to support the minority, and to request of the Polish government that it recognize by treaty the existence of a German minority that was many times larger than the official propaganda allowed. In addition, the German authorities, together with the support of the Polish government and a younger generation of BdV activists offered an alternative to earlier unrealistic expectations. They put forward the idea that (the ethnic Germans of) Silesia should develop a bridging function between Germany and Poland and in that way play a pivotal role in promoting economic recovery and reconciliation. Reluctantly, German community leaders agreed, thus allowing real progress to be made. The extent to which the German minority has been able to act as such a bridge is debatable. The vast majority of well-educated Germans either fled or were expelled or killed in the period 1945–1949. During the intervening years, the remaining intellectual elite opted for Germany. Of those who are left, it is extremely rare to find a member of the German minority born before 1980 who has received a university education (Ociepka 2004). On top of that, at national level the German minority is not numerically significant, and neither is Opole Silesia of any great economic importance. In addition, as the results of the Polish census of 2002 show, another process of consciousness shift, this time towards a Silesian identity may be under way in the area (Stadtmüller 2004). The idea of the area serving as some kind of bridge was nevertheless a good public relations exercise (Sakson 2004).

Within this context, there has never been any clarity over what is meant by Silesia, and too often the term 'Silesia' is incorrectly and misleadingly used as a synonym for Opole Silesia (see, for example, Koschyk 1993).

Aside from its German and Czech fragments, Silesia lies today almost wholly within Poland. Importantly, it is divided administratively, and to a great extent culturally, between Lower, Opole and Upper Silesia. It is only in the second of these three provinces, and more specifically within three of the counties that make up the *Opolskie* voivodship (province), that substantial numbers of Germans are to be found. There are negligible numbers of Germans in Lower Silesia, and in the neighbouring *Śląskie* voivodship numbers are dwindling rapidly. Certainly in terms of interpersonal family contacts, the Germans of the *Opolskie* voivodship continue to perform a bridging role. However, given their lack of domestic political and economic capital, the grander plans for Silesia, no matter how vaguely defined, have not been realized.

The German minority in post-communist Poland

In general, the situation of the German minority in Poland has significantly improved since the end of communism. They enjoy full minority rights in accordance with the norms established by the Copenhagen criteria and other international agreements (Góralski 2004). Well over a hundred thousand Germans still live there, the vast majority of them in the *Opolskie* and *Śląskie* voivodships. Others are scattered throughout the country, with larger concentrations only to be found in Lower Silesia, Masuria and Ermland.

Unfortunately, confusion reigns concerning the total number of Poland's German minority. The umbrella organization of the German minority the *Verband der Deutschen Gesellschaften* (Association of German Societies/ VdG) currently estimates the total to be in the region of 400,000, although most Polish academics believe that figure to be too high. The VdG also claims that a total membership of some 276,000 individuals. The results of the Polish census of September 2002 failed to clarify the issue. This census was important because it was the first since the 1930s in which respondents were asked whether or not they were ethnic Poles. Prior to the census, by common consent it was held that between 96 and 97 per cent of the total population was ethnically Polish. Indeed, the result showed that 96.74 per cent of respondents declared themselves to be Polish citizens of Polish ethnicity. The results also showed that there were in fact only 152,900 Germans, a figure that simply does not square with either the VdG's figures or those of most Polish researchers. Then again, a further 173,200 people, overwhelmingly from the *Opolskie* voivodship replied that they were in fact neither German nor Polish, but Silesian. This combined figure of 326,100 although not corresponding to the VdG's estimate of the total number of Germans in Poland does at least come close to many Polish estimates and makes the VdG's membership figures more comprehensible. However, it does so, only if one works on the assumption that the overwhelming majority of declared Silesians have a German orientation. The census results also showed that a total of 279,600 Polish citizens resident in Poland have dual Polish–German citizenship. In order for a Polish citizen, resident in Poland to qualify for a German passport, certain strict criteria must be fulfilled. Possession of German citizenship prior to May 1945 is one obvious criterion, but one that affects fewer and fewer people. In all other cases, applicants born before 1 January 1994 must prove either that both parents, or an applicant's father either possessed a German passport or was entitled to one according to contemporaneous German nationality law. Matrilineal descent alone is not sufficient. On top of that, no-one born in Poland after 1 January 1994 is entitled to a German passport on grounds of descent.

The result of this mélange of qualifications is that a large number of people in Poland who consider themselves to be partly or wholly German are not entitled to German passports. This provides further grounds for treating the census figures with caution. Then again, for decades many Poles have held the view that many of those who claim to be German emphasize their rather tenuous connections with Germany as an economic insurance policy. Given the huge discrepancy between the total number of declared Germans in the census and declared German passport holders, this hypothesis may possibly have been borne out by the results themselves.

However, there is one major caveat. A total of 774,900 people are missing from the statistics on ethnic background. They either refused to answer the question or gave ambiguous answers that could not be classified according to the set criteria. Given the total number of Poles weighed in at the predicted figure, and persistent problems since 1918 between the ethnic Polish population and its minorities, it is not unreasonable to assume that members of the various minority groups are over-represented in the above-cited figure. Nor is it unreasonable to assume that Germans (and Silesians) are among their number. In sum, no-one knows how many Germans live in Poland. For some German observers the official figures are far too low. They point to the fact that older people in particular may have been worried that in telling the truth they might have been inviting discrimination. They also claim more controversially, that the term Silesian should be taken in the same way that a Saxon or Bavarian would use the analogous terms, and not as a marker of a non-German identity (Rossmanith 2004). Whatever the case, the census of 2002 could have important ramifications for the VdG, as funding is in part contingent upon numbers. Not unreasonably, governments need a reliable base upon which to calculate financial provision for cultural and other programmes. The official figures show there to be far fewer Germans than was previously thought. It is not unreasonable to assume that both the German and Polish governments will now further cut support for ethnic Germans according to the census results.

Regardless of just how many Germans there are in Poland, the minority is relatively well organized at the national level, even though the focus of its activities is on the *Opolskie* voivodship. The minority has benefited from financial, material, and human resources made available to them by the German government. These have enabled the minority, with the consent and support of Polish authorities, to restore in part the German-language education system that existed in areas that were German before 1945, to revive a German cultural life for ethnic Germans, and to participate actively in the economic reconstruction of their homeland.

Of equal importance is the fact that at the local level relationships between ethnic Germans and Poles have improved. After a period of inter-communal tension in the early 1990s, much of which resulted from the activities of the German expellee organizations, inter-ethnic co-operation has prevailed. In fact, such tension usually existed between local Germans and Poles from outside the area, as opposed to their neighbours. This is broadly the case today, where apart from indigenous Silesians with a Polish orientation, the majority of the Polish population in Upper Silesia are either refugees or deportees from eastern Poland, or the descendants of such people.

Today, Poland's minorities policy, like that of the Czech Republic, is governed by the Framework Convention for the Protection of National Minorities. The ministries of the interior and culture have a dedicated staff that deals with minority questions and, among other things, co-ordinate the activities of other government departments in this particular field. There are over 600 *Deutsche Freundschaftskreise* in Poland. They in turn combine to form ten regional organizations. These organizations, alongside a further seven functional societies are federated to the VdG that possesses a small full-time bureaucracy. Immense strides have been made in recent years in a variety of fields. The German (and Polish) governments have contributed towards infrastructural projects, the revival of German language education, initiatives aimed at combating stereotypes and towards renovating German cultural monuments. Bilingual signage in areas of German residence is also becoming more common, although one hears occasional complaints from the German side that Poles are some-times unduly sensitive with regard to the issue (Rossmanith 2004). A large number of schools, particularly in the *Opolskie* voivodship, provide a German-language curriculum, except for the core subjects of Polish, History and Mathematics. In terms of media representation the contrast with the Czech Republic is apparent. There is a weekly newspaper, two monthly, and one quarterly magazine, all of which are bilingual. In addi-tion, one television station and five radio stations in Opole and Upper Silesia have some German language output.

Parallel to the improvement of relationships at the local level, the rela-tionship between the minority and the Polish state also became more constructive. A sincere effort has been made by Polish authorities to imple-ment also those aspects of the Treaty on Good Neighbourliness and Friendly Co-operation that were aimed specifically at the German minority. From the mid-1990s this has included the previously cited rapprochement with the expellee organizations. Since the 1970s, the joint German–Polish educational textbook commission aims have been to achieve consensus on the interpretation of disputed parts of the two countries' history, the enacting of regulations that make minority radio and TV broadcasts as well as the publication of minority print media possible, and the co-spon-sorship of the scholarly Eichendorff journal. Despite that, a number of problems remain. They include an insufficient number of well qualified teachers of German and of a curriculum for the teaching of German (Paweltziki and Kirstein 1998: 16). German-language knowledge among the minority is somewhat patchy (Sułek 2004). With regard to the pre-war generation, this is because many of them never learned *Hochdeutsch*. Those born in the 1940s and 1950s had no legitimate opportunity to learn any form of German. Nevertheless, improve-ments in the overall situation of the minority have been significant, which is also evident from the fact that since 1992 rates of emigration have declined considerably.[7]

In the early 1990s, through a combination of fortuitous circumstances, the German minority achieved a remarkable degree of success in the polit-ical sphere. This was particularly true of the first post-communist general election of 1990. The German minority succeeded in having seven MPs and one senator elected to parliament. Since then, their political fortunes have ebbed somewhat. Their representation at national level has fallen at each general election. They now only have two MPs in the *Sejm* and no sena-tors. Similarly, in terms of representation at the regional and local level, after early successes they have effectively retreated to their heartlands in the *Opolskie* voivodship. Here they have a total of 304 councillors sitting in various local authorities and actually control 34 of the 71 communal coun-cils. Within the voivodship, they control 3 out of 12 district/county coun-cils, and are the largest faction in a further 4. Curiously enough, today German political representation is in fact greater than it was before 1939, despite the minority's reduction in size in both relative and absolute terms (Tomala 2004). Yet, since the early 1990s, there has in fact been a decline in electoral support for the VdG, impressive though these figures may sound. The reasons for this are not difficult to identify. First, there was a further massive wave of emigration to Germany in the early 1990s just as the wave of democratization was getting into full swing. Second, successive reforms to the national Polish electoral system have been designed to pro-mote consolidation and put and end to party political fragmentation. One consequence has been that smaller parties have been disadvantaged. Third, the ageing process has taken its toll. As older activists die or retire, so it becomes more difficult to fill vacancies. The younger generation is less numerous and indeed less alienated from wider Polish society. Finally, some are disappointed at the lack of support received from the German government and at the fact that they are not a major item of interest in Germany. Taken together, all of these factors have combined to reduce support for VdG candidates at election times.

We must also consider the attitude of the German population at large together with that of the German government. For most Germans born and raised in post-war Germany, *Spätaussiedler* together with the minority in Poland are not considered to be German. Rather, they are viewed as Poles who by virtue of some tenuous family or ancestral link have simply taken advantage of the special migration regimes that existed for ethnic Germans from former communist Europe to come to Germany. The fact that when these people arrive in Germany, Polish tends to be the lingua franca simply serves to re-enforce that belief. Such attitudes come as a great disappointment to Germans from Poland, who in fact have come to view themselves as people who exist between two worlds, not fully at home in either.

As for the German government, VdG activists are disappointed with the lack of priority they are accorded. Berlin is characterized as being parsimonious, disinterested and much more concerned with preserving good relations with Warsaw at their expense. There is probably some truth in this. In the early 1990s expectations of Germany were far too high. For instance, German community activists in Poland, spurred on by the BdV, sought to convince the German government to persuade Poland into accepting the South Tyrol package as a model for Opole Silesia (Hajnicz 1995: 114). Given prior German involvement in internal Polish politics from the 1770s until 1945, and the recently achieved freedom from Soviet tutelage, such ideas were unsustainable.

Memory, family ties and the BdV, none of which proved to be particularly useful prisms, mediated knowledge of German political realities. However, difficulties in the relationship are not simply due to these factors. They apply more to the current government than to its right-of-centre predecessor. Primarily they do not result from the clash between the cosmopolitanism of the Greens and the SPD with the narrow parochialism of the Germans of Upper and Opole Silesia. In fact, as much as anything else, the current divide is the latest manifestation of a rift between the German political and cultural centre and its eastern periphery that has been apparent for at least 250 years.

A comparative assessment

If we assess the situation today we find that in terms of bilateral Czech–German relations, the remaining German minority is not an issue. It is too small to have any political weight in either country. In addition, the Czech government's attitude towards this minority does not fuel controversy over the wider 'Sudetenland question'. As we have seen, by virtue of its size and contested provenance, the role and place of Poland's German minority has been more of an issue in Polish–German relations, than has that of its Czech counterpart in dealings between Berlin and Prague. Having said that, we have also seen how since 1990 successive German and Polish governments have sought to accommodate the minority without letting it dominate the political agenda. Although many minority activists are disappointed with this stance, the fact of the matter is that much has been achieved since 1990, and less would have been achieved, had Poland's German minority been allowed to dictate to either Warsaw or Berlin. Whether the much vaunted 'bridging function', has brought all the benefits envisaged or promised in the early 1990s is another question. In fact, it is fair to say that in the 1990s both hopes and fears of where this bridging function would lead were misplaced. It is not the case that any part of Silesia became the centre of gravity either in terms of German–Polish relations, or Poland's EU integration strategy. Nor has it led to Poland's territorial integrity being put in question (Starr 1993: 243), except in the minds of those who failed to come to terms with the post-Second World War order, let alone the post-Cold War order. While there has been positive change, difficulties do still exist. Rather than the minorities *in situ*, they centre upon the activities and attitudes of the *Landsmannschaften* (Sułek 2004). In Poland the government and the expellees/refugees have attempted to understand and come to terms with one another's respective positions. As should be clear by now, the extent to which such an understanding has been reached is a matter of debate. Unfortunately, as we have seen in the previous chapter, attempts by their Czech counterparts to replicate this limited success continually stumble on the rock of intransigence concerning the years 1938–1948.

The situation of German minorities in Poland and the Czech Republic evolved in dramatically different ways after 1989. The minority in Poland has been reconstituted as a conscious group and now plays a part in regional political, social and economic life. On the other hand, there are far fewer Germans in the Czech Republic and they lack the capacity to become any kind of meaningful actor in the way in which their Polish counterparts have. In addition, their future prospects have been heavily determined by events outside their control and not always to their advantage. From this perspective, the German minority in the Czech Republic has become caught between Germany, the Czech Republic and the Sudeten German expellees. Whereas an almost identical constellation has worked to the advantage of the minority in Poland, historical and current events have prevented ethnic Germans in the Czech Republic from achieving similar acceptance in society. For both groups, this difference illustrates that ethnic minorities 'are doubly historical in the sense that not only are historical memories essential to their continuance but each such ethnic group is the product of specific historical forces and is therefore subject to historical change and dissolution' (Smith 1991: 20).

8 Ostpolitik

Continuity and change

At the beginning of our investigation stood at an interesting paradox. Although guided by seemingly identical norms and pursued in the same context, at the beginning of the twenty-first century German–Czech and German–Polish relations displayed rather different dynamics, and what is commonly referred to as the German question, in many of its different dimensions, appeared to be at very different stages of solution in each of these two sets of bilateral relations.

Despite the fact that over more than three decades a very specific German Ostpolitik had been in operation vis-à-vis Poland and the Czech Republic (and before 1993, Czechoslovakia) the outcomes have been remarkably different. Proceeding from the assumption that Ostpolitik, as a distinct instance of German foreign policy, could be best explained in a constructivist framework of foreign policy analysis, we set ourselves a dual objective for the subsequent examination. The first was to show that, in this particular instance and without making broader claims, German Ostpolitik is a norm-consistent foreign policy and that the norms that guide its formulation and implementation have remained by and large the same since the late 1960s. If this was indeed the case, and our assumption of a constructivist explanation of German foreign policy in this instance therefore viable, we realize that we would have to account for differences in the state of German–Polish and German–Czech relations within the same constructivist framework of foreign policy analysis. We would also have to demonstrate how, at different levels of analysis, different norms have shaped dissimilar policy outcomes. In other words, Ostpolitik, because of its goals and therefore because of the way in which its success can be measured, is not a policy area in which specific policy outcomes can be willed into existence by the actions of one country alone. Rather, outcomes depend on responses to that country's policies as much as they depend on the initiation of these policies in the first place. Merely pointing to the existence of different norms that can help us understand the different outcomes of German Ostpolitik in relation to Poland and the Czech Republic would only be convincing and satisfying if we could also provide an explanation as to what the causes of these differences in norms were.

With these considerations in mind, the final two chapters of our book will address several issues that shall enable us to answer the various questions we have raised in the course of our examination of bilateral relations in the German–Czech–Polish triangle of fate. We will begin by summarizing the previous discussion to demonstrate the norm consistent nature of Ostpolitik since the 1960s and into the post-Cold War period. We will then answer the question why German–Polish (re)conciliation has been somewhat less difficult to achieve than its German–Czech counterpart. By way of conclusion, we will assess the impact of the various strategies employed since the early 1990s that seek to draw a line under the events that shattered German–Polish and German–Czech(oslovak) relations between 1938 and 1950 and offer some assessment as to the direction in which we believe bilateral relations in this triangle of fate are heading.

German Ostpolitik since the 1960s

Little doubt exists in the academic literature on the subject that from the 1960s onwards, a gradual re-orientation of German foreign policy occurred towards more proactive engagement with Central and Eastern Europe. The reasons for this are varied, but most significantly for our own analysis, they include the consolidation of Germany's links with the West through membership in NATO and the predecessor organizations of today's European Union, the completion of the social, political and economic integration of about 10 million refugees and expellees primarily from Poland and Czechoslovakia, and a generational change in the German political class with younger and more pragmatic leaders rising to the top. In addition, the 1960s were a time of socio-political upheaval in the midst of growing economic prosperity in the Federal Republic, and the student movement and so-called extra-parliamentary opposition contributed to an environment in which Germany's more recent past came under renewed scrutiny, including its relations with Central and Eastern Europe.

In this context, first, between 1966 and 1969, in the grand coalition of the CDU and SPD, and then in an SPD-led coalition government with the liberal democratic FDP, Willy Brandt and a close-knit circle of his foreign policy advisers around Egon Bahr implemented a new policy towards the countries of Eastern Europe that preceded from the recognition of the political and territorial status quo and the acknowledgement that this status quo could not be changed through force or a policy of isolation. Rather, the premise of this new Ostpolitik was that stable peace, reconciliation, and regime change in Central and Eastern Europe could only be achieved by means of rapprochement. After twenty years of marginal relations with the East while prioritizing political, economic and military integration into the West, this shift in foreign policy orientation had a quite revolutionary impact. In a domestic and governmental context in which fear and distrust of the East's intentions had been the order of the day for so long, rapprochement could not but meet initial significant resistance.

Yet, both the governmental and international, as well as to some extent the bilateral contexts of Ostpolitik enabled Brandt and his team to reshape underlying societal norms at the domestic level. Concluding treaties with the Soviet Union, Poland, East Germany and Czechoslovakia, as well as other countries in Central and Eastern Europe, had been possible because of an international climate that presented a window of opportunity in the form of détente between the superpowers, because of a governmental context in which the SPD/FDP coalition had a secure parliamentary majority as of November 1972 and because of a bilateral context in which coalitions of interest emerged that were able to respond positively to the opportunities that arose.[1]

In turn, the success of the new Ostpolitik had a profound impact on the content of societal norms in the domestic context of foreign policy-making. Not only did a majority of the population recognize that Ostpolitik was the only way forward in relations with the East under the conditions of Cold War geopolitics, but, more importantly, previously dominant norms that were most obviously embodied in Adenauer's *Politik der Stärke* very quickly lost credibility. Over time, they became relegated to smaller and smaller constituencies who became increasingly unimportant in electoral terms. This is not to say that the SPD's main political opponent in the domestic arena, the CDU/CSU, did not always keep an eye on its traditional constituency of expellees. Yet unlike in the 1950s, 'expellee issues' of either a domestic or foreign policy nature did no longer dominate party platforms and election manifestos. Ostpolitik had been too successful and the norms become too deeply ingrained. Its policies aimed at peace, reconciliation and regime change were so embedded within the overall political culture of the Federal Republic that it would neither have been worthwhile, nor possible for any mainstream party in the Federal Republic to depart from a long-established consensus. Consequently, the change in government in 1982 did not mean a return to an Adenauer-style *Politik der Stärke*. The new CDU/CSU-FDP coalition in Bonn continued the course of change through rapprochement, initiated as an 'official' foreign policy over a decade earlier. This was helped, in part, by the political and bureaucratic continuity in the German Foreign Office, which, since 1969, had been in the hands of the FDP.

While one could argue, from a (neo-)realist perspective that none of this suggests that German Ostpolitik was indeed norm-consistent, i.e. pursued following a logic of appropriateness rather than one of consequentiality,[2] the preservation of the basic direction of this specific instance of German foreign policy in the post-Cold War era suggests otherwise. A (neo-)realist prediction, of which there were several quite influential ones at the time, would have assumed that Germany's power gains, both relative and absolute, as a consequence of the end of bipolarity, the collapse of communism in Central and Eastern Europe and German unification would inevitably lead to a more assertive foreign policy, including in relation to its eastern neighbours. Yet, none of this occurred. Germany remained committed to the project of European integration and its ties to its Western partners in the various regional and international organizations in which it was a member, while at the same time continuing its Ostpolitik in pursuit of peace, reconciliation and regime change.

The important point to bear in mind in this discussion is that our argument is about the norm-consistent character of Ostpolitik and the fact that the norms guiding its formulation and implementation have by and large remained identical since the 1960s and beyond the end of the Cold War. In other words, neither a change in the content of the policies that were part of Ostpolitik nor different policy outcomes are inconsistent with our argument. That policy content has changed over time while its underlying norms have remained the same should have become clear by the analysis in the previous chapters. Changing dynamics in the international context, in particular, can explain this. Take the example of regime change. Always one of the guiding norms of Ostpolitik, the opportunities to realize it were obviously more limited during the Cold War than they were after the collapse of communism. The more intriguing issue, therefore, that we still have to explore is the difference in policy outcome, i.e. the question why German–Polish and German–Czech relations remain, almost stubbornly, at qualitatively different levels, especially in terms of the degree to which the residual issues stemming from the Second World War and its aftermath have been dealt with in a conciliatory and satisfactory manner. To answer this question is the task that remains to be accomplished.

The Czech and Polish cases: similarities and differences

Having in a broad sense established the pattern of relations between Germany on the one hand and Poland and the Czech Republic on the other, let us now examine the causes in a little more detail. First, as we have seen, some in Germany and Poland have taken a closer interest in one another, than have Czechs and Germans, although the extent to which this is the case is a matter of some dispute. Such engagement is particularly apparent at elite level, but it also true for the practitioners of the liberal arts, and rapprochement has also occurred in the shape of a whole host of governmental and non-governmental initiatives. The extent to which these initiatives have permeated the consciousness of ordinary Poles and especially Germans is another question. For the most part, the operational field is Poland, as opposed to Germany, and, areas in which Germans live to one side, the benefits of such infrastructural and other programmes are not immediately obvious to all Poles. Nevertheless, the sheer breadth and depth of such activity cannot be denied. Whereas similar initiatives have taken place in the Czech Republic, the general consensus is that they have not yet received the same prominence as their German–Polish counterparts. In part, this is due to the disparities in population, size and political and economic weight between the two countries. In the economic sphere the question of German investment and presence in the Czech Republic is still more sensitive than in Poland, despite the largely successful example of the Volkswagen takeover of Czech car manufacturer Škoda.

The reasons for this state of affairs are varied. Poland, because of its sheer size, is of more importance to Germany than is the Czech Republic (Žák 2004).[3] Second, there is the rumbling debate on the Sudetenland, which has no parallel in German–Polish relations. Third, it could be argued that Czech politicians need to rid themselves of a certain parochialism (Žák 2004). At another extreme, some argue that until more Czechs lose their inferiority complex with regard to Germany, full-scale reconciliation will never occur (Schröter 2004). Having said that, the example of Volkswagen and Škoda, where the German parent did not substitute the indigenous management with 'German imports', shows that Czech–German relations can be enhanced through economic co-operation (Žák 2004). In fact, a wide number of commentators point to the continued successful bilateral economic co-operation and its steady growth (Schwall-Düren 2003).

Another cause of differentiation between Poland and the Czech Republic is the fact that there are huge numbers of people in Germany, primarily in the west of the country, who have first-hand experience of Poland, including wide-ranging family ties. This includes not only the refugee and expellee generation, but also subsequent waves of migrants. Among them are ethnic Poles who migrated to escape the combination of economic chaos and political repression of the 1980s. We also find among this number ethnic Polish family members of those who left Poland by claiming their right to settle in Germany as ethnic Germans under German law. It also includes those who have migrated to Germany on the basis of claimed German ancestry. Although there has been a more or less steady trickle of German migration to the Federal Republic from Czechoslovakia/Czech Republic since 1949, the numbers simply do not come close to those who have migrated from Poland to Germany. The fact that in the 1980s and 1990s many of ethnic German emigrants from Poland had ties to Germany that only a lawyer could identify is unimportant. What is of importance is that they can and do act as a bridge between the two societies (Góralski 2004). Thus, for significant numbers of Germans, Poland is a country with which they have connections, where they have family, Polish is a language they speak, and Poland is a country whose concerns they understand. This engagement and these facts have percolated into some of the 'Polish' *Landsmannschaften*, whose engagement with Polish society is correspondingly greater than that of their Sudeten German equivalent. Encounters occur at an everyday level through family visits, which are a much rarer occurrence in the Czech Republic. In other words, much more so in Poland than in the Czech Republic, everyday contact has reduced the importance of the post-war experience, and facilitated projects that deal with the here and now. Most commentators agree that fear of the 'Other' is correspondingly less prominent between Poles and Germans than between Czechs and Germans. Of course, mistakes and misunderstandings do occur. It is also true to say that stereotypes and unidimensional views of past experiences are still present. In order to understand this fact, we shall now further examine contemporary insecurities and how they relate to perceptions of the past.

Refining the differences

We have already noted how the German occupation regimes in Poland and Czechoslovakia differed markedly from one another. However, in this volume we are not concerned with examining these differences in any great detail. Rather, we are concerned with identifying how perceptions of wartime occupation impact upon contemporary society by shaping the norms that regulate bilateral relations. In both Poland and Czechoslovakia the German occupation from 1938/1939 to 1945 was presented as the culmination of over 1,000 years of German aggression towards peaceful peoples. In the historiography of both countries, Germans came to be presented as barbarians who had to be fenced in and held down lest they wrought further havoc. History itself was distorted in such away that it was reduced to a chronicle of survival in the face of unprecedented oppression. It was also presented as a struggle between modern nations and nation-states. In so doing, in Czechoslovakia both the Beneš government and the communist regime immediately succeeding it sought to employ history as a legitimizing device.

In the case of Poland, elements of Roman Dmowski's integralist nationalism were selectively grafted onto the local variant of Marxist-Leninist ideology. The Polish communist party, much like its Czechoslovak counterpart, presented itself as the sole guarantor of national independence, and sought to establish continuity between the past and the present. The People's Republic of Poland represented itself as the heir to the Polish Piast kingdom of the Middle Ages. In a sense, this was quite logical as the borders of the two entities happened to be broadly identical (Holohan and Ciechocinska 1996: 160). Germany was portrayed as the eternal aggressor, with Poles as the consistent objects of its unwelcome interest. Similarly, in the Czech case, history was re-written in such a way that the Czech/Bohemian relationship with Germany was presented as a tireless struggle for national liberation. It is worth repeating that this applied not only to the communist authorities, but also to the short-lived post-1945 Beneš-led government from which the current authorities in Prague derive their legitimacy. Beneš himself saw the twentieth-century Czechoslovak state as having its origins in the seventh-century Kingdom of Sámo, and as having been engaged in a civilizational struggle with the Germans stretching back well over a thousand years (Gordon 1990: 108ff.). Curiously enough, one can also find claims that in 1918 Czechs had more in common culturally with Germans than they did with Slovaks (Auer 2000: 25). Such statements are intriguing and rest upon the supposed absence of widespread ethnically related conflict in Bohemia and Moravia until the nineteenth century. Having said that, if differentiation from the 'Other' is an essential tool of nation-building, then anti-German sentiment was pivotal for the post-1945 Czech(oslovak) nation-building project. After all, what better way was there to present (pan-)Slavic credentials than through the prism of anti-German propaganda? When the communists came to power in 1948 all they did was to refine the picture somewhat by attempting to equate all Germans with the Sudeten German expellees and therefore a (state-sponsored) desire for revenge (Kunštát 2004).

Whereas such projects may have been the product of dubious scholarship, they were, given the circumstances, extremely effective (Meckel 2004). In both countries, the immediate post-war regimes needed to legitimize both themselves and their actions. They both sought to complete the nation-building project and engineer widespread social reform. In particular, the German threat was used in an attempt to keep the population in line (Fiszer 2004). In Poland it was argued that the Polish–Soviet alliance was essential in order to keep the German threat at bay (Czapliński 2004). In the media, the Federal Republic and its citizens were presented as unreconstructed and unreconstructable revisionists, and it has proven difficult to eradicate this caricature (Czapliński 2004). In other words, a society was created in which legitimacy rested upon nationalism and social reconstruction. Once the latter ground to a halt, the former began to lose credence. This was especially so from the 1970s, as official and non-official contacts with Germans increased. Increasingly, official portrayals of Germany grew more contradictory and confused. Thus, the Czech and Polish communist regimes were in part undermined by their own inconsistent attitudes towards Germany. Obviously, the employment of such stereotypes ebbed and flowed with the passing of time, and in Poland in particular, from the 1970s as civil society grew apace, the portrait of the historical engagement between Poland and Germany became somewhat more balanced.

If we examine the nature of contemporary politics in both the Czech Republic and Poland, we find that they are both liberal democracies. This is an important, if obvious point. The very exposure of what occurred between 1945 and 1949 has been part and parcel of the democratization process (Rossmanith 2004). The fact that the outstanding issues have not brought the process of reconciliation to a halt does credit to all sides. Moreover, we find that even the post-communist *Sojusz Lewicy Demokratycznej* (Democratic Left Alliance/SLD) in Poland disavows the actions of its communist ancestors *Polska Zjednoczona Partia Robotnicza* (Polish United Workers' Party /PZPR) and the *Polska Partia Robotnicza* (Polish Workers'

Party/PPR). This includes condemnation of the nature of the expulsions, although all Polish parties are quick to point out that the principle, if not the manner of expulsion was sanctioned by the Allies. On this point they are absolutely correct, and it applies as much to the Czechoslovak as it does to the Polish case. It is also pointed out that the expulsions have to be seen within the overall context of the war and its consequences, which included Poland's westward shift, and the expulsion of Poles from former eastern Poland. These qualifications to one side, no serious party in Poland claims it derives legitimacy from the (actions of the) vanished People's Republic, and all parties recognize that the post-war 'coalition' between communists and non-communists was a short-lived, Soviet-imposed stepping stone on the way to building a pro-Soviet communist regime.

In this sphere Poland contrasts sharply with the Czech Republic. The Czech Republic possesses a barely reconstructed communist party that has a reasonable level of public support. In part it derives this support by playing upon fears concerning the SdL, who inadvertently thereby act as a recruiting sergeant for the Czech communists (Kovanic 2004). Not only that, the state itself derives its legitimacy from the post-war Beneš government that in February 1948 was overthrown by its erstwhile communist partners. Ultimately, it derives its legitimacy from the immediate post-war liberal democratic strand of Czech politics, and thus from the inter-war republic which was destroyed by the Munich Agreement of 1938. Within this context, the crucial point is this: by early 1948 the bulk of the expulsions had occurred (officially they were completed later that year). They had been accomplished and sponsored by a broad coalition of Czechoslovak political forces. The communists did not promulgate the Beneš Decrees. Although supported by the communists, they were instigated above all by those forces to which current Czech political elites trace their origins. Small wonder then that many Czechs find the question of the Sudeten Germans difficult to deal with. To condemn it in the terms that post-communist Polish governments have condemned the Polish experience would in effect beg more questions than it answers. Such a condemnation might even serve to undermine the legitimacy of those parties that seek to establish their liberal democratic credentials by referring to the inheritance of Beneš and the Masaryks. Thus, the difficulty, from a constructivist point of view, is that not only do societal norms in the domestic context make it difficult for political elites to take a more pragmatic approach towards the German question but also that norms at the governmental level itself almost entirely rule out such a possibility.[4] An illustration of just how emotionally charged this whole issue is came in July 2003, after the Czech referendum on EU accession. In that same month, the German foreign minister Joschka Fischer spoke in favour of the Czech–German Future Fund making a symbolic humanitarian gesture towards the expellees. The response among Czech politicians was uniform, and the position of the Czech government was clear. Any such payment would simply put obstacles in the way of Czech–German reconciliation. Cyril Svoboda, the Czech foreign minister did not rule out compensation for Czech citizens of German descent who had been adversely affected by the Beneš Decrees, but that is the extent of 'concession' the Czech side seems to be able and willing to make. The responses of Czech opposition parties ranged from support of the government's position to those of blatant anti-German posturing. Some see this as primarily a matter of Czech internal politicking, and as such nothing much to worry about (Lintzel 2004). Others would view it as the cheap instrumentalization of a potentially explosive issue that capitalizes upon and re-enforces pre-existing societal norms in the domestic arena, rather than attempting to change them. Having said that, the position of Polish political parties with regard to maximum demands emanating from Germany is little different. This is not to say that we equate Fischer's proposal with the kind of demands for the return of property, land and territory occasionally still issued by extremist fringe groups. What it does show, however, is the difference of what is considered a maximum demand in German–Czech compared to German–Polish relations. The difference between the two cases is not that the expulsion and their consequences are not as much of an issue in Polish–German relations as they are in Czech–German relations but that neither the German nor the Polish side finds it difficult to agree on a formula of words with regard to the nature of the expulsions, precisely because the societal norms that exist in the relevant domestic and governmental arenas in both countries allow the two governments meaningful and broadly acceptable compromises. To put it simply, although all sides co-operate fully within a variety of supranational institutions, the different legacies account for why a large section of Polish society, particularly at elite level, has been able to change its view of Germany and the Germans while the same has not been possible in the Czech Republic.

In addition, given the different experiences of the two countries, it has been relatively easy for Polish historians and others to attempt to debunk communist historiography and present a more balanced analysis of the past – and not only with respect to Germany. It has been controversial, and often painful, but nevertheless it has been done. For example, Poland's acquisition in 1945 of eastern German territories is increasingly presented as the price Germany paid for launching total war, and then having lost it totally (Stadtmüller 2004). The 'recovered territories' thesis previously applied in almost equal measure by the communists and Catholic Church has been discarded. It is freely admitted in some circles that on the whole 'the recovered territories' in fact had a wholly German character (Fiszer 2004). The extent to which this fact has been transmitted to groups other than the socially and politically engaged is a matter for some debate (Schwall-Düren 2003). Yet, importantly the transition to democracy which began in the 1980s has also meant that the new political elites in Poland have made a conscious effort to reshape societal norms in terms of what is permissible in the country's relationship with Germany, a significant accomplishment, comparable to the efforts of Willy Brandt and his team in the 1960s when a similar change began to take place in West Germany with regard to relations with the East in general that provided the domestic and eventually governmental environment in which the new Ostpolitik became an appropriate course of foreign policy.

The Polish example of norm change since the late 1980s has a parallel in developments in the Czech Republic, but as ever there is divergence. In Poland, the communists re-invented history after shunting their non-communist opponents out of the way. The Czech communists and the short-lived post-war Beneš government jointly engaged in the systematic re-presentation of history by incorporating the war and its aftermath within a historiography that presented the expulsions as a final reversal of centuries of German repression. After the non-communists had outlived their useful-ness, the communist project alone came to be identified with its national counterpart. We saw in Chapter 2 how the Protestant reformer Jan Hus was transformed into both a proto-socialist and wider national hero (Auer 2000: 249). In turn, the defeat and expulsion of the Germans was seen as expunging the memory of the defeat of the armies of the Protestant Bohemian nobility, re-invented as the Czechoslovak nation, by the Habsburgs at the Battle of the White Mountain in 1620. The fact that the Catholic Habsburg armies actually defeated the Protestant nobility of Bohemia, both German and Bohemian, is once again not the point. It is how people perceive the past that governs their perception of current reality and contributes to creating and sustaining the very norms that deter-mine what is deemed an appropriate course of action in Czech–German relations and what is not.

With regard to the Second World War itself, the Czechoslovak experi-ence was re-interpreted in such a way that no major differences in terms of occupation regimes in Poland and Czechoslovakia became apparent – contrary to the historical facts. The purpose of the German invasion and subsequent occupation of both countries was to exterminate the Jewish population and to incorporate territory into the *Großdeutsches Reich*. However, for the non-Jewish element of the population, the occupation regime was by no means identical. It was much more cruel in Poland than in Czechoslovakia. The Germans sought not only to exterminate the Polish intellectual elite, but also to enslave the overwhelming remainder of society. Moreover, whereas the Czech armed forces did not resist either the German aggression of 1938 or 1939, the Poles did so in 1939. It is a significant understatement to say that 'the invasion by the Germans of Czechoslovakia in 1938 after the Munich Agreement and the creation of the Protectorate of Bohemia and Moravia in the year 1939 were perhaps less bloody than was the German invasion of Poland . . .' (Vollmer 1997). Moreover, resistance to German occupation was more constant and fierce in Poland than it was in Czechoslovakia. The policy of mass intellectual decapitation and enslavement that took place in Poland did not occur in Czechoslovakia. Some argue that for Czech society to come to terms with the post-war expulsions in the same way that Poland has, these facts have to be confronted (Pick 2003). It is claimed this must be done not only because such facts are true but also because they contain the answer to understanding just why this whole issue is more sensitive to Czechs than it is to Poles. Similarly, the post-war expulsion of German-speaking Jews from Czechoslovakia needs to be acknowledged in the same way that the Polish government has accepted Polish culpability for anti-Jewish pogroms that occurred during and after the war (Schröter 2004). Within this context we should also mention that for many Poles, Germany's perceived emphasis on the anti-Jewish as opposed to the anti-Polish elements of Nazi racial theory can be seen as problematic (Stadmüller 2004). Yet, sometimes, talk is cheap. In Germany itself, the Allied-led selective de-Nazification campaign of the late 1940s aside, it was not until the late 1960s that a more honest self-assessment of ordinary peoples' roles in the Nazi regime began. In the (former) GDR, the record is equally, if not more, ambiguous. The official communist doctrine of an anti-fascist and 'progressive' state identity sat uneasily with a Nazi past from which the East German state could not so easily divorce itself and its population. Thus, show trials and cover-ups were about as frequent as they were in West Germany. Elsewhere in Europe, it was not until the 1970s that French society was able to confront the reality of the Vichy regime, and of the complex relationship between resistance and collaboration. Coming to terms with the past is part and parcel of the process of internal democratization. The current debate in Spain concerning the nature of the civil war and the mass executions that followed it may provide another useful example (Lintzel 2004). The contemporary debate in Spain shows, as did its French counterpart, that the past can be dealt with in a dispassionate and honest manner. However, both examples show that it takes time for emotions to become secondary to the need for clarity.

No-one should deny the brutality of the German occupation regime in either country, nor should the crimes of the occupiers be minimized, trivialized or relativized. Nor should we pretend that it is easy for any society collectively to face up to the actions of some of its ancestors. For example, how many contemporary English people are aware of the behaviour of Oliver Cromwell's troops in Ireland? How many Swedes know the extent of the carnage wrought by the armies of Gustav Aldophus during the Thirty Years War? Yet, we have to face history in order to ensure that we do not repeat it.

Within the context of our study, and to return to our main theme, we should not ignore the violence of the language on all sides. For example, in a radio broadcast on 27 October 1943 Beneš warned: '. . . the end of the war in our country will be written in blood. The Germans will be paid back mercilessly and in multiples for everything they have done' (Staněk 2001: 216). Naturally enough, he was not alone in using such language, before, during or after the war. It could be argued that Beneš was simply trying to rally the Czechoslovak population during a period when it faced brutal oppression. Such words do, however, raise questions concerning intent, incitement and culpability. This, in turn, highlights another problem that the Czech political elite must deal with. It is one of how to present an alternative view of the German occupation and its aftermath that does not simultaneously create an institutional and social psychological crisis within the Czech Republic itself. It must also be done in such a way that it does not inadvertently give ammunition to those who would seek either to relativize or minimize the brutality of the German occupation regime.

A final factor in determining differences that we must take into account is that substantial numbers of Poles are either surviving expellees and deportees, or the descendants of such people. They were forcibly uprooted from former eastern Poland towards the end of the Second World War by a bloody civil war, and one between Poles and the Soviet army against Ukrainian insurgents. Many of the Poles affected by warfare eventually ended up on former German territory. Sometimes they had quite literally travelled halfway around the world in circumstances that are scarcely credible, but nevertheless true. Whereas, especially in the aftermath of war, they might have had little sympathy for Germans, a kind of community of fate now exists between the two. The common experience of expulsion has led to a great deal of mutual understanding of the processes that lead to destitution, pauperization and recognition that they affect the innocent as well as the guilty. Again, we find this experience to be largely absent in the Czech Republic. There were indeed Czechs from former Polish Volhynia, Romania and elsewhere who were forcibly re-settled in Czechoslovakia after the war. However, in comparison to the Polish and German cases they were very few in number. Several tens of thousands of Czechs were evicted from their homes by the Germans at various times after the Munich Agreement, and many thousands were murdered. However, once again the cases are comparable only in the broader sense, and, for reasons that should now be clear, it is more difficult for contemporary Czech political elites to deal with this issue constructively at the bilateral level and simultaneously maintain domestic credibility than it is for their Polish counterparts. The dissimilar legacies underlying these dynamics stem first of all from the divergence in the wartime treatment of Czechs and Poles by the Germans. Second, the nature of society in Poland and Czechoslovakia during the period of communist rule was also very different. Contemporary differences stem also from the different ways in which the post-communist regimes in Prague and Warsaw have used the period of German occupation as a frame of reference through which they seek to legitimize current actions. In other words, different pasts and different perceptions, interpretations and instrumentalization thereof have established very different sets of social norms in Poland and the Czech Republic with regard to the range of appropriate (and hence, from an elite perspective, permissible) courses of action vis-à-vis Germany. For Germany, therefore, reconciliation has become easier to achieve with Poland where the democratic transformation process has accelerated at elite level a reorientation of foreign policy towards Germany that had, to some extent, been initiated by the democratic opposition years earlier. In relation to the Czech Republic, a very different norm consensus applies at the domestic and governmental levels that crucially shape the chances of achieving reconciliation at the bilateral level.

Yet, we must not turn a blind eye to the impact that the 'German factor' has had in this context. It has been much more obvious for Polish elites and the interested wider public to see that the Federal Republic of Germany that actually existed in the late 1980s and early 1990s was very different from the image that the communist regime had portrayed of it. This even extended to the much dreaded expellees and their organizations which, a small number of problems aside, took a much more conciliatory and constructive approach to the democratizing Poland than they had done at any time in the past. These processes fed off each other in the Polish case as much as their equivalents did in the Czech case – the crucial difference being that in the latter pre-existing norms were reinforced rather than changed. Moreover the norms that existed precluded anything beyond superficial declarations of good neighbourly relations, and at times endangered even the rhetorical commitment to come to terms with a complex and painful legacy of mutually inflicted pain. The intransigence of the SdL and of leading CSU politicians contributed as much to this as did the at best careless, at worst deliberate and manipulative way in which the Czech political class has handled the reconciliation complex. Bearing in mind the constraints that the relevant elites faced in the domestic, governmental and bilateral contexts of their relationship and from which they were either unwilling or unable to free themselves, much hope was vested in the European integration process that became part and parcel of the social, political and economic transformations that have engulfed Central and Eastern Europe since the early 1990s.

The 'return to Europe' and its consequences

For a variety of reasons, Poland and the Czech Republic sought western integration and membership of NATO and in particular the EU. Both states became members of NATO in 1999. The importance of this event cannot be understated for either Poland or the Czech Republic. For the Czech Republic, it signified not only that it was allied to Germany, but that they had achieved a kind of equality at a political and military level (Kovanic 2004). For the Poles, an important psychological barrier, i.e. entering into permanent military alliance with (a united) Germany, was overcome (Tomala 2004). In neither case did NATO accession stir up emotions concerning the past. Membership of this organization was above all a question of collective security, which for the first time since the advent of the nation-state resulted in Germans, Czechs and Poles becoming allied with one another (Meckel 2004). NATO membership and the American guarantee was therefore seen as a means of guaranteeing peace in Europe and offering protection from further (Russian or German) aggression (Žák 2004). Although a common political framework had been enjoined (Handl 2004), residual questions arising from the Second World War simply did not enter into anybody's equation (Schröter 2004).

Matters were much different in the case of EU accession. Rather than becoming members of a political and military *alliance*, negotiation of entry into the EU meant determining the terms under which the two countries could join a *value community* with very strong legal foundations (Posselt (interview) 2003). This did not only imply implementing the vast body of existing regulations and laws known as the *acquis communautaire* but also to subscribe to the values and principles upon which the EU and its various predecessors had been founded. Crucial among these were some of the very norms that came to guide Ostpolitik in the 1960s in an attempt to replicate the ensuing success of Franco-German understanding, peace and reconciliation. Given the complexity, and number of residual issues stemming from the past, it cannot come as a much of a surprise that accession negotiations quickly became embroiled in renewed bilateral controversy suggesting that the German question was far from completely resolved.

What then were the apparent advantages of EU membership that made the political elites on all sides persist and eventually succeed in the negotiations? From the German perspective, following Hyde-Price (2000: 182–183), we can say that the country's commitment to EU enlargement derives from four key factors. First, there is the desire to ensure stability along its own eastern frontier. EU membership is seen as a means through which the ghosts of the past can finally be laid to rest. Provided that membership brings the expected economic benefits, migratory flows from the Czech Republic and more especially Poland should be kept to a minimum. Within this context political stability should also be secured. Second, it is believed that enlargement will bring substantial economic benefits to Germany itself by facilitating trade and investment. Third, by embedding its bilateral relations with these East-Central European countries within the overall framework of the EU, Germany hopes to dispel fears that it seeks to re-create a German-led *Mitteleuropa*. Finally, there has long been widespread agreement within Germany that EU membership has been beneficial to all member-states. Therefore Czech and Polish accession was supported in full, as it was seen as being virtuous in itself. Above all, EU membership was identified with being European and as a means of achieving psychological parity with existing member-states (Kafka 2004).

The latter reasoning applied in equal measure to Poland and the Czech Republic. In addition, it was and is felt in both countries that an additional western anchor, apart from NATO membership, will enhance the sense and actuality of security. Third, it is hoped that membership will help close the technology and prosperity gap that exists between east and west. Finally, it is felt that the integration process will minimize the chances of a slide back towards dictatorship and the command economy (Aniol 1996: 7). From the point of view of the EU, it was important to avoid the creation of a political vacuum in East-Central Europe that could result in continent-wide instability. The question was not so much of whether or not to associate with post-communist Europe, but rather about what form institutional co-operation should take (*Forschungsgruppe Europa* 1996: 59).

As soon as it became clear to emergent non-communist political elites that the Soviet Union, and subsequently Russia, could not and would not, stand in their way, preliminary negotiations on accession began. At this point it is useful to acknowledge the work played in Poland and the Czech Republic by the foundations that are affiliated to each of the major German parties. Since the early 1990s they have been prominent in various ventures aimed at boosting civil society and at increasing awareness of the practicalities and consequences of the European venture. Neither should we forget the work of the joint German–Polish Viadrina University in Frankfurt an der Oder, nor of the Willy Brandt Institute at the University of Wrocław, which in fact is partly sponsored by the SPD-linked *Friedrich-Ebert-Stiftung*. A wide cross section of commentators single out both institutions for particular praise with regard to what co-operation can actually achieve (Ociepka 2004). Similarly neither should we forget the efforts of the German–Polish reconciliation centre at Krzyżowa (Czapliński 2004).

Given the widespread praise that the Viadrina University has received, it is worthy of mention that as of 2004, no direct equivalent institution had been established between Germany and the Czech Republic. Instead, there is a large number of student exchanges, as there is between Poland and Germany. In addition, Charles University, Prague, has been particularly active in promoting links with German universities and academics. In part, some of these activities are funded by the Czech–German Future Fund (Lintzel 2004).

As for the various research institutions and other NGOs, it could possibly be argued that some have not been active enough in promoting inter-regional co-operation among the emerging democracies of East-Central Europe. The fact is, however, that structures and plans for regional co-operation, such as the Central European Free Trade Association (CEFTA), were in effect swept away in the desire to 'return to Europe'. In order to complete the first stage in the integration process, Poland joined various second-level West European institutions, such as the European Bank for Reconstruc-tion and Development (EBRD) in 1990, the Council of Europe (CoE) in 1991, and the Organization for Economic Co-operation and Development (OECD) in 1996 (Sanford 1999: 85). Czechoslovakia and then the Czech Republic trod an identical path, with the same goal in mind.

Importantly, these overtures towards Western Europe were taking place in a wholly novel geopolitical environment. If we first deal with Poland, we find that for the first time in 500 years, Poland was not faced either by a hostile Russia and/or Germany. Russia was debilitated and Germany had made a conscious decision to pool its sovereignty within various supranational frameworks, principally the EU. The issue, from the Polish point of view, was how to embed Poland within the process in such a way that the drive towards 'European unity' would be sustained, while simultaneously continuing to ensure that Russia would not become a hostile power. The example of how EU membership seemed to have been instrumental in establishing liberal democracy in Portugal, Spain and Greece was another important factor.

In turn, the Special Accession Programme for Agriculture and Development (PHARE) acted as a pioneer in the field of post-communist co-operation between Western and Eastern Europe. Originally aimed at Hungary and Poland, it was later extended to most of the transition countries (Jovanović 1998: 25). Another important programme, particularly for Poland, was the Programme of Community Aid to the Countries of Central and Eastern Europe (SAPARD) that was designed to support agricultural and rural re-development. In 1992, the European Agreements created formal trade links between Poland, Hungary and Czechoslovakia (Cichowski 2000: 1243). The year 1992 was of particular importance, as it was in December of that year that following the European Council meeting the pre-accession Copenhagen criteria were established. Formal EU entry negotiations commenced in March 1998, and were completed in November 2002. In the referenda of June 2003, in both countries overwhelming majorities, albeit on low turnouts, voted in favour of accession which duly occurred in May 2004. The result is that the Czech Republic and Poland are now enmeshed within the same supranational policy community as Germany. This new relationship throws many of the issues we have dealt with into sharp relief. Let us now examine how accession might bring about a mutually acceptable resolution of outstanding issues between Germany and its two Slavic neighbours.

Helmut Kohl saw the collapse of communism not simply as an opportunity to unite Germany, but also to promote the eastward expansion of the EU (Ingram and Ingram 2002: 55). In fact, in the case of Poland, Kohl attempted to develop a strategy that sought to replicate post-1949 Franco-German rapprochement and incorporate Poland within the Franco-German axis through the creation of the 'Weimar Triangle' of regional co-operation (Ingram and Ingram 2002: 59). As we noted in Chapter 3, whether or not full replication can ever occur is open to question. For some, Franco-German rapprochement was a unique series of events that led to the evolution of a unique partnership (Rossmanith 2004). That to one side, the overall strategy was designed to ensure that if countries such as Poland and the Czech Republic were able to accede to the EU, then membership could and should offer a resolution to most if not all of the residual issues arising from the Second World War. After all, the EU operates on the principle of shared sovereignty, regional co-operation, the malleability of borders and the freedom of movement. Yet equally importantly, the EU is a community of shared values and norms, and membership in it effectively requires subscribing to these norms and values.

The 'Weimar Triangle' attracted a great deal of media and scholarly attraction, as did the idea that (an ill-defined notion of) Silesia could become a bridge between Germany and Poland. Most importantly, the circumstances of Poland and Germany in the early part of the twenty-first century are not directly comparable to those that existed between West Germany and France in the 1950s (Schwall-Düren 2003). First, the personal commitment that Adenauer showed towards France and that which Kohl showed towards Poland are gone. Second, the memory of war has faded. Third, and following on from this, the issues faced by all three countries are different. Finally, the intemperate remarks made by President Chirac of France shortly before the onset of the third Gulf War (1980–1988) reduced France's political stock in Poland to approximately zero. Nor did the stance of the Schröder government on Iraq impress Polish public opinion, even though, given the depth of pacifist sentiment in Germany, the German government's stance was more acceptable to the Poles than was French grandstanding. Having said that, the former Polish ambassador to Germany, Janusz Reiter, believes that this episode has done real long-term damage to Polish–German relations. From this perspective, Poland had little choice but to align itself with the US: Polish history and psychology dictated that it must be so (Reiter 2004). Others share Reiter's broad assessment of the situation, but feel Poland, despite the changes that have occurred since the late 1980s, still to be a victim of its geo-political situation (Fiszer 2004). The furore caused by the row over voting rights in the recently expanded EU has served to make matters even worse. Whatever the merits of this argument, it is clear that the German–Polish honeymoon is over. Although Poland and Germany now share sovereignty within a range of supranational organizations, these disagreements showed that the two countries do not possess identical views on Europe's relationship with the US. Neither is there a common view on the future shape of 'Europe' except at the most abstract of levels (Stadtmüller 2004).

Even if we put to one side the claim that the Weimar Triangle was in fact the child of political expediency (Anon. 2004b), it clearly is not functioning as the public was led to believe it could and would. The culmination of factors and events mentioned in the previous paragraph when married to the whiff of political expediency, means that in the near future there is no realistic possibility of the Weimar Triangle developing any kind of policy-generating or policy-making capacity. If it is so to do, it will only come about following the realization on the part of Germany and France that within the EU they cannot continue indefinitely to act as the locomotive of change (Góralski 2004). This in turn would necessitate the Polish side coming to terms with the fact that the political class in France is instinctively wary of the US's attitude towards 'Europe'. For the Weimar Triangle to become an effective locus of power within the EU, Polish politicians will have to accept that France does not share Poland's vision of a benign US (Byrt 2004). These developments reaffirm on the one hand the greater significance of Poland within the EU and for German foreign policy calculations compared with the Czech Republic. On the other, they form the general background against which the dynamics of the residual dimensions of the German question are played out at the beginning of the twenty-first century.

The German government has made it clear that it regards eastward expansion as necessary in order to right a historical injustice and in order to promote harmony, growth and stability throughout Europe. They have also made it crystal clear to the BdV, and to the Czech and Polish governments, that Berlin does not support demands that expellees be compensated, be given special privileges with regard to re-settlement in their former homes, or have passports restored en masse. For conservative opponents of the current Red–Green coalition, this attitude masks a general disinterest in issues that are regarded as inconvenient irritants to the task of creating a united Europe (Rossmanith 2004). By the same token, Berlin has made it clear that, once the transition periods have been completed, all EU citizens must be allowed to exercise their rights as such, regardless of where they once lived.

This has proven to be a thorny issue in both the Czech Republic and Poland. Of course, during the Cold War, the issue was more theoretical than real. However, it was recognized early on in the reform process that land reform, privatization and a land ownership regime less hostile to foreigners would have to be established. In the Polish case, early draft legislation on the privatization of state lands was held up by President Jaruzelski, who feared German intentions and purchasing power (Prybyla 1991: 16), and the matter has proven to be contentious ever since. The ability of France and Germany to stop any far-reaching reforms to the EU's Common Agricultural Policy (CAP) simply fuels Polish suspicions. As parties such as *Samoobrona*, the PSL and the *Liga Polskich Rodzin* (League of Polish Families/LPR) point out, a large majority of Polish farmers will receive no substantial benefit from the CAP. While it is primarily the responsibility of the Polish government to reform its own agricultural sector, few would deny that the CAP itself is in urgent need of radical surgery. Franco-German intransigence on this issue simply adds fuel to the fire of those in the Czech Republic, and more particularly Poland, who argue that as soon as the transition periods are over, richer

Germans will use their purchasing power to persuade hard-up farmers to part with their land. Taken to its furthest extent, the doomsday scenario is that after a period of time re-colonization will become evident, whole areas will start to assume a German hue and eventually demand unification with the 'Fatherland'. Such thinking is of course fanciful. However, given that elements of the population give such views widespread credence, we need to examine the issue in a little more depth.

During the accession negotiations, in Poland fears of German economic power were so great, that the Polish government insisted on a twelve-year transition period during which strict limitations would be placed on foreign investment. What is perhaps of greater significance is the fact that anti-German elements were not able to make greater political capital during the 2003 EU referendum campaign (Ociepka 2004). Whether or not, either by accident or design after 2016 there will be a German take-over of Polish land is not the point. The point is that such a belief is not uncommon in Poland (Góralski 2004). One problem with the CAP is that it is protectionist, and as such does little to encourage good practice on the part of farmers. During the accession negotiations, this entire issue was deliberately underplayed. It appears that, with accession an established fact, a decision has been taken to ride out whatever storm was generated by the (non-)application of the CAP to large sections of the Polish agricultural sector. Quite how politicians intend to deal with the resultant social dislocation is anyone's guess. Moreover, from the perspective of the Polish farmer, the head start enjoyed by their West European counterparts will have reduced them to penury by 2016, rendering the lure of the (German) Euro a matter of necessity.

Education, or the lack of it, is one factor that helps explain the popularity of the populist right among sections of Polish society and its ability to capitalize on the German question. In Poland, parts of the peasantry live in Dickensian squalor, with corresponding levels of education. In rural areas, young men begin to drift out of the education system from the age of fourteen. Their knowledge of Germany is not that great, and their knowledge of the EU is not much better. All too often they have developed a picture of Germany that has been constructed by folk memory, and according to the perception of groups whose place in Germany is marginal, namely the *Landsmannschaften*, or by those who are (wilfully) ignorant or worse. Through assiduous use of the Polish (and Czech) media, the BdV is able to present itself as a more important player in German politics than in reality it is. It is widely agreed that the president of the BdV, Erika Steinbach, has greater name recognition in Poland and the Czech Republic, than in Germany, where she also happens to be a CDU member of the Bundestag (Meckel 2004). Fears generated by the failed campaign on the part of the BdV that their demands be seen central to the accession process are in turn fuelled by aggressively nationalist politicians in the Czech Republic and Poland. In Poland in particular, the populist right has incorporated the fear of Germany within a distinctive anti-modernist and parochial programme.

Another factor that causes problems is the aforementioned link between history and political legitimacy. To acknowledge unequivocally that all EU citizens have the same rights calls into question the nature of contemporary legitimacy, precisely because it revives issues that are rooted firmly in past historical experience. It does so because here we are specifically referring to Germans and in particular to Germans who once lived in the Czech Republic and Poland, many of whom were collectively and without due process found guilty of treason. An early problem that Warsaw and Prague had to confront is that EU law does not allow permanent exclusions of EU citizens from any part of its territory. To this end during the accession process, both the Polish and Czech governments agreed that following the completion of the accession process no exclusions can and shall be permitted (Schwall-Düren 2003). In fact, in both countries such exclusions effectively ceased to operate shortly after the fall of communism. As we have noted throughout this book, however, under no circumstances will the Czech government collectively offer Czech citizenship to (former) Sudeten Germans, and neither government is prepared to pay compensation or offer restitution to the expellees.

Finally, we must consider the issue of economics. The comparative gap in purchasing power of Germans vis-à-vis Czechs and Poles is huge. Prima facie at least, Germans could be tempted to buy huge swathes of agricultural land and property in both countries because it is cheap. Of course, the basic economics of the situation cannot be completely disentangled from the politics of the situation, as scare stories in the Czech press about the return of Germans thirsting for land at bargain prices have shown (Tampke 2003: 154). Having said that, transition periods are in place, by the end of which some levelling off of incomes hopefully will have occurred. Furthermore, there is no requirement on the part of the EU for any country to tailor its land and property acquisition procedures specifically to suit Germans or anyone else. The purchase of land and property in Poland and the Czech Republic is by no means straightforward. It becomes more complex when the would-be purchaser has no working knowledge of either Czech or Polish. Of course, reputable legal and translation services can mitigate these issues, but they cannot in themselves solve them. Research in Germany has repeatedly shown that there is no special desire among Germans to purchase land in either the Czech Republic or Poland. In addition, any would-be purchasers would have to satisfy the authorities of their ability to tend to property and land and also that they would not be a burden on the state. However, we are once again faced with the question of perceptions, and a belief in both Slavic countries that the possibility of this kind of 'invasion' is much greater than its actual likelihood. From the evidence available of the impact of German investment in the Czech Republic and Poland, the issue of individual land purchases need not prove to be too controversial (Sułek 2004), any more than the issue of the restoration and renovation of German objects of cultural value has proven to be. By the same token, even some responsible Polish commentators appear to be convinced that a kind of German land hunger still exists (Fiszer 2004). The fact that such attitudes are evident among informed observers illustrates just how difficult is the task of breaking down stereotypes among less well-educated members of society.

Various other economic factors are about to come into play as well. For example, there is the question of penetration of the domestic market by German capital which had already taken place in the absence of EU membership. Experience here has shown that in both the Czech Republic and Poland people tend to be more concerned about earning a decent wage than being worried about the provenance of their employers. Another issue we have to consider is that of labour mobility. We have put forward the case that with regard to the Czech Republic, and more particularly Poland, fears of renewed German interference are exaggerated. Similarly, we should now point out that Germans are themselves not free of overstated concerns when it comes to their eastern neighbours. During the accession negotiations, one of the fears articulated by the German side was that Germany might be overwhelmed by cheap Polish labour. This argument was based around the following set of circumstances. Up to 500,000 Poles annually seek work in some capacity in Germany, usually either as seasonal workers or on the fringes of the legitimate economy (Byrt 2004). Their reasons are many. First, there is high unemployment in Poland. Second, although there is also high unemployment in Germany, there are many unfilled vacancies, and for less money Poles often work harder than Germans. Paradoxically, although there is a general call for the opening of borders, and the dissolution of national barriers, there is equally a fear that in border areas in particular, Polish commuters could undercut German labour (Rossmanith 2004). To the east of Berlin, there is also concern that these economically depressed areas could lose whatever investment they have in labour-intensive industries. The argument is that investors will simply relocate to the Polish side of the Oder (Schröter 2004). In sum, Germany may prove to be an attractive destination for Poles, who earn more doing badly paid work in Germany than they would in Poland, and Poland may provide a safe haven for unscrupulous employers who place profit ahead of any real notion of welfare. Indeed, German fears were so great in this direction, that as with land purchase in Poland and the Czech Republic, a transition period was negotiated during which the German labour market would not be fully open to citizens of the new EU member states. Whether cheap Polish labour will ever 'flood' over the border is another question. Then again, according to some, a single market should tolerate no 'protectionist' restrictions. Similarly, some argue that a united Europe within which national borders have become permeable should not be prey to national sensitivities. What this whole argument illustrates is the fact that in all three countries economic considerations are intimately bound to their political equivalents, and that political questions become easily exacerbated in the context of their economic consequences.

Of course, all of the above-mentioned issues have arisen since the first flush of rapprochement wore off in the mid-1990s. That the enthusiasm would wane was to be expected. Nor should anyone be surprised that the aforementioned difficulties still sometimes cloud relationships between the three countries. Such issues have inevitably had an impact upon public perceptions of the EU. The result was growing support for Eurosceptic parties in Poland and the Czech Republic, and a general cooling down in 'Euroenthusiasm' on the part of the wider population as accession loomed in terms of practical policy as opposed to a series of symbols and slogans. Having said that, as the referenda results showed support for membership proved to be stronger than was thought, particularly in Poland, earlier unrealistic expectations of the benefits that membership will bring have been dampened. As much as anything, this change came about because throughout the 1990s as Poland and the Czech Republic developed greater first-hand contacts with Western Europe in general. Such contacts attuned both members and would-be members to one another. With regard to Germany, which presented itself above all as Poland's partner, closer bilateral contact provoked a realization that Germany (like all other societies) is not necessarily as liberal as the official media sometimes portrays it to be. On top of that, as we mentioned earlier, a large cross-section of German society is in fact disinterested in Poland (Sakson 2000). After the initial burst of enthusiasm in the early 1990s, bilateral relations between the two states have been largely stable. There is, however, the question of residual social prejudice that exists on either side of the border (Czapliński 2004). In Germany, only those with family links to Poland (itself not an inconsiderable number), together with a rather narrow group of specialists keep a weather eye on Poland (Ociepka 2004). Although, as noted earlier in the chapter, they constitute a more significant group than do those who have regular contact with the Czech Republic, they are by no means a majority nor do they have a big share in the public discourse. The majority of society, if it cares at all, only shows concern when the rougher edges of the EU integration process and residual questions arising from the Second World War manifest themselves. This may mean that for many Germans, traditional negative stereotypes of Poles still exist (Lintzel 2004). From the Polish perspective, this interest may harbour darker motives on the part of the Germans. It can also be seen to strengthen inadvertently both the populist right in Poland as well as the forces of popular apathy. Apparent German disinterest can easily be repackaged as German condescension or worse and manipulated accordingly. Yet once again we must avoid the trap of indulging those who wish to accentuate such stereotypes. Neither is it sufficient to say that the persistence of such stereotypes is down to German failure to do more to overcome them (Sułek 2004). Negative stereotypes of Germany are all too commonplace among some sections of Polish society. For example, during his failed presidential campaign of 2000, Marian Krzaklewski, the chairman of the now defunct *Akcja Wyborcza Solidarność* (Solidarity Electoral Action/AWS), made great play of the threat to Polish interests posed by Germany in general and the BdV in particular (Ociepka 2004). He came third with 15.6 per cent of the vote thereby demonstrating that such atavistic sentiments can only go so far in today's Poland.

German disinterest/ignorance was vividly illustrated at the highest level in the 1990s. On one occasion it involved Chancellor Kohl, and on the other President Roman Herzog. On the former occasion, in 1989, the chancellor sought to stage an act of reconciliation on St Ann's Mount in Upper Silesia. In the twentieth century this traditional place of inter-communal Catholic pilgrimage assumed huge symbolic significance to both Germans and Poles. During the third Silesian Uprising (1920), it became a literal battlefield and marked the spot where the *Freikorps* halted the Polish advance. Unsurprisingly from 1939 the Nazis turned part of the area into a shrine, and similarly the Poles when they recovered the area in 1921 and 1945 did the same. For Kohl and his advisers to insist on staging an act of 'reconciliation' on this part of the mount as opposed to the religious site was for many Poles an unbelievably crass act. Worse was, however, avoided when this act of reconciliation was staged at the Polish–German centre in Krzyżowa. Similarly, in 1997 in an interview with the German magazine *Stern*, prior to making an official state visit to Poland, President Herzog conflated the liquidation of the Jewish ghetto in Warsaw with the uprising of 1944 (Góralski 2004). From a Polish perspective such acts at best were insensitive. Whatever the case, they vindicate the point that German knowledge of Poland is not what it could or should be.

From our constructivist perspective on the foreign policy dynamics in this German–Czech–Polish triangle of fate, disinterest is an important factor, and one that, once it has been put into the context of a larger picture, assumes some explanatory value. As we have seen in relation to German–Polish relations, in Germany disinterest among a large part of the population is matched with more proactive engagement on the part of those who are genuinely committed to reconciliation. The situation in Poland is more differentiated with fear and prejudice more widespread, but making political capital out of either has its clear limits as illustrated by the 15 per cent share of the vote for Krzaklewski and his decidedly anti-German platform in the 2000 presidential elections. With regard to German–Czech relations, the situation is quite different. Here, widespread German public apathy meets with Sudeten German activism; the relatively low priority accorded to the Czech Republic in Berlin meets with the strong tangible and intangible links between the SdL and the CSU, the long-term governing party in Bavaria and former partner in several CDU-led coalition governments. While this mix does not bode too well on its own for resolving outstanding issues in German–Czech relations, the prospects for the latter are by no means improved once we add to this mix the united front that the Czech political class and public have, for the most part, displayed when it comes to dealing with the complex past and present of the two countries' bilateral relations.

The crux of the matter, therefore, is this. In the German Polish case, by and large in both societies and government institutions norms exist that make dealing with each other, and the past, possible in a largely constructive way. These norms may not be shared in all detail by everyone, but there is no significant counter-discourse that would seriously or success-fully challenge the norm consensus in either country that allows, for the most part, constructive engagement. In the case of German–Czech rela-tions, this picture is turned upside down. Apart from the occasional flurry of activities at the highest political levels, the field is largely left to those whose norms dictate courses of action that are unlikely to result in a similar normalization of relations as between Germany and Poland. Be it the no-vote of the CSU's MEPs on Czech accession to the EU or Vladimír Špidla's suggestion that the expulsion of the Sudeten Germans contributed to a stable European peace order after the Second World War. 'Norm-consistent' as these policies may be from the perspective of each side, there is no bargaining space left between the parties in which accommo-dation could be achieved that remained within the boundaries prescribed by these underlying norms. In other words, the crucial change that has occurred in German–Polish relations since 1989/1990 – in terms of level of interest among the German political elite, in the *Landsmannschaften* and the BdV, in the Polish public and successive Polish governments – is still missing in the German–Czech context.

9 Towards a common future?

Although outstanding issues still colour Polish–German relations, as we have seen, Czech–German relations are more problematic. Several milestones have been erected, each of which is designed to point the way to a better future. We shall now consider the more important of these. The bedrock of the contemporary relationship is formed by The Treaty on Good Neighbourly and Friendly Co-operation (with Czechoslovakia) of 1992. The primary objective of the treaty was to break with the past and pave the way for bilateral co-operation within a pan-European framework (Tampke 2003: 144). Prior to that in 1990, a joint Czech–German Historical Commission was established with a brief to investigate many of the themes that have been covered in this volume.[1] Havel's speech of February 1995 constitutes another milestone in the process of reconciliation (Vollmer 1997). Also in 1995, work began on a joint Czech–German parliamentary declaration designed to hammer out a common position on all that had occurred between 1938 and 1948. This proved difficult to achieve. To this day large sections of Czech society feel that the Germans got their just desserts in 1945 and 1946, and that is that. This attitude is reflected in support for the communist and (other) nationalist parties. On top of that, during the accession process, the SdL seized the opportunity to embark on a typically inopportune campaign to have the Beneš Decrees declared to be incompatible with European and international law. Eventually the hardliners on both sides were marginalized when more reasoned voices came to a compromise concerning the exact terminology to be used as a means of describing the expulsion process (Tampke 2003: 147ff.). In 2003, a further joint parliamentary resolution was passed that sought to re-enforce and re-iterate the position taken in 1997.

At this point it is worth emphasizing the German–Czech Future Fund established in 1997 as part of the German–Czech Declaration which has since proven to be a valuable mechanism promoting German–Czech reconciliation (Kunštát 2004). The fund, which is due to operate for ten years, seeks to achieve various objectives. It promotes cultural exchanges, provides compensation for the victims of Nazi violence, supports the German minority in the Czech Republic and seeks to preserve the joint

Czech–German heritage (*Auswärtiges Amt* 2003). Its remit is to further promote co-operation and reconciliation. Since its inception it has worked in a highly efficient manner, and is taken by some to serve as a role model for similar programmes (Žák 2004). In Germany, both the goals and operation of the Fund are similarly placed in high esteem (Vollmer n.d.).

However, these aforementioned initiatives and others have sometimes inadvertently contributed to polarization and the radicalization of some hardline elements in both countries. This situation has from time to time come about precisely because of the sensitivity of some of the issues dealt with. This is not surprising given the complexity of German–Czech relations past and present. It is noticeable that when the wider public in both countries takes notice of each other, they often do so through the prism of stereotypical views of the previous relationship, no matter how marginal they might be to reality. The assessment of the extent to which negative stereotypes of Czechs are embedded within the German psyche is a matter of some conjecture. The record of various Czech governments in this field is patchy. There are few votes to be had in the Czech Republic by assuming a 'pro-German' stance on matters such as compensation, and the smouldering debate over 1938–1948 makes it difficult for politicians to steer a middle course. Among wide sections of Czech society there is still a residual distrust of overall German objectives with regard to the Czech Republic (Kovanic 2004). We have already noted Markus Meckel's observations on the matter. In another vein, Antje Vollmer is keen to point out that for (many) Germans, Czechs were highly valued neighbours (Vollmer 1997). Yet, the long-term consequences of the damage wrought during the nineteenth and twentieth centuries cannot be denied.

Everyday encounters and joint workshops, particularly between young people, cannot sweep away decades of fear and distrust in a matter of months or even years. Ventures such as the joint textbook commission can and do help (Brod 2004), but they have to battle against competing negative influences. Perhaps more attention should be paid to everyday encounters through such media as the tourist industry (Kovanic 2004). Given the mutual intransigence of the SdL and of much of the Czech political class, wider societal reconciliation, although clearly observable, has been halting and somewhat limited. Many expellees remain inflexible in their attitudes towards Prague, and the SdL refused to support the 1992 Treaty on Friendship and Co-operation (Seibt 1997: 408). Others, although more accommodating in their attitudes, are disappointed at the refusal of the Czech government to rescind those of the Beneš Decrees that legalized the collective victimization of the Sudeten Germans and gave amnesty to anyone who committed a crime in the course of their expulsion. Such disappointment is sometimes echoed on the Czech side where some claim that it would be quite possible in law for the contemporary Czech government to disavow the Decrees in much the same way that in the 1970s

Bonn disavowed the Munich Agreement (Handl 2004). Within this context, we should reiterate that it is difficult to ascertain exactly what the SdL desires of the Czech government (Meckel 2004). Its demands are couched in suitably vague terms. Various German politicians with an interest in the field have repeatedly pleaded with the SdL to clarify its position, all to no avail (Vollmer n.d.). It may well be the case that what is desired is Czech agreement to a formula of words as proposed by the SdL. Indeed in the early 1990s, this is what former President Havel seems to have been close to agreeing. For a majority of Czech politicians progress with the SdL will not be possible until it finally and explicitly states its terms for a final 'settlement' (Lintzel 2004) and simultaneously drops all threats of legal action against the Czech state. On a more positive note, despite this incessant wrangling, initiatives have begun in the Czech Republic that at the local level address many of these unresolved issues, in the towns and villages where the expulsions actually happened. The SdL has also, with a degree of modest success, attempted to forge links with Czech museums and cultural institutions (Brod 2004). Such initiatives are to be welcomed, as they reduce the scope for hardliners on both sides give one other the pretext to sabotage a comprehensive process of reconciliation.

An excellent, albeit inadvertent illustration of mutual Czech–German sensitivities came with the Czech–German Declaration of 1997. The purpose of the Declaration was to cement bilateral co-operation and finally to agree on a formula of words that adequately expressed official German regret for the occupation and subsequent destruction of Czechoslovakia, whilst allowing the Czech government to do the same with regard to the post-war expulsions (Vollmer n.d.). It was constructed with the participation and support of a broad constellation of political forces in both countries. On the Czech side, President Havel, and his special adviser on foreign affairs, Alexandra Vondra, actively participated in drawing up the document. On the German side, Chancellor Kohl had been one of the prime movers, and even Edmund Stoiber gave it his blessing (Vollmer n.d.). The belief in Prague was that the Declaration would finally put this matter to rest at an official level at least. Thus, when Chancellor Kohl subsequently revealed to the Bundestag that despite the Declaration, certain matters remained open, horror and disappointment was widespread throughout Czech society (Žák 2004). The failure of Kohl to confront the CSU and SdL over the declaration may be regarded not only as indicative of the CDU's wider relationship with the CSU, but also as a badly botched opportunity to move on from the events of 1938–1948.

If we wish to further compare and contrast the Czech and Polish cases, there are a number of factors that we must also take into account and that help us understand how especially societal norms shape the options available to politicians in a particular policy area. The controversy caused in Czechoslovakia by President Havel's personal apology for the expulsions in March 1990 to his German counterpart Richard von Weizsäcker, contrasted sharply with the comparative calm that reigned in Poland when foreign minister Władysław Bartoszewski (himself an Auschwitz survivor) offered a similar apology to the German parliament. Furthermore, both the Czech Republic and Poland agree that compensation cannot (on financial grounds), and possibly should not (on moral grounds), be paid to German expellees/refugees. Yet, mainstream Polish politicians readily recognize that within the context of EU expansion, Germans from areas of Poland that were once German, and former *Volksdeutsche* Polish citizens must in principle have the same rights as in Poland any other EU citizen. Apart from anything else, the Polish government recognizes the rules of the game, and knows that in reality 'returnees' will be overwhelmingly elderly, wealthy and few in number.

In the case of the Czech Republic the principle is the same, but the situation is a little more fraught. This is despite the fact that since 1993 Germans, including individual Sudeten Germans, have exactly the same rights as other foreigners to live, work and own real estate in the Czech Republic. Therefore, the Czech government has conceded that all Germans must have the same rights as all other EU citizens (Kovanic 2004). For Vollmer, it is important that this right applies in full to the *Sudetendeutsche* as much as it does to other Germans (Vollmer 1997). By encountering the reality of the situation in the Czech Republic, the Sudeten Germans may come to realize that their former homes are precisely that, and that co-operation with the newly-indigenous inhabitants presents the only way forward. However, as we have already noted, what the Czech government will not concede is the SdL's continued demands for even symbolic compensation and their insistence on the bestowal of Czech citizenship on the basis that the contemporary Czech state is the successor state to Czechoslovakia. Neither is the repeal of the Beneš Decrees on the agenda. The EU is satisfied with the position of the Czech government as are the authorities in Berlin. Having said that, there still remains the possibility that a class action on the part of expellees through the international courts could re-open the debate.

For most commentators the case is closed. Others point out that the whole question of German collective guilt, and consequent expropriation and expulsion has yet to be tested in international law, particularly in the European Court of Human Rights. The actions of the German government following unification, the successful claims by former slave labourers and by Jews against the German government could in theory add weight to any such action (Schröter 2004). Indeed, in the Czech Republic some intellectuals have also questioned the notion of collective guilt and the way in which it was applied in 1945 (Brod 2004). In particular, this may be the case if they are couched within a narrow discourse of human rights that ignores a number of factors. These include the fact that expellees have in fact received compensation from the German government, in the form of the *Lastenausgleich* (Lintzel 2004). Second, the majority of the expellees have since died, so the question of to whom compensation is paid immediately arises. Third, the political damage that would result from such a judgement would be catastrophic. Fourth, how does one establish culpability over sixty years after the fact? Fifth, neither the Czech nor Polish governments could afford to pay billions of dollars in compensation. Sixth, exactly which property is being referred to here? In the Czech context, would such claims refer to property that was owned by Germans before or after Munich? After all, that agreement is null and void in international law. Finally, is a point of legal principle so valuable that it should be allowed to cause potential distress to those, many of whom in the Polish case especially experienced maltreatment and destitution at the hands of the Germans, who in good faith had at some point after the Second World War acquired or inherited such property (Kovanic 2004)?

In 2003, a potentially explosive series of legal steps was initiated by elements of the BdV. Members of the various 'Polish' *Landsmannschaften* banded together to form the *Preußische Treuhand* (Prussian Claims Society). This collective legal entity takes the Jewish Claims Conference as its role model, and has already begun utilizing the American legal system in order to pursue its claims. The demand for compensation against the Polish and Czech governments by the *Preußische Treuhand* and the SdL runs into billions of dollars (Meckel 2004). Ironically, the success of the Jewish Claims Conference has acted as a spur for this latest attempt to assert a legal 'solution' to what is above all a political and emotional issue. Both the Czech and Polish governments reject the claims and re-affirm that formerly German property confiscated under the terms of international and domestic law, cannot and will not be returned either to its former owners or their 'legal heirs' (Barcz 2004). Significantly, the BdV has now also disowned the *Preußische Treuhand*. Instead, the BdV leadership is now calling for clarification of the issue, and compensation where the *Lastenausgleich* was 'insufficient'.

Unsurprisingly, the issue exploded onto the Polish political scene in late summer of 2004. In September 2004, by way of retaliation to the actions of the *Preußische Treuhand* the *Sejm* passed a resolution demanding compensation from the German government for destruction wrought upon Poland during the Second World War. Neither Chancellor Schröder's visit to Poland in August 2004, where he explicitly stated that the German government rejected all claims against either the Polish state or private firms or individuals, nor Erika Steinbach's unexpected distancing of the BdV from the demands of the *Preußische Treuhand*, did anything to calm the situation. Similarly, statements by the Polish government to the effect that the whole matter was closed did little to assuage an incensed Polish public.

In Germany, the general reaction was one of puzzlement. Most Germans were simply unaware of Polish sensitivities on this issue. Neither do they understand how the government could be called upon to interfere in what is an explicitly legal matter. After all, regardless of the nature of its claim, the *Preußische Treuhand* has broken no laws, either domestic or international. The German attitude contrasts vividly with the reaction of Polish public opinion and the Polish media, and demonstrates the extent to which it is largely unable to comprehend the fact that in Germany the *Preußische Treuhand* is an insignificant actor (*The Economist*, 6 November 2004). What is clear from this whole episode is that just as with Czech–German relations, in this matter at least, the situation between Germany and Poland is more fragile than some would like to think.

A further clarification of the situation in Polish domestic law concerning the property deeds of former German real estate could prevent interference in these matters on the part of the international judiciary (Barcz 2004). As it currently stands, the *Preußische Treuhand* may have been presented with a window of opportunity by virtue of the fact that the 'recovered territories' were exempted from the post-communist re-privatization legislation, and that in many land registries, the last registered owner, as opposed to perpetual lessee, is in fact a German who fled or was expelled in 1945 or shortly thereafter (Anon. 2004b). In other words, as Polish law stands at present, legal title to (some) former German property is in urgent need of clarification, and belatedly is in fact being so clarified (Czapliński 2004). Indeed, in the wake of Schröder's visit, a joint Polish–German legal commission was appointed to investigate the *Treuhand's* claims. In the autumn of 2004 it presented its findings. These were that the claims were unfounded in German, Polish and international law. Whether or not this finally brings the matter to a close remains to be seen. What is of real interest here is not a hypothetical successful claim for compensation, but rather the apparent Polish over-reaction to potential German claims. It has been stated that in the event of being dragged through the international courts, the Polish government would rest its defence on the fact that no such analogous claims are being made against Russia (as a successor state to the Soviet Union), or against either the US or the UK for the wholesale destruction of German cities by their airforces (Sakson 2004). Some go even further and simply state that should the international courts rule against Poland then no Polish government would ever pay compensation, regardless of the consequences to the wider international system and Poland's place within it (Byrt 2004). Yet, not all share such apocalyptic vision. Others in Poland argue that the *Preußische Treuhand's* claim is built upon such shaky legal foundations that it is nothing more than an unwelcome irritant (Góralski 2004), and that both Polish domestic law and the application of the Allied Communiqué of the Potsdam Conference in Poland are sufficient to rebut any claims made. Regardless of arcane legal intricacies, such demands have a negative impact upon German–Polish relations (Sułek 2004). To say that in Poland the *Preußische Treuhand* does not receive a sympathetic hearing is a classic case of under statement. On the other hand, one is

sometimes left with the impression that many in Poland fail to understand that in a liberal democracy particular points of view cannot be
deemed illegitimate simply because they articulate an alternative perspective
with regard to the consequences of the past. There is perhaps an argument for saying that in Poland this whole issue receives greater attention
than it merits. Whether or not the proposed joint German–Polish commission that if established will have the brief of settling this issue once and
for all, will succeed in its mission, only time will tell.

Just as curiously, or perhaps worryingly, there has been widespread
condemnation in the Czech Republic and Poland over the BdV's plan to
establish a Centre against Expulsions in Berlin. The idea behind the centre
is to illustrate the wrongful nature of such activities regardless of to whom
they occur, and is closely identified with Erika Steinbach herself. For many
Czechs and Poles, for Berlin to give its assent to the project would be
tantamount to recognizing the legitimacy of the actions of the *Preußische
Treuhand*. The fact that such a tenuous connection can be made, illustrates just how sensitive a matter the past is to some on all sides. Even
for some Poles, the fact that an issue such as the planned centre, which,
in essence, is of secondary importance, has received such prominence in
the Polish media says more about Polish neuroses concerning Germany
than anything else (Stadtmüller 2004). Claims that such a centre would
automatically be 'a disaster' for Polish–German relations (Barcz 2004) do
in part vindicate this observation.

In addition, as at least one Polish commentator points out, the impact
upon the European political scene of this proposal was approximately
zero, until certain Polish political forces decided to turn it into a domestic
political issue that impinged upon German–Polish relations (Tomala 2004).
For other Polish commentators (Sakson 2004), the opposite is true. From
their perspective the plans demonstrate the centrality of the BdV to contemporary German politics. In turn, this supposed centrality is evidence that
since the early 1990s German–Polish relations have gone backwards
(Sakson 2004).

Until fairly recently, a further issue that clouded relations between the
three sides was that of compensation for former slave labourers and others
who were forced to work for the German occupation regime. During the
period of communist rule, they received no compensation either from
the German government or from their former 'employers'. With the collapse
of communism, the prospect of compensation finally appeared on the
horizon. Talks began in 1993, and after much argument, coupled with
threats of further legal action, a compensation fund was eventually established. The tardiness of both the German government and business in
agreeing to establish the fund left a sour taste in both Poland and the
Czech Republic, where around 12,000 people had lodged claims (Handl
2004). Although the passage of time had reduced the number of potential
claimants, in the end, a significant number of them were still registered

and compensation is now distributed through the foundation 'Memory, Responsibility, Future'. The fact that so many people had died in the intervening years before the fund was finally operational, was itself something of an emotional problem that had a political spill-over. So did the fact that many German companies seemed to be reluctant to pay anything but the absolute minimum they thought they could get away with. The problem is that, individually, the sums of money are not great. Moreover, problems of certification and proof of exploitation caused controversy and added to the feeling that this was an issue the German side would rather forget about. From the Czech and Polish perspective, the reluctance of the German side in this respect did not sit comfortably with German demands for more understanding of the position of German expellees and refugees. From the perspective of German expellees, and on the part of former forced labourers in particular, once again their concerns were being ignored and sacrificed for reasons of high politics.

How then do we assess the future pattern of Germany's relationship with Poland and the Czech Republic? Despite the various caveats that punctuate our analysis, there is little reason to be gloomy. The basic infrastructure that was established in the early 1990s is still in place (Barcz 2004) and has been complemented by Czech and Polish accession to NATO and the EU. The majority of commentators agree that bilateral relations are more positive than at any time since the modern nation-state came into being (Byrt 2004). In light of those comments let us present our final balance sheet.

If we first deal with Poland, it could be argued that bilateral relations are at something of a crossroads. Whether they are in a state of 'crisis' (Reiter 2004), is an entirely different matter. Reiter points to the obvious fact that the 'grand designs' of the early 1990s have not been achieved. He also highlights the short and medium term issues that exist in Polish–German relations and the difficulty of creating administrative structures that have the ability to make the Euroregions function to full capacity, that create better transportation links and in general draw the two societies closer together. He also stresses the waning of interest in Poland among Germans, even at elite level. He is not alone in his assessment. Andrzej Sakson also talks of a state of crisis, and compares the situation in the early part of the twenty-first century unfavourably with that which existed in the early 1990s (Sakson 2004). On a less melodramatic note, Elżbieta Stadtmüller talks of 'rising coldness and indifference (Stadtmüller 2004). Perhaps most accurately in our view, Beata Ociepka characterizes them quite simply as having entered the phase of normalization. She points to the fact that the early 1990s were by necessity a time of grand gestures. This phase is now over, and since 1995 the two states have entered into a relationship that is, or at least should be corresponding to the norms that pertain to allies (Ociepka 2004).

Differences do of course exist, and differing geopolitical perspectives and priorities play a role here. What is curious about negative evaluations is that themes and issues that play only a peripheral role in either German domestic or foreign policy are so prominent in Polish domestic politics and in perceptions of Germany and the Germans. These include the planned Centre against Expulsions, the demands of the BdV, and anxieties concerning financial claims on the part of German refugees and expellees for material damage and the violation of human rights. Given that Poland is the potential object of such claims, the reasons why large sections of Polish society are worried should become clearer. On the other hand, it could be argued that on occasion some elements of the Polish political class act in a precipitate manner whenever the BdV proposes something that is not to their taste. In fact, one could even argue that a 'German syndrome still exists in the Polish consciousness' (Góralski 2004). At one level, the claim that Polish society should simply ignore a lot of the utterances of the BdV (Ociepka 2004) may be correct, yet the fact of the matter is that much of Polish society blows the importance of the BdV beyond all reasonable proportion. Whereas all of the aforementioned factors may carry some weight in explaining contemporary German–Polish relations, it could be argued that such problems are not the consequence of political will, or indeed the lack of it. The fact that Germans do not have the same level of interest in Poland as Poles do in Germany, may be, as much as anything else, further testimony to the success of Adenauer's Westpolitik. Interestingly enough, Polish commentators often cite the need to replicate the intensive programme of youth exchanges that took place between France and the old Federal Republic, as a means of combating stereotypes (Czapliński 2004). In fact, some go so far as to argue that such programmes between the communist former German and Polish states were more effective and developed than they are today (Sułek 2004). Perhaps what is lacking on both sides, apart from cash, is a politician with Adenauer's single-mindedness, commitment and vision. By the same token, the needs of Europe as a whole in the early part of the twenty-first century are not identical to those of the continent in 1945.

In sum, since the mid 1990s, by which time all major issues had in effect been settled and the major German–Polish initiatives had been established (Góralski 2004), bilateral German–Polish relations may have simply settled down to a level of mundane normality. This may be unwelcome to those Poles who in the 1990s saw Germany has either having some special obligation towards Poland, or who felt that within a 'New Europe' the alliance structures could be re-cast. The fact of the matter is that from a German perspective, good relations with Poland are of the utmost importance, but that in terms of strategic partnership they cannot supplant either the US or France. In addition, there is a tendency to over-react to changes in the German political spectrum. For instance, at the time of Gerhard Schröder's accession to the chancellorship in 1998, the Polish media and political class engaged in a furious debate about the potential damage that such a step could have for Polish–German relations (Fiszer 2004). The root cause seems to have been Schröder's rather mundane admission that as German chancellor he would seek to pursue German national interests. For many Poles such statements equated to some kind of threat to revive German nationalism (Stadtmüller 2004), which once again illustrates the difficulty in demolishing a wall of prejudice that was in part built upon two hundred years of German expansion that began with Friedrich the Great's acquisition of Silesia in the 1740s. In other words, historical legacies have a profound impact on the way in which societal norms can be reshaped and thus on how successful the Ostpolitik project can eventually be.

One way in which these problems could be overcome is for both sides, and more especially Poland, to proceed from the fact that they and Germany are now partners within the common institutional and policy-making community of the EU that is predicated on a common set of norms and values (Góralski 2004). Thus, Poland is no longer pitted against Germany on a nation-state versus nation-state level. Through the act of accession to the EU, bilateral German–Polish relations have entered a qualitatively different epoch. For this new relationship to work, Poland will have to proceed from the basis of partnership and use the EU as a platform from which to articulate common interests (Góralski 2004), and not as a forum for the articulation of purely national interests.

With regard to the Czech Republic, bilateral relations with Germany may best be described as stable (Kovanic 2004). For example, in terms of economic relations, residual border questions play no role with regard to Czech–German co-operation. That includes economic co-operation within the border area itself (Handl 2004). On both sides, there are of course those who reject the hand of friendship. In some cases, they do so because of ideology and in others through sheer blind prejudice. A greater number, principally those who experienced the war and its aftermath, although desiring reconciliation, seem to be unable to develop a balanced view of the past that will bring about such reconciliation. It is not difficult to see why. The wounds are too deep, and the memories too painful. Indeed, we should be careful when using the word 'reconciliation' with regard to the Czech Republic and Germany. From the Czech perspective reconciliation means developing a working relationship with contemporary Germany and those who, from the Czech perspective, have themselves become reconciled to the results of the Second World War. In other words, there can never be any reconciliation with those who supported the dismemberment of Czechoslovakia, or who seek to rationalize and qualify that experience (Kovanic 2004). In other words, as long as the SdL continues in its demands, reconciliation between Czech society and one section of its German counterpart can never take place. In order for the past finally to be laid to rest, both Czechs and Germans have to come to understand one another's perspectives on their common history. Moreover, Czech–German relations are not a major priority in Berlin. Residual questions regarding the Second World War and the Czech Republic are correspondingly not that important to most Germans. Neither are they perhaps as important to a sufficient number of leading German politicians (Kafka 2004). For the Czech Republic, given the obvious importance of such a large neighbour to such a small state, the reverse is true (Kovanic 2004).

We have seen how moving beyond the nation-state may provide a means of 'finally laying the ghosts of the past to rest and breaking still existing impasses' (Schröter 2004). German economic engagement in Poland and the Czech Republic can create new synergies, break down barriers, create functional co-operation and enmesh all three countries with one another (Góralski 2004). No matter how the EU progresses, member states must continue to have a vision of the future, as well as a keen tactical awareness. If Germany, Poland and the Czech Republic continue to build upon what has been achieved since 1990, there is no reason to assume that mutually beneficial co-operation will not continue to grow, and that the innocent victims of the past will not have died in vain.

Notes

1 The German question and German foreign policy: a conceptual introduction

1 White (1989: 8) also includes in this list disciplinary problems of approaches favouring an International Relations or a Political Science approach, assuming that the former would take factors in the international environment as key determinants of foreign policy, whereas the latter would see those in the domestic environment as decisive. In our own approach we consider foreign policy analysis to be distinct from both approaches, and one that usefully combines the relevant tools into an analytical framework that does not prejudge the pre-eminence of either environment, but enables the analyst to reach conclusions on a case-by-case basis in order to determine which factors are decisive.

2 The distinction between bilateral and international contexts makes sense from the perspective of the focus of our study – the comparison of German–Czech and German–Polish relations in the post-Cold War period – and from the perspective that Germany, Poland and the Czech Republic form a 'triangle of fate', i.e. a regional substructure 'in which interactions [are] more intense than at the global level' (Allen 1989: 68).

3 We should note at this stage that we are not concerned with a general testing of neo-realist, liberal institutionalist and constructivist theories in the case of Germany. Our analysis is limited to exploring the extent to which Ostpolitik can be explained within a constructivist framework.

4 Gutjahr (1994: 34) notes in this context that the Helsinki conference and subsequent meetings of the CSCE confirmed the (bilateral) results of Ostpolitik in a multilateral setting. Yet, as Kreile (1980: 141) emphasizes as early as 1980 as we do with regard to our point on the mutual sustainability of *Ostpolitik* and the CSCE process, '[t]he future of *Ostpolitik* therefore depends on the future of détente'.

2 A usable past? German–Czech and German–Polish relations before the Second World War

1 In German law, ethnic Germans from post-communist Europe and Asian successor states of the Soviet Union who have migrated to Germany since 1 January 1994 are referred to as *Spätaussiedler*.

3 An insurmountable legacy? Invasion, occupation, expulsion and the Cold War

1 We are not trying to infer that the partial or wholesale extermination of Germans was pursued as a policy of state, but rather that the everyday conditions

and levels of random and organized brutality were little different. This was especially so as the war drew to a close, and in the immediate aftermath of of the war.

2 The extent of the involvement of the GDR's armed forces in the invasion of Czechoslovakia in 1968 is still a matter of dispute. Helmut Ziebart, the GDR's former ambassador to Czechoslovakia, claims that no more than 20 to 25 GDR soldiers entered Czechoslovak territory as part of the invasion force and that they were gone by October of that year. Other commentators insist that the number was higher, but there is no common agreement concerning overall numbers. See, for instance, Prieß, Kural and Wilke (1996).

4 German–Czech and German–Polish relations since the end of the Cold War: an overview

1 So-called because they involved the two German states and the four occupying powers. Poland was brought in after the inception of the negotiations.

2 Apparently, in the villages concerned some Germans were convinced that with the collapse of communism, the pre-1945 border with Poland would be restored, and it was therefore necessary to have some means by which the 'indigenous' German inhabitants could be distinguished from post-war Polish immigrants.

3 The Germans also argued that a majority of Poles who during the twentieth century emigrated to Germany, were either in fact (partly) German in terms of culture and/or ethnicity, and that they actively sought assimilation into German society. It was also pointed out that there were no legal restrictions upon the activities of Polish associations in Germany. The number of Poles in Germany is a matter of dispute and classification.

5 Foreign policy and its domestic consumption: the German political parties and Ostpolitik

1 It also happens that his father was an ethnic German expellee from Hungary.

6 Domestic constituencies and foreign audiences: the *Landsmannschaften* and their impact on German–Polish and German–Czech relations

1 By 1949, about 7.6 million refugees and expellees had arrived in the western zones of occupation; by 1953, the total was 8.4 million. The total number of refugees and expellees was around 12 million, with approximately 3.5 million of them being resettled in what was to become the GDR.

2 On 28 May 1995, the UN High Commissioner for Human Rights, José Ayala-Lasso, affirmed in a message to the German expellees that 'the right not to be expelled from one's ancestral homeland is a fundamental human right'. Translated from Ayalo-Lasso (1995).

3 While this may seem to be self-promotional propaganda by the BdV, it is actually an almost verbatim translation from a speech by the German Minister of the Interior, Otto Schily, of the SPD, delivered on the fiftieth anniversary of the BDV on 29 May 1999. Cf. Schily (1999).

4 Banat Swabians; Berlin – Mark Brandenburg; Bessarabian Germans; Bukowina Germans; Carpathian Germans; Danube Swabians; Dobrudscha and Bulgarian Germans; East Prussians; German Balts; Germans from Danzig; Lithuanian Germans; Lower and Upper Silesia; Pomerania; Russian Germans; Sathmar

Swabians; Sudeten Germans; Transylvanian Saxons; Upper Silesian Germans; Weichsel-Warthe; and West Prussia.

5 Industrialists, youth, students, women, athletes, the deaf, and farmers.

6 The agreements between West Germany and some of the host-states for the repatriation of ethnic Germans included financial arrangements setting 'per capita fees' to be paid by the federal government. Average figures of annual emigration of ethnic Germans after 1950 are as follows: 1955–1959: 64,000; 1960–1964: 18,000; 1965–1969: 26,000; 1970–1974: 25,000; 1975–1979: 46,000; 1980–1984: 49,000; 1985–1986: 41,000; 1987: 78,000.

7 This, however, solved only a part of the problem as it included only the Germans of the northern territories of former East Prussia, the so-called Memel Germans, and those ethnic Germans who, in the aftermath of the German–Soviet treaty of 1939, had been resettled to the then German territories from the Baltic states, Galicia, Volhynia, Bessarabia, and the Northern Bukovina but found themselves again on Soviet territory at the end of the war. Thus, it did not cover the by far largest group of ethnic Germans who had migrated to Tsarist Russia, mostly in the eighteenth and nineteenth centuries.

8 In 1988, over 200,000 ethnic Germans 'returned' to Germany. The figure for 1989 was 377,000, and in 1990, a figure of 397,000 was recorded. Between 1950 and 1988, the annual average of ethnic German immigrants was well below 40,000 per annum (cf. note 6 above).

9 This fall has two further explanations apart from legal restrictions. Many ethnic Germans who have successfully applied for citizenship have not yet exercised their option to migrate to Germany, but keep it as a fall-back position. In addition, the majority of people from Romania and Poland who wanted to leave had already done so in the late 1980s and early 1990s so that demand from these two countries is now greatly reduced.

10 The key international agreements in this context are the 1990 Copenhagen document of the CSCE and the Council of Europe's Framework Convention on Minority Rights. Bilateral treaties exist between Germany and Poland, the Czech and Slovak Republics, Hungary, Romania and Russia. Major bilateral agreements were concluded with Ukraine and Kazakhstan.

11 The total of the various budget titles peaked in 1997 at almost 115 million Deutschmark, not including the payments made to various expellee organizations in support of their activities in the host-countries (DM 5.1 million) and also not including institutional funding for the BdV (DM 24.8 million) before it was cut to DM 85 million in 1998 and DM 75 million in 1999. From 1998 to 1999 there was, however, a significant increase in institutional funding for the BdV to DM 42 million.

12 This (*Deutsche Kultur des östlichen Europas*) is the title of a special subgroup in the Federal Chancellor's Department of Culture and Media created only in 1998. The former term, German Culture of the East (*Deutsche Kultur des Ostens*) is no longer used.

13 Thereafter the BdV started two further initiatives. One was for the Europeanization of the Oder–Neiße territories, the other to enable members of the German minority in Poland to participate in parliamentary elections in the Federal Republic. Both failed.

14 Indeed, it is impossible to get any detailed information on this matter from the BdV or any of its affiliated organizations.

15 While the legal situation of both groups of claimants is different, their action was, to some extent, triggered by a resolution of the US House of Representatives (1998).

7   The role of the minority populations

1   In January 1991, the 1968 Law on the Status of National Minorities was superseded by the Charter of Fundamental Rights and Freedoms which, in December 1992, became part of the Czech constitution according to Article 3 of the Constitutional Law of the Czech National Council. Apart from general non-discrimination clauses in Articles 3 and 24, the Charter also details specific minority rights: autonomous cultural development; mother-tongue communication and reception of information, the right to form ethnic associations, education in the mother tongue, use of the mother tongue in public affairs and participation in the handling of affairs concerning national and ethnic minorities.

2   The Report also notes that Czech history text books largely ignore the fact that the Czech lands for centuries had been jointly and peacefully inhabited by large populations of Czechs, Germans and Jews, and that the contributions of the latter two to the development of the area are widely disregarded.

3   Just how the Polish authorities could actually differentiate Germans from *Volksliste* 1 from those on *Volksliste* 2 is a matter of conjecture. The corresponding identity card made no mention of grade, and in both cases the identity card was the same shade of blue.

4   Smaller numbers of designated Germans lived elsewhere in Poland, primarily in and around the Pomeranian city of Koszalin.

5   At the time both German states employed the 1913 Reich Citizenship Act.

6   Between 1950 and 1956, less than 60,000 ethnic Germans had been allowed to leave Poland, but in 1957, 98,290 emigrated, and in 1958, 117,550 did so. During the following two decades until 1979, over 300,000 ethnic Germans left, and by 1990, another more than 800,000 came to Germany, almost two-thirds of them between 1988 and 1990 (*Infodienst* 1997: 2–5).

7   After emigration had peaked in 1988–1990, with almost one million ethnic Germans leaving in just three years, numbers went down to around 100,000 emigrants per year for the second half of the 1990s.

8   Ostpolitik: continuity and change

1   In the case of the German–Czech treaty of 1973, it was also, and perhaps primarily, Soviet pressure put on the Czech communist regime that made a successful conclusion of the negotiations possible.

2   As constructivists we would, of course, make an argument that the very fact that Ostpolitik was initiated bears witness to the fact that German foreign policy in this instance was guided by a normative conviction that peace, reconciliation and regime change were the necessary and normatively justifiable goals of German foreign policy vis-à-vis Central and Eastern Europe because of the country's moral obligations towards its neighbours. In other words, the realist perspective falls short in explaining why *Ostpolitik* was initiated, even though it can explain its timing.

3   This betrays a distinctly (neo-)realist view of international relations on the part of this informant, and we do not deny that this is a legitimate view. A constructivist explanation, and one that bears relevance at different levels of our argument as we will demonstrate below, is that (in addition to its strategic relevance) German atrocities in Poland were of a significantly graver nature and therefore required a greater and more consistent policy effort to address them.

4   We will come back to this issue and show that it is not only that societal norms at the domestic and governmental levels in the Czech Republic constantly

mutually reinforce themselves but that there is also a significant 'contribution' to this, primarily from Germany in the form of the SdL and the Bavarian CSU.

9   Towards a common future?

1 The Bavarian delegation to the *Bundesrat* voted against the treaty. All others voted in favour.

Bibliography

Adomeit, H. 1990. 'Gorbachev and German Unification', *Problems of Communism*, vol. 17, no. 3, 1–23.

Allen, D. 1989. 'The Context of Foreign Policy Systems: The Contemporary International Environment', in Clarke, M. and White, B. (eds) *Understanding Foreign Policy*, Aldershot: Edward Elgar, pp. 60–83.

Allen, D. and Webber, M. 2002. 'The New Europe: Germany and Poland', in Webber, M. and Smith, M. (eds) *Foreign Policy in a Transformed World*, Harlow: Prentice Hall, pp. 179–214.

Aniol, W. 1996. *Poland's Migration and Ethnic Policies: European and German Influences*, Warsaw: Friedrich Ebert Foundation.

Auer, S. 2000. 'Nationalism in Central Europe-A Chance or a Threat', *East European Politics and Societies*, vol. 14, no. 2, 213–267.

Ayala-Lasso, J. 1995. *Grußbotschaft an die deutschen Vertriebenen vom 28. Mai 1995*, Frankfurt: BdV.

Bender, P. 1986. *Die 'Neue Ostpolitik' und ihre Folgen*, München: dtv.

Berger, P. and Luckmann, T. 1966. *The Social Construction of Reality*, New York: Anchor Books.

Bielasiak, J. 2002. 'Determinants of Public Opinion Differences on EU Accession in Poland', *Europe-Asia Studies*, vol. 54, no. 1, 1241–1266.

BK-Pressemitteilung 9 March 1999

Blanke, R. 2001. *Polish-speaking Germans*, Köln: Böhlau Verlag.

BMI-Pressemitteilung 18 May 1999.

BMI-Pressemitteilung 14 June 1999.

BMI-Pressemitteilung 25 June 1999.

BMI-Pressemitteilung 2 July 1999.

BMI-Pressemitteilung 10 August 1999.

BMI-Pressemitteilung 1 September 1999.

BMI-Pressemitteilung 21 October 1999.

Boekle, H., Rittberger, V. and Wagner, W. 2001. 'Constructivist Foreign Policy Theory', in Rittberger, V. (ed.) *German Foreign Policy since Unification: Theories and Case Studies*, Manchester: Manchester University Press, pp. 105–137.

Born, K. 2000. 'The Articulation of Identity in Silesia since 1989', in Cordell, K. (ed.) *The Politics of Ethnicity in Central Europe*, Basingstoke: Macmillan, 112–126.

Břach, R. 2001. 'Die Bedeutung des Prager Vertrags von 1973 für die deutsche Ostpolitik', in Hoensch, J. and Lemberg, H. (eds) *Begegnung und Konflikte*, Essen: Klartext, pp. 285–303.

Brandt, W. 1967a. *Deutsche Politik in europäischer Verantwortung (Sonderdruck aus dem Bulletin des Presse- und Informationsamtes der Bundesregierung)*, Bonn: Bundespresseamt.

Brandt, W. 1967b. 'Entspannungspolitik mit langem Atem', *Bulletin des Presse- und Informationsamtes der Bundesregierung*, No. 85/1967, 729.

Brandt, W. 1993. *My Life in Politics*, London: Penguin.

Brubaker, R. 1992. *Citizenship and Nationhood in France and Germany*, Cambridge, MA: Harvard University Press.

Bulletin der Bundesregierung 1970.

Bulletin der Bundesregierung 1973.

Bundestagsdrucksache 13/1116.

Bundestagsdrucksache 13/3195.

Bundestagsdrucksache 13/3428.

Bundestagsdrucksache 13/10845.

Charta der deutschen Heimatvertriebenen, gegeben zu Stuttgart am 5. August 1950. Kulturelle Arbeitshefte 22, Bonn: Kulturstiftung der deutschen Vertriebenen.

Cichowski, R. 2000. 'Western Dreams, Eastern Realities', *Comparative Political Studies*, vol. 33, no. 10.

Council of Europe, www.humanrights.coe.int/Minorities/Eng/frameworkConvention/ State Reports/[Czech Republic], accessed 27 January 2003.

Croan, M. 1982. *Dilemmas of Ostpolitik*, in Merkl, P. (ed.) *West German Foreign Policy: Dilemmas and Directions*, Chicago: Chicago Council on Foreign Relations.

Curp, T. D. 2001. 'The Politics of Ethnic Cleansing: The PPR, the PZZ and Wielkopolska's Nationalist Revolution, 1944–1946', *Nationalities Papers*, vol. 29, no. 4, 575–604.

Czech Census, March 2001, www.czso.cz/, accessed 4 April 2003.

Dialog, No. 61, 2002.

Dialog, No. 62/63: 2003.

Dobrosielski, M. 1992. *Deutsche Minderheiten in Polen*, Hamburg: Lit.

Dora, S. 1997. 'Eastern Europe and the European Union: the Accession Negotiations', *International Relations*, vol. 13, no. 6.

Eberhardt, P. 2003. *Ethnic Groups and Population Changes in Twentieth-Century Central-Eastern Europe*, London: M. E. Sharpe.

The Economist, 6 November 2004.

Eibicht, R.-J. (ed.) 1991. *Die Sudetendeutschen und ihre Heimat. Erbe – Auftrag – Ziel*, Wesseding: Gesamtdeutscher Verlag.

Erb, S. 2003. *German Foreign Policy: Navigating a New Era*, Boulder, CO: Lynne Rienner.

Ermacora, F. 1992. *Die Sudetendeutschen Fragen*, München: Langen Müller.

Forschungsgruppe Europa. 1996. 'Europas Neue Ostpolitik', *Internationale Politik*, no. 10, 59–63.

Franzen, K. 2001. *Die Vertriebenen*, München: Ullstein Verlag.

Fure, J. 1997. 'The German–Polish Border Region. A Case of Regional Integration?' *ARENA Working Paper* 97/19, http://www.arena.uio.no/publications/wp97_ htm, accessed 27 January 2003.

Geiss, I. 1990. 'Die deutsche Frage im internationalen System', in Schröder, H.-J. (ed.) *Die deutsche Frage als internationales Problem*, Stuttgart: Steiner, pp. 15–37.

Görgey, L. 1972. *Bonn's Eastern Policy 1964–1971*, Hamden, CT: Archon Books.

Gordon, H. 1990. 'Die Beneš Denkschriften: Die Tschechoslowakei und das Reich 1918/19', *Kommentar und Kritik*, Verlagsgemeinschaft Berg.

Grill, W. 2002. 'A Conversation with David Rock', in Rock, D. and Wolff, S. (eds) *Coming Home to Germany? The Integration of Ethnic Germans from Central and Eastern Europe in the Federal Republic*, New York and Oxford: Berghahn.

Guérin-Sendelbach, V. and Rulkowski, V. 1994. 'Euro-Trio Frankreich-Deutschland-Polen', *Aussenpolitik*, no. 11, 246–253.

Gutjahr, L. 1994. *German Foreign and Defence Policy after Unification*, London and New York: Pinter.

Hahn, E. 2001. 'Die Sudetendeutschen in der deutschen Gesellschaft' in Hoensch, J. and Lemberg, H. (eds) *Begegnung und Konflikte*, Essen: Klartext Verlag, 249–269.

Hajnicz, A. 1995. *Polens Wende und Deutschlands Vereinigung*, Paderborn: Schöningh.

Harris, E. 2003. 'Management of the Hungarian Issue in Slovak Politics: Europeanization and the Evolution of National Identities', paper presented at the PSA Annual Conference, University of Leicester.

Henning, F. 1982. *F.D.P.: Die Liberalen. Porträt einer Partei*, München: Günter Olzog Verlag.

Herman, C. F., Kegley, C. W. and Rosenau, J. N. (eds). 1987. *New Directions in the Study of Foreign Policy*, London: HarperCollins Academic.

Hilf, R. 1986. *Deutsche und Tschechen*, Opladen: Leske und Budrich.

Hill, C. 2003. *The Changing Politics of Foreign Policy*, Basingstoke: Palgrave.

Hirsch, H. 1998. *Die Rache der Opfer*, Berlin: Rowohlt.

Historikerkommission (Gemeinsame deutsch-tschechische Historikerkommission). 1995. *Konfliktgemeinschaft, Katastrophe, Entspannung*. München: Oldenbourg.

Hochfelder, H. 1991. 'Über die Ziele sudetendeutscher Politik', in Eibicht, R.-J. (ed.) *Die Sudetendeutschen und ihre Heimat. Erbe – Auftrag – Ziel*, Wesseding: gesamtdeutscher Verlag.

Hoffman, R. 1996. *Die Anfänge der Emigration aus der Tschechslowakei 1948*, Prague: Insitute for Contemporary History.

Holohan, W. and Ciechowski, M. 1996. 'The Recomposition of Identity and Political Space in Europe: The Case of Upper Silesia', in O'Dowd, L. and Wilson, T. (eds) *Borders, Nations & States*, Aldershot: Avebury, pp. 155–178.

Hupka, H. 1971. 'Der Warschauer Grenzvertrag', in Brandt, W. (ed.) *Ostpolitik im Kreuzfeuer*, Stuttgart: Seewald Verlag.

Hyde-Price, A. 2000. *Germany and European Order*, Manchester: Manchester University Press.

Ihme-Tuchel, B. 1997. *Die DDR und die Deutschen in Polen*, Berlin: Helle Panke.

Info-Dienst Deutsche Aussiedler. 1997. Berlin: Federal Ministry of the Interior.

Ingram, H. and Ingram, M. (eds). 2002. *EU Expansion to the East*, Cheltenham: Edward Elgar.

Ivaničková, E. 2001. 'Die Krise der ČSSR im Zusammenhang mit der Intervention von 1968', in Hoensch, J. and Lemberg, H. (eds) *Begegnung und Konflikte*, Essen: Klartext Verlag, pp. 270–284.

Jovanović, M. 1998. 'Does Eastern Enlargement Mean the End of the European Union?', *International Relations*, vol. 14, no. 1, 23–39.

Kacíř, P. 2000. 'Upper Silesia 1918–1945', in Cordell, K. (ed.) *The Politics of Ethnicity in Central Europe*, Basingstoke: Macmillan, pp. 112–126.

Kárný, M. 2001. 'Die tschechoslwakischen Opfer der deutschen Okkupation', in Hoensch, J. and Lemberg, H. (eds) *Begegnung und Konflikte*, Essen: Klartext Verlag, pp. 136–205.

Kersten, K. 2001. 'Forced Migration and the Transformation of Polish Society in the PostWar Period', in Ther, P. and Siljak, A. (eds) *Redrawing Nations*, Lanham: Rowman & Littlefield, pp. 75–86.

Köcher, R. 1997. 'Vertriebene der Erlebnis- und Nachfolgegeneration. Ergebnisse einer Sekundäranalyse,' *Deutschland und seine Nachbarn. Forum für Kultur und Politik*, 21: 3–67.

Kořalka, J. 2001. 'Nationsbildung und die nationale Identität der Deutschen, Öster-reicher, Tschechen und Slowaken um die Mitte des 19. Jahrhunderts', in Hoensch, J. and Lemberg, H. (eds) *Begegnung und Konflikte*, Essen: Klartext Verlag, pp. 38–55.

Koschyk, H. 1993. 'Schlesien als verständigungspolitisches Schlüsselgebiet in und für Europa', plenary paper presented at the Haus Schlesien, Königswinter.

Kotzian, O. 1998. *Die Sudetendeutschen*, Bonn: BdV.

Kramer, M. 2001. 'Introduction', in Ther, P. and Siljak, A. (eds) *Redrawing Nations*, Lanham, Rowman & Littlefield, pp. 1–42.

Kreile, M. 1980. '*Ostpolitik* Reconsidered', in Krippendorff, E. and Rittberger, V. (eds) *The Foreign Policy of West Germany: Formation and Contents*, London and Beverly Hills, CA: Sage, pp. 123–146.

Krüger, H. 1998[1958]. 'Leitartikel in der Erstausgabe des Deutschen Ostdiensts'. Reprinted in *Deutscher Ostdienst*, vol. 40, no. 1/2, 9 January 1998, 3–4.

Kubů, E. 2001. 'Die brüchigen Beziehungen: Die Weimarer Republik und die Tschechoslowakei', in Hoensch, J. and Lemberg, H. (eds) *Begegnung und Konflikte*, Essen: Klartext Verlag, pp. 71–84.

Kučera, J. 2001a. 'Der Hai wird nie wieder so stark sein', paper presented at the Hannah-Arendt-Institut für Totalitarismusforschung e.V., Dresden.

Kučera, J. 2001b. 'Statistische Berechungen der Vertreibungsverluste: Schlusswort oder Sackgasse?', in Hoensch, J. and Lemberg, H. (eds) *Begegnung und Konflikte*, Essen: Klartext Verlag, pp. 230–248.

Kulczycki, J. 2001. 'The National Identity of the "Natives" of Poland's "Recovered Lands"', *National Identities*, vol. 3, no. 3, 205–219.

Leff, C. 1997. *The Czech and Slovak Republics*, London: Westview Press.

Lemberg, H. 2001. 'Die Entwicklung der Pläne für die Aussiedlung der Deutschen aus der Tschechoslowakei', in Hoensch, J. and Lemberg, H. (eds) *Begegnung und Konflikte*, Essen: Klartext Verlag, pp. 190–204

Leonhard, E. 1999. 'Die Verantwortung der Politik für die gesamtdeutsche Kultur' (Festrede aus Anlass des 25 jährigen Bestehens der Kulturstiftung der deutschen Vertriebenen am 14 Juni 1999).

Löffler, H. 1997. *Sudetendeutsche Siedlungen und Gemeinschaften in aller Welt – von 1827 bis heute*, Vienna: Österreichische Landsmannschaft.

Loth, W. 1989. *Ost-West-Konflikt und deutsche Frage*, München: dtv.

Mayall, J. 1994. 'Sovereignty and Self-Determination in the New Europe', in Miall, H. (ed.) *Minority Rights in Europe*, London: Pinter.

Mezihorák, F. 1998. 'Chancen der Versöhnung aus tschechischer Sicht', in Wichard, R. (ed.) *Deutsche, Polen, Tschechen: Chancen der Versöhnung*, Frankfurt: Verlag der Aktion.

Modelski, G. 1962. *A Theory of Foreign Policy*. London: Pall Mall Press.

Müller, R. 1999. 'Nichts als Erinnerung? Wie die Bundesregierung das kulturelle Erbe der Vertriebenen tilgen will', *Frankfurter Allgemeine Zeitung*, 23 September 1999.

Müller, U. 1993. 'Die deutsche Volksgruppe in der Tschechoslowakei – Chancen und Perspektiven', *Deutschland und seine Nachbarn*, no. 6 (February 1993), pp. 20–26.

Myant, M. R. 1981. *Socialism and Democracy in Czechoslovakia*, Cambridge: Cambridge University Press.

Otter, J. 1994. *Das Los der Deutsch-Tschechischen Nachbarschaft*, Heršpice: HU Verlag.

Paweltziki, R. and Kirstein, H. 1998: *Oberschlesien*. Bonn: BdV.

Posselt, B. 2003. *Presseerklärung*, 9 April 2003.

Prieß, L., Kural, V. and Wilke, M. 1996. *Die SED und der Prager Frühling 1968*, Berlin: Akademie Verlag.

Prybyla, J. 1991. 'The Road from Socialism', *Problems of Communism*, vol. 17, no. 1, 1–17.

Report submitted by the Czech Republic Pursuant to Article 25, Paragraph 1 of the Framework Convention for the Protection of National Minorities, 1999. www.riga.lv/minelres/reports/czech/czech.htm, accessed 3 December 2000.

Rogall, J. 1993. 'Die deutschen Minderheiten in Polen heute', *Aus Politik und Zeitgeschichte* 48/93, pp. 31–43.

Rosenau, J. N. 1987. 'Introduction: New Directions and Recurrent Questions in the Comparative Study of Foreign Policy', in Herman, C., Kegley, C. W. and Rosenau, J. N. (eds) *New Directions in the Study of Foreign Policy*, London: Harper Collins Academic, pp. 1–10.

Rossmann, A. 1999. 'Der kalte Krieger. Unter Ideologieverdacht: Naumann und die Vertriebenenkultur', *Frankfurter Allgemeine Zeitung*, 28 August 1999.

Rouček, L. 1990. *Die Tschechslowakei und die Bundesrepublik Deutschland*, München: tuduv-Verlag.

Sakson, A. 2000. 'Crisis or Normalcy? Reflections on Contemporary Polish–German Relations', www.msz.gov.pl, accessed 27 January 2000.

Sanford, G. 1999. *Poland: The Re-Conquest of History*, Amsterdam: Harwood Academic.

Schily, O. 1999. 'Die Erinnerung und das Gedenken findet ihren Sinn in dem Willen für eine bessere Zukunft' (Rede auf der Festveranstaltung zum 50. Jahrestag des Bundes der Vertriebenen am 29. Mai 1999 im Berliner Dom).

Schnürch, R. 1991. 'Konsequenzen sudetendeutscher Heimatpolitik', in Eibicht, R.-J. (ed.) *Die Sudetendeutschen und ihre Heimat. Erbe – Auftrag – Ziel*, Wesseding: Gesamtdeutscher Verlag.

Seibt, F. 1997. *Deutschland und die Tschechen*, München: Piper.

Skilling, H. G. 1976. *Czechoslovakia's Interrupted Revolution*, Princeton, NJ: Princeton University Press.

Smith, A.D. 1991. *National Identity*, London: Penguin.

Staněk, T. 2001. 'Vertreibung und Aussiedlung der Deutschen aus der Tschechoslowakei 1945–1948', in Hoensch, J. and Lemberg, H. (eds) *Begegnung und Konflikte*, Essen: Klartext, pp. 230–248.

Starr, R. (ed.). 1993. *Transition to Democracy in Poland*, New York: St Martin's Press.

Steinbach, E. 1999. 'Tschechen und Deutsche – Der Weg in die Zukunft' (Vortrag vor Studenten der Karlsuniversität in Prag, 17 März 1999), www.bund-der-vertriebenen.de/politik.htm.

Strobel, G.W. 1997. 'Die polnische Preussenkrankheit und ihre politische Instrumentalisierung', *Aus Politik und Zeitgeschichte*, 53/97, pp. 21–33.

Süddeutsche Zeitung. 8 August 2003.

Tampke, J. 2003. *Czech–German Relations and the Politics of Central Europe*, Basingstoke: Palgrave.

Tewes, S. 2002. *Germany, Civilian Power, and the New Europe: Enlarging NATO and the European Union*, Basingstoke: Macmillan.

Ther, P. 2001. 'A Century of Forced Migration: The Origins and Consequences of "Ethnic Cleansing"', in Ther, P. and Siljak, A. (eds) *Redrawing Nations*, Lanham: Rowman & Littlefield, pp. 43–74.

Urban, T. 1994. *Deutsche in Polen*, München: Beck'sche Reihe.

US House of Representatives.1998. 105th CONGRESS, 2nd Session, H. RES. 562 (HRES 562 IH).

Vollmer, A. 1997. *'Ende der Zweideutigkeiten': Rede in der Karls-Universität Prag*. Manuscript in authors' possession.

Vollmer, A. 2002. Interview with Neue Zürcher Zeitung. 11/12 May 2002.

Vollmer, A. n.d. *Aufbruch der Vergangenheit, die Deutsch-Tschechische Erklärung von 1997*. Manuscript in authors' possession.

Walicki, A. 2000. 'The Troubling Legacy of Roman Dmowski', *East European Politics and Societies*, vol. 14, no. 1, pp. 12–46.

Wallace, W. 1978. 'Old States and New Circumstances: The International Predicament of Britain, France and Germany', in Wallace, W. and Paterson, W. E. (eds) *Foreign Policy making in Western Europe*, Westmead: Saxon House, pp. 31–55.

Wanka, W. 1991. 'Mit dem Blick auf eine wahre Lösung. Anmerkungen zur Sudetenfrage', in Eibicht, R.-J. (ed.) *Die Sudetendeutschen und ihre Heimat. Erbe – Auftrag – Ziel*, Wesseding: Gesamtdeutscher Verlag.

Webber, M. and Smith, M. 2002. 'Frameworks', in Webber, M. and Smith, M. (eds) *Foreign Policy in a Transformed World*, Harlow: Prentice Hall, pp. 7–104.

Wendt, A. 2001. 'Constructing International Politics', in Brown, M. E., Coté, O. R., Lynn-Jones, S. M. and Miller, S. E. (eds) *Theories of War and Peace*, Cambridge, MA: MIT Press, pp. 416–426.

White, B. 1989. 'Analysing Foreign Policy: Problems and Approaches', in Clarke, M. and White, B. (eds) *Understanding Foreign Policy*, Aldershot: Edward Elgar, pp. 1–26.

Wichard, R. 1998. 'Deutsche, Polen, Tschechen: Chancen der Versöhnung', in Wichard, R. (ed.) *Deutsche, Polen, Tschechen: Chancen der Versöhnung*, Frankfurt: Verlag der Aktion.

Windsor, P. 1971. *Germany and the Management of Détente*, London: Chatto & Windus.

Wiskemann, E. 1967. *Czechs and Germans*, London: Macmillan.

Ziebart, H. 1999. *Bilanz einer deutsch-tschechischen Alternative*, Stuttgart: GNN Verlag.

List of interviews

Anon. (a), supplied to the authors, 2004.
Anon. (b), interview with A. Dybczyński, 2004.
Anon. (c), interview with A. Dybczyński, 2004.
J. Barcz, School of Trade, Warsaw, interview with A. Dybczyński, 30 April 2004.
P. Brod of the Czech–German Future Fund, interview with Z. Hausvater, 18 February 2004.
A. Byrt, Polish Ambassador to Germany, interview with A. Dybczyński, 11 March 2004.
W. Czapliński, Director of the Institute of Law, Polish Academy of Science, interview with A. Dybczyński, 10 March 2004.
Sibylle Dreher, 5 June 2002.
J. Fiszer, Polish Academy of Science, interview with A. Dybczyński, 25 March 2004.
W. Góralski, interview with A. Dybczyński, 9 March 2004.
V. Handl, The Institute of International Relations, Prague, interview with Z. Hausvater, 19 January 2004.
H.-J. Hansen, electronic interview, 8 December 2003.
V. Houžvička, The Czech Academy of Science, interview with Z. Hausvater, 20 January 2004.
T. Kafka, Director of the Czech–German Future Fund, interview with Z. Hausvater, 12 January 2004.
J. Kovanic, of the Circle of Czech Expellees, interview with Z. Hausvater, 18 January 2004.
H. Koschyk, MdB, electronic interview, delivered 4 December 2003.
J. Křen The Czech–German Future Fund, interview with Z. Hausvater, 19 January 2004.
M. Kunštát, The Institute of International Studies, Prague, interview with Z. Hausvater, 18 February 2004.
K. Larischová, The Friedrich-Ebert-Stiftung, Prague, interview with Z. Hausvater, 4 February 2004.
A. Lintzel, Office of A. Vollmer, MdB, 2004, interview with K. Cordell, 11 February 2004.
M. Meckel, MdB, interview with K. Cordell, 13 February 2004.
B. Ociepka, Institute of International Studies, University of Wrocław, interview with A. Dybczyński, 4 May 2004.
O. Pick, Czech–German Future Fund, interview with Z. Hausvater, 8 January 2004.
Bernd Posselt, MEP, interview with S. Wolff, 21 November 2003.

J. Reiter, President of the Centre for International Relations, Warsaw, interview with A. Dybczyński, 9 March 2004.

K. Rossmanith, MdB, interview with K. Cordell, 12 February 2004.

A. Sakson, Polish Western Institute, interview with A. Dybczyński, 10 March 2004.

K. M. Schröter, FDP Referent für Europapolitik, interview with K. Cordell, 16 February 2004.

A. Schwall-Düren, MdB, electronic interview received, 14 December 2003.

E. Stadtmüller, Institute of International Studies, University of Wrocław, interview with A. Dybczyński, 30 March 2004.

U. Stemke, electronic interview, 25 November 2003.

Erika Steinbach, MdB, interview with S. Wolff, 6 June 2002.

J. Sułek, Former Political Director of the Polish Foreign Ministry, interview with Dybczyński, 13/21 April, 2004.

M. Tomala, Former Polish Deputy Ambassador to the GDR, interview with A. Dybczyński, 15 March 2004.

P. Uhl, Human Rights Commissioner of the Czech(oslovak) Government, 1991–2001, interview with Z. Hausvater, 20 January 2004.

V. Žák, The Czech–German Future Fund, interview with Z. Hausvater, 4 February 2004.

Index

Adenauer, Konrad 37, 38, 39, 67, 72, 73, 74, 75, 83, 133, 147, 163
Allied Powers 7, 24, 25, 27, 31, 32, 33, 35, 41, 42, 46, 54, 63, 66, 74, 79, 82, 84, 108, 109, 110, 138, 141, 143, 144, 160, 162
assimilation 18, 113, 115, 118, 122, 167
Aussiedler 17, 88, 92, 129, 166, 173
Austria 3, 5, 18, 21, 24–26, 107, 111
Austro-Hungarian Empire 3, 4, 23
autonomy 7, 26, 36, 65

Basic Law (Grundgesetz) 88
Bavaria 47, 58, 74, 76, 77, 84, 94, 95, 126, 153, 170
BdV (Union of Expellees) 46, 48, 50, 52, 55, 56, 66, 69, 71, 86, 88, 89, 92, 96, 97, 100–104, 112, 123, 124, 129, 148, 149, 153, 154, 159, 161, 163, 167, 168, 171, 174, 175
belonging 93, 93
benefits 26, 43, 53, 68, 134, 144, 152
Berlin 1, 4, 14, 38, 40, 41, 42, 43, 47, 48, 53, 57, 60, 66, 67, 70, 72, 75, 94, 103, 118, 120, 124, 129, 130, 148, 151, 153, 158, 161, 165, 167, 173, 175
bilingual 118, 123, 127
Bohemia 18–22, 29, 64, 116, 136, 137, 140
borders 3–5, 8, 16, 18, 22, 25–29, 34, 35, 38, 39, 41–43, 48, 49, 51–55, 57, 61–63, 65, 66, 75, 78, 83, 87–90, 92, 93, 100, 102–105,

107–110, 123, 124, 136, 147, 151, 152, 164, 167, 172, 173
Brandt, Willy 1, 13, 30, 41–44, 46, 50, 66, 67, 73, 88, 115, 123, 132, 133, 140, 145, 172, 173

CDU 40, 41, 44, 48, 68, 69, 72–76, 78, 80, 88, 89, 98, 106, 132, 133, 149, 153, 157
census 25, 112, 114, 116, 118, 119, 124, 125, 126, 172
Central and Eastern Europe 1, 3–5, 7, 10, 12, 17–19, 23–25, 32, 37, 50, 67, 75, 82, 87–90, 97, 104, 105, 107, 108, 111, 132, 133, 134, 143, 169, 173
Central Europe 2, 3, 19, 20, 30, 39, 41, 44, 67, 75, 89, 106, 144, 145, 171, 173, 176
citizenship 12, 16, 17, 33, 34, 36, 49, 66, 69, 76, 77, 83, 89, 94, 97, 102, 113, 118, 119, 121, 126, 150, 158, 168, 169, 172
Cold War 2, 5–15, 18, 30–61, 63, 67, 77, 82, 88, 89, 103, 130, 132–134, 148, 166, 167
collective identity 93
communism 12, 26, 27, 31–36, 38–42, 45, 48, 50–52, 54–59, 64, 82–84, 87, 92, 97, 101, 102, 104, 106, 110, 112–114, 116, 118, 125, 128, 129, 134, 136–143, 145, 146, 150, 155, 160, 161, 163, 166, 167, 169, 171, 175
conflict 3, 6, 17, 19, 20, 90, 107, 110, 137

consciousness 17, 20, 124, 134, 163
cross-border 55, 65, 88, 92, 105, 107
CSCE 11—7, 104, 166, 168
CSU 47, 48, 68, 72—4, 78–80, 89,
    94, 98, 104, 133, 143, 153, 154,
    157, 170
culture 5, 9, 22, 23, 55, 64, 78, 84,
    89–92, 96, 104, 109, 111, 113–116,
    118, 127, 133, 167, 168
Czech Republic 2, 5, 6, 8, 9, 11,
    13–18, 35–37, 41, 44, 45, 49, 53,
    57–60, 62, 64, 65, 68–74, 76–80,
    82, 93–102, 104, 106, 107,
    114–118, 127, 130, 131, 134–140,
    142–153, 155–158, 161, 162,
    164–166, 169, 172, 175
Czechoslovakia 2, 11, 16, 17, 21,
    23–28, 30–32, 34–45, 47, 49–51,
    53, 56, 57, 59, 60, 64–67, 72, 73,
    77, 78, 82, 87, 88, 93, 95, 97, 98,
    103, 104, 106, 109–111, 114–120,
    131–133, 135, 136, 140–142, 146,
    155, 157, 158, 164, 167, 175

Danzig 29, 167
democracy 44, 56, 60, 86, 89, 90, 96,
    105, 139, 146, 161, 175
demographic change 39
deportation 33, 107, 111, 113, 121
dialect 84, 123
difference 13–17, 22, 31, 34, 35, 46,
    49, 52, 57, 62, 94, 101, 103, 106,
    107, 130, 131, 134, 136, 139, 140,
    142, 143, 162, 163, 171
discrimination 17, 22, 23, 25, 70, 83,
    89, 113, 122, 126, 169
distinction 7, 8, 74, 76, 119, 149,
    166

East German 45, 59, 83, 93, 115, 133,
    141
East Germany 93, 133
East Prussia 3, 24, 29, 101, 102, 167,
    168
Eastern Europe 1, 3, 4, 5, 7, 10, 12,
    16, 17, 18, 19, 23–25, 32, 37, 38,
    50, 67, 75, 82, 85, 87, 88–90, 92,
    97, 104, 105, 107–109, 111,
    132–134, 143, 146, 169, 172, 173

education 23, 31, 56, 114, 117, 121,
    122, 124, 127, 128, 149, 169
ethnic minorities 106, 130, 169
ethnicity 4, 16, 21, 26, 32, 118, 125,
    167, 171, 173
EU 1–5, 7, 9–14, 16–20, 22–25, 27,
    30–33, 36–48, 50–55, 57, 61, 63,
    64, 66–80, 82–94, 96–100,
    102–109, 111, 112, 114, 116,
    118–120, 124, 125, 127–130,
    132–134, 138, 140, 141, 143–152,
    154, 155, 157–166, 168, 169,
    171–178
European integration 51, 64, 134,
    143
exclusion 26, 150
expellees 8, 36, 37, 44–46, 49, 57,
    58, 65, 66, 71, 74, 75, 77, 82–88,
    92–94, 96, 97, 99–105, 117, 130,
    132, 133, 137, 138, 142, 143, 148,
    150, 156, 158, 159, 162, 163, 167,
    177

family 34, 36, 40, 58, 63, 82, 115,
    123, 125, 129, 135, 152
FDP 41, 42, 72, 73, 74, 89, 132, 133,
    178
Federal Republic of Germany 8, 10,
    12, 17, 34, 37–45, 47, 48, 50, 51,
    66, 72–74, 80, 82–84, 86–90, 93,
    102, 106, 114, 115, 122–124, 132,
    133, 135, 137, 143, 163, 168,
    173
First World War 4, 23, 24, 25, 29–31,
    82, 110
Fischer, Joschka 70, 138, 139
funding 3, 10, 12, 58, 60, 69, 71, 85,
    88, 90, 91, 115, 117, 126, 138, 145,
    155, 156, 161, 162, 167–169, 177,
    178

Galicia 108, 168
GDR 38, 40, 42, 45, 47, 48, 55, 56,
    59, 62–64, 67, 71, 75, 79, 80, 92,
    106, 113, 114, 120, 121, 123, 124,
    141, 167, 178
Genscher, Hans-Dietrich 52, 73, 74
German constitution 12, 88
Gorbachev, Mikhail 46, 68, 171

Görlitz 52, 63
Green Party (Germany) 68, 70–72, 88, 89, 129

Habsburg 20, 22, 23, 140
Havel, Václav 50, 80, 81, 97, 155, 157
Heim ins Reich policy 98, 107
Heimat 27, 71, 76, 85, 94, 100, 102, 103, 172, 173, 175, 176
Himmler, Heinrich 107
Hitler, Adolf 17, 28, 38, 43, 98, 103, 108, 109, 111
home 17, 27, 33, 37, 38, 72, 75, 82, 84–87, 91–93, 96, 99, 102, 111, 117, 118, 120, 127, 129, 142, 148, 158, 167, 173
homeland 27, 37, 82, 84–87, 92, 93, 96, 99, 102, 111, 127, 167
Honecker, Erich 43, 62, 106
Hungarian 3, 4, 23, 25, 26, 36, 97, 99, 110, 111, 173
Hungary 28, 97, 110, 146, 167, 168

identity 4, 5, 17, 19, 20, 24, 25, 36, 37, 84–86, 93, 94, 113, 114, 116, 118, 124, 126, 141, 169, 171, 173–175
inclusion 85
integration 27, 31, 38, 51, 61, 64, 73, 83–87, 91, 104, 105, 130, 132, 134, 143, 145, 152, 172, 173
irredentism 23, 92
ius sanguinis 16

Klaus, Václav 57, 81
Kohl, Helmut 44–48, 52, 73, 74, 78–80, 88, 93, 146, 147, 153, 157

land reform 26, 148
Landsmannschaften 43, 45–48, 53, 56, 64, 65, 70, 76, 79, 80, 82, 84–88, 90, 93, 95, 100–103, 124, 130, 135, 149, 154, 159, 167, 174
language 19, 22, 23, 26, 36, 55, 76, 78, 88–90, 113, 114, 116, 117, 120, 127, 128, 135, 141, 142
language test 90
League of Nations 24, 26, 28

Lebensraum 29, 107–109
legitimacy 23, 28, 36, 48, 99, 136, 137, 138, 150, 161

Meckel, Markus 51, 55–57, 59, 64, 69, 76, 88, 137, 144, 149, 156, 157, 159, 177
memory 57, 60, 86, 106, 116, 129, 140, 147, 149, 162
migration 4, 16–19, 21, 22, 25, 32, 36, 37, 87, 89–91, 93, 107, 110, 113–115, 120–123, 128, 129, 135, 168, 169, 171, 173, 174, 176
minority rights 36, 125, 168, 169, 174
Mitteleuropa 54, 144
Moravia 18–22, 29, 64, 110, 116, 137, 140
Munich 5, 27, 34, 43, 45, 57, 60, 64–66, 77, 94, 110, 117, 138, 140, 142, 157, 159

nationalism 4, 16, 20, 21, 23, 28, 110, 121, 136, 137, 164, 171
national minority 36, 120
National Socialists (Nazis) 1, 17, 24, 28–33, 43, 57, 59, 65, 71, 72, 78, 83, 88, 107–109, 111, 141, 153, 155
NATO 1, 5, 64, 65, 71, 87, 104, 115, 128, 132, 143–145, 153, 162, 176

Opole 55, 124, 125, 127, 129
orientation 10, 12, 13, 19, 20, 54, 78, 122, 126, 127, 132, 143
OSCE 11, 13, 37, 152
Ostgebiete 37, 39, 45, 66, 70, 73, 74
Ostpolitik 2, 3, 5–15, 30, 38, 40–42, 44, 52, 62–82, 87, 88, 131–154, 164, 166, 167, 169, 171–174
Ostverträge 1

PDS 62, 63, 64, 65, 70, 71
Poland 1, 2, 5, 6, 8, 9, 11, 13–18, 21–57, 59, 60, 62–74, 76–83, 87, 88, 89, 91, 93, 95–97, 99–104, 106–110, 115, 118–120, 121–127, 129–154, 158–169, 171, 174, 175
Polish Corridor 24, 29

Pomerania 18, 20, 29, 92, 119, 167, 169
Posselt, Bernd 78, 144, 175, 177
Potsdam Conference 5, 32, 33–35, 37, 52–54, 67, 83, 84, 119, 160
Prague Treaty 43
Prussia 3, 19–24, 29, 92, 101, 102, 159, 167, 168

reconciliation 2, 7, 8, 12, 13, 34, 39, 45–47, 53, 58, 60, 66, 67, 70, 76, 80, 82, 86, 90, 92, 94, 99, 100, 103–105, 124, 132–135, 137, 139, 143–145, 153, 155–157, 164, 169
refugees 34, 36, 38, 44, 46, 47, 65, 66, 74, 75, 79, 80, 82–84, 86, 100, 103, 104, 112, 127, 130, 132, 158, 162, 163, 167
region 2, 4, 7, 9, 14, 20, 21, 24, 28, 46, 50, 80, 85, 86, 90–93, 102, 108, 116, 125, 127, 128, 130, 134, 145–147, 162, 166, 172
religion 19, 20, 46
reparations 5, 23, 83
resettlement 102, 107–109
reunification 12, 13, 93
revanchism 70, 96
revisionism 37
Russia 3, 4, 19–24, 28, 29, 34, 51, 71, 84, 91, 92, 101, 102, 108, 144–146, 159, 160, 167, 168

Scheel, Walter 41, 72, 73
Schmidt, Helmut 44, 67, 73
SDL 47, 49, 59, 69–71, 76, 78, 94–96, 100, 102, 103, 116, 117, 138, 143, 153, 155–159, 164, 170
Second World War 1, 2, 6, 9, 16–32, 37, 39, 42, 51, 56, 57, 61, 68, 96, 99, 103, 107, 130, 134, 140, 142, 144, 147, 152, 154, 159, 164, 165, 166
settlement 4, 5, 18, 22–24, 31, 33, 83, 87, 102, 107–109, 113, 148, 157
Silesia 16, 18–20, 24–26, 29, 34, 35, 48, 54, 55, 63, 88, 92, 93, 102, 110, 116, 119, 120, 122, 124–127, 129, 130, 147, 153, 164, 167, 168, 171, 173

Slovakia 2, 11, 16, 17, 21, 23–32, 34–45, 47, 49–51, 53, 56, 57, 59, 60, 64–67, 72, 73, 77, 78, 82, 87, 88, 93, 95, 97, 98, 103, 104, 106, 109–111, 114–120, 131–133, 135, 136, 140–142, 146, 155, 157, 158, 164, 167, 175
Soviet Union 18, 29, 32, 34, 38, 40–42, 44, 46, 47, 65, 71, 74, 75, 89, 92, 107–111, 133, 145, 160, 166
SPD 40–42, 44, 46, 65–75, 78, 89, 96, 98, 129, 132, 133, 145, 167
Staatsangehörigkeit 16, 17
Staatsbürgerschaft 17
stability 4, 68, 99, 118, 144, 145, 148
Stalin, Joseph 34, 35, 75, 108, 109, 121
Stoiber, Edmund 76, 77, 79, 80, 98, 157
Sudeten Germans 17, 27, 28, 35, 41, 43, 57, 58, 60, 65, 68, 69, 76, 78, 93–95, 98, 102, 103, 111, 112, 117, 130, 135, 137, 138, 150, 153, 154, 156, 158, 168
Sudetenland 28, 59, 60, 65, 72, 76, 83, 92–95, 116, 129, 135

Third Reich 33, 65
transition 38, 46, 56, 69, 77, 89, 101, 139, 146, 148, 149, 150, 151, 175

Ulbricht, Walter 41, 43, 62, 106
Umsiedler 45, 83
unification 10, 12, 13, 32, 36, 37, 48, 49, 51, 52, 55, 56, 60, 63, 66, 68, 73, 74, 79, 86, 92, 93, 123, 134, 149, 158, 171, 173
Upper Silesia 16, 20, 24, 25, 29, 34, 35, 93, 102, 110, 119, 120, 122–125, 127, 153, 167, 168, 173

Verheugen, Günter 99
Versailles 5, 18, 23, 24, 28, 31
Vertriebene 46, 84–86, 171, 172, 174–176
Volksliste 54, 108, 118, 169
Volkszugehörigkeit 17

Vollmer, Antje 20, 25, 55, 57, 71, 140, 155–158, 176, 177
War Consequences Conciliation Act 89
Wende 56, 71, 76, 80, 173
West German 7, 10, 12, 13, 30, 34, 39, 41, 43, 46, 47, 66, 68, 83, 85, 86, 89, 115, 122–124, 140, 141, 147, 168, 172, 174

West Germany 7, 10, 34, 39, 83, 85, 122, 124, 140, 141, 147, 168, 174
West Prussia 19, 92, 168
Western Europe 23, 70, 146, 152, 176

Yalta 67, 84, 109

Zeman, Miloš 68, 98, 99

9 780415 499576